The Seven Ages of One Man

or
How one man started the Museum of Science and Industry in Manchester

Richard L. Hills MBE

Ph.D., M.A., D.I.C., Dip.Ed., C.I.Mech.E., F.M.A.

2018

Richard L. Hills

15 april 2018

First published in the United Kingdom in 2018 by The Choir Press
in association with Seven Ages Publishing

ISBN 978-1-911589-67-9

Designed and typeset by

Tony Kershaw
tony@tkershaw.co.uk

Contents

In memory of
Margaret Magdalen Hills

The mother whom I never knew
But
Who has left so much to me.

And in memory of
Bernice Pickford Hills

Whom I knew for
Far too short a time.

Richard Leslie Hills   John Henry Hills   Margaret Muriel Hills

1936 –   1933 – 2014   1931 –

My siblings

W. Shakespeare

All the world's a stage,
And all the men and women merely players.
They have their exits and their entrances:
And one man in his time plays many parts,
His acts being seven ages. At first, the infant,
Mewling and puking in his nurses arms.
And then the whining schoolboy, with his satchel,
And shining morning face, creeping like snail
Unwillingly to school. And then the lover,
Sighing like the furnace, with a woeful ballad
Made to his mistress' eyebrow. Then a soldier,
Full of strange oaths, and bearded like the pard,
Jealous in honour, sudden and quick in quarrel,
Seeking the bubble reputation
Even in the cannon's mouth. And then the justice,
In fair round belly, with good capon lin'd,
With eyes severe, and beard of formal cut,
Full of wise saws and modern instances;
And so he plays his part. The sixth age shifts
Into the lean and slipper'd pantaloon,
With spectacles on nose and pouch on side,
His youthful hose well sav'd a world too wide
For his shrunk shank; and his big manly voice,
Turning again towards childish treble, pipes
And whistles in his sound. Last scene of all,
That ends this strange eventful history,
In second childness, and mere oblivion,
Sans teeth, sans eyes, sans taste, sans everything.

Acknowledgements

'All things work together for good to them that love God.' (Romans 8, 28)

My dear Bernice passed away on 15 August 2016 in Willow Wood Hospice having suffered bravely from cancer. The two most important people in my life both died from this scourge. Both I knew for far too short a time. At Willow Wood, I found a leaflet of Macmillan Cancer Support offering 'to record your own unique life story with one of our experienced history team'. I contacted them and Val Harrington came and was impressed with my career. She felt that perhaps I should make a longer version.

At the same time, Willow Wood offered a bereavement counselling service so I went to see Sarah Ellenbogen. She also was surprised that I had led so varied a career with its many ups and downs. She felt that I ought to write a proper biography. So I stared the present work. For me, one surprising outcome has been that I learnt a great deal about my mother and through that perhaps a better understanding of myself. I have been able to reflect more about the mysterious way in which pieces of the jigsaw have fitted together and have been used by God to enable me to fulfil his will.

I must thank all the family members and others who have contributed their memoirs and copies of photographs and paintings, in particular Peter Bishop and Duncan Robertson who have shared their family archives. To my step-daughter, Alison Ashworth, I am especially grateful for her willingness to share her computer skills and correct all my mistakes. To Callum Boothroyd who also has tried to teach me the inner complexities of computers and this digital age. To Tony Kershaw, who wrestled with my manuscripts and pictures, and made the book finally come to fruition, also Claire Bibby who proof-read the text, and has made sure that there are not too many errors. The many others who have helped me in my career, and in the production of this book, I thank them all.

Richard L. Hills.

'Rejoice in the Lord always; and again I say rejoice.' (Phillipians 4.4)

We the willing,
Led by the unknowing
Are doing the impossible
For the ungrateful.
We have done so much
With so little for so long
We are now qualified
To do anything with nothing.
(The impossible takes a little longer)

The First Age
A Tale of Three Families

A Way of Life Shattered by the Advent of War

The jerky black and white picture on the screen featured a chubby baby boy crawling across a lawn with a wicked grin on his face. This confirms my only memory of that early period of my life, being in a garden with some adults around me. These were probably my father, the Rev. Leslie Hills, and my mother, Margaret called Peggy. My elder siblings, Margaret and John, could have been there also.

BIRTHS

CUDDIGAN.—On Sept. 2, 1936, to JANET (*née* Redfern), wife of DR. JAMES CUDDIGAN, of New Ollerton, Notts—a son.

DYKES.—On Aug. 25, 1936, at Murree, India, to JOYCE (*née* Todd), wife of CAPT. O. C. T. DYKES, 6th Gurkha Rifles—a daughter.

FARMER.—On Sept. 6, 1936, at 14, Rotherwick Road, Golders Green, to JOYCE, wife of DAVID STAHEL FARMER—a son.

GILROY.—On Sept. 4, 1936, at Elmbank, Woking, to MARGARET, wife of DONALD GILROY—a son.

GODBY.—On Aug. 14, 1936, at Cordoba, Argentina, to JOSEFINA, wife of NOËL VANRENEN GODBY—a daughter.

HAWORTH-BOOTH.—On Sept. 4, 1936, at a nursing home, Salisbury, to MYRTLE (*née* Knight), wife of SQUADRON LEADER R. HAWORTH-BOOTH, R.A.F.—a son.

HILLS.—On Sept. 1, 1936, at the Vicarage, Handen Road, Lee, S.E.12, to MARGARET, wife of the REV. LESLIE HILLS—a son.

Above: Announcement of my birth
Left : Rev. Leslie Hills
Below: The Vicarage 47, Handen Road, Lee

This film suggests something else, that here was a relatively well-off middle class family able to afford an 8mm. cine camera and projection apparatus. This was a world and way of life that would soon be shattered. I, Richard Leslie, was born on 1 September 1936. My birth was registered on 14 September 1936 with Godparents Major General D. Ian Robertson and the Rev. Selwyn.

That I was crawling around points to the film being shot in the spring or early summer of 1937, so before my mother became ill and died of cancer in the West Sussex Hospital, Chichester, aged only 40 on 6 May 1938.

The Second World War would intervene between the shooting and showing of that film which was discovered in a cabinet in the vicarage of the Church of St. Peter and St. Paul at Seal, near Sevenoaks, after my father had set up home again on being demobbed from the army. When war against Germany was declared on 3 September 1939, he offered and was accepted as Chaplain to the armed forces.

He had been born at Maidstone and fought in the First World War in the Royal Field Artillery, being awarded the Military Cross. On cessation of hostilities, he gained a place at Queens' College, Cambridge, where he obtained his Bachelor and then Master of Arts Degrees followed by training for ordination at Ridley Hall, Cambridge. He served a curacy at St. Helens, Lancashire, where he was ordained priest at Liverpool Cathedral. For a time, he worked in the Sudan. Then he was Curate at St. James, Sussex Gardens, where he must have met my mother. Their engagement was announced on 19 February 1930, being married on 10 July 1930 at that church. It was quite a posh affair with the Rt. Rev. Bishop Eden officiating. Father became Vicar of Christ Church, Rotherhithe, moving to the Church of The Good Shepherd, Lee, London, SE12, in 1935. He was one influence in my life and he always hoped that I would be ordained, perhaps in the Victorian tradition

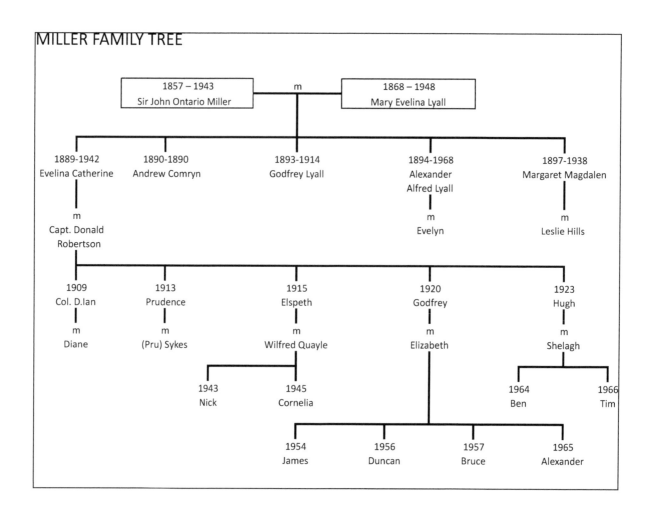

of the eldest son becoming squire inheriting the estate, while a younger son would go into the church.

My mother's parents were Sir John Ontario Miller and Lady Evelena born Lyall. Her father was Sir Alfred Comyn Lyall, 1835 – 1911, who trained at Haileybury for service in the old East India Company. He arrived in India in 1856 shortly before the outbreak of the Indian Mutiny in which he was nearly killed when his horse was shot beneath him. He served in India with distinction in administrative posts such as Home Secretary to the Governor of India, Governor General's agent, Chief Commissioner of Oudh (North West Province) and much more. He founded the University of Allahabad. On retirement to England, he was made a member of the Privy Council in 1902 and also Knight Commander of the Order of the Star of India. But his importance for me lay in his literary output. Amongst other writings, he was noted for his poetry, his Asiatic Studies, but above all for his *Rise of the British Dominion in India*. What I learnt when later I read his works was the importance of the power of the pen which reached so many more people than either lectures or sermons.

Sir John had also served with distinction in the Indian Civil Service holding many administrative offices such as Chief Secretary to the North West Provinces and Oudh. He was involved in the Government of India Revenue Department and became a member of the Viceroy Executive Council of India and Commissioner of Legyrai Province. In 1901, he was made a Knight Commander of the Order of the Star of India. On retirement to England, he became the London County Council representative on the Port of London Authority and a Founder of the London School of Economics in 1895. He married Mary Evelina Lyall in 1888. They had five children, Evelina who died of cancer in 1942, Andrew who died as a baby in India, Godfrey who was killed at the start of the First World War

Peggy on the left and Mrs. Whitefield on the right.
Probably taken in Kashmir.

in the army, my Uncle Alexander or Sandy, 1894 - 1968, who joined the navy in the First World War and was the only one of her children to survive Lady Miller. Last of all came my mother.

My mother was familiarly known as Peggy. While she was born in India, she spent part of her childhood in England and Scotland. In the later part of World War I, she served in the Voluntary Aid Detachment for nursing at Devonshire House. She was in

Boulogne from November 1919 to April 1920. She had wide interests such as poetry in which circles she must have been well-known because authors presented copies of their books to her. Then there was botany. The black tin flower box for collecting specimens mentioned in a letter of July 1927 sadly rusted beyond further use but I still have the tin cases for paint brushes and her small watercolour paint box. She was quite a respectable watercolour artist.

She went to India in 1927. A batch of her letters home from that July to March 1928 has survived. They show her interest in botany as well as the many contacts she had. She spent most of the late summer and autumn of 1927 in Kashmir until well into October through fear of catching malaria in the hotter, lower parts of India. There she enjoyed the outdoor life, walking and camping as well as the colourful array of flowers. She wanted to go to Burma and made her way through India by Rawal Pindi, Dehli, Lucknow, Agra and so to Bombay. She sailed on to Rangoon, visiting Mandalay. In the middle of February, she was at Colombo before coming home through the Suez Canal. In the final letter she had reached Marseilles, presumably arriving home soon after to meet the handsome new Curate, Leslie Hills.

Although I never knew her, I am surprised at so many traits I seem to have inherited from her, her love of the outdoors, walking in the mountains, and interest in botany and drawing. In fact, I seem to have more affinity with the Millers than the Hills. Losing a mother at the age of two must have been some sort of bereavement but I have no recollection of that. Presumably some housekeeper or nanny was engaged. At that time, the Millers were living at 6 Sussex Place, Hyde Park. When I first remember Sir John and Lady Miller, they had retired to live at Robson's Orchard in the village of Lavant, just to the north of Chichester. Sir John died in 1943. This side of the family was always rather romantic, perhaps because we could see them so rarely.

Robson's Orchard

Robson's Orchard lay rather inconveniently alongside the Chichester to Midhurst road. The grounds were extensive enough for two or three properties to be built on it recently. At the end nearest Chichester was the tennis court with a wooden summer house which could be rotated to face the sun, much to our joy. Closer to the house were the vegetable garden, potting shed and greenhouse. The main entrance was here and there was a lawn beside the

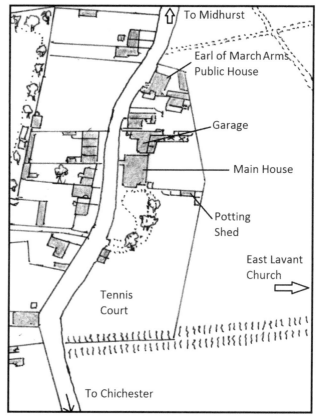

Map of Robson's Orchard

Entrance to Robson's Orchard

Side View of Robson's Orchard

The tennis lawn at the bottom of the garden

house with views that reached down to the little Lavant stream, past East Lavant Church, before rising up to the South Downs and Goodwood Race Course. The garden and house finished in a courtyard with large garage below a couple of empty rooms above – a suitable den for children.

The front door opened into a rather gloomy long passage. Sir John's study was by the front door at the bottom of stairs which we never normally used. The dining room was on the left with high windows so that passers-by could not see in. The drawing room had windows down to ground floor level giving access to the garden. Lady Miller, a rather austere figure, had her own room on the garden side. Communication with the kitchens might be by speaking tube! The back stairs led up to the bedrooms where we children slept, well away from our grandparents.

<u>The Hills Family</u>

War against Germany was declared on 3 September 1939 when I was just three. Father was soon called up. My two elder siblings went to live with Grandpa Henry Hills, and Granny Charlotte Oldacre, at Kingsmead near Matfield, Kent. I was sent to my Aunt Kathleen who lived with her husband, Robert Eve Tomson, at Littlehurst, Tunbridge Wells. The Hills family consisted of Kathleen, Leslie, Olive or Poll, Stanley, Freda or Bee, Muriel, and Ruth. This outlines the people involved in my three families as they were at the beginning of the Second World War.

Grandpa Hills had risen up from being office boy to chairman of Fremlin's Brewery in Maidstone whose motto was, 'Take a little elephant home with you'. Kingsmead was a

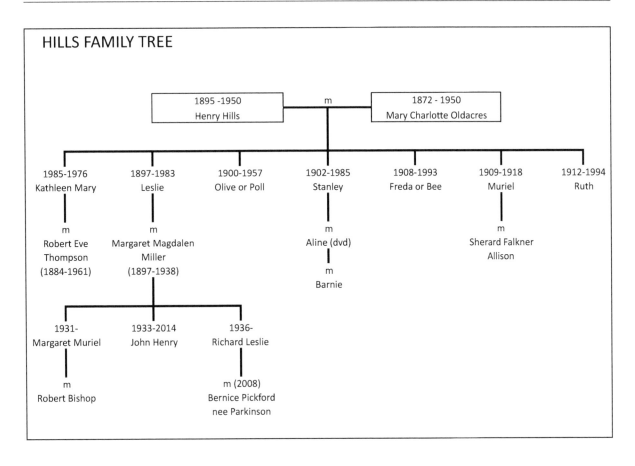

HILLS FAMILY TREE

| 1895 -1950 Henry Hills | m | 1872 - 1950 Mary Charlotte Oldacres |

- 1985-1976 Kathleen Mary — m — Robert Eve Thompson (1884-1961)
- 1897-1983 Leslie — m — Margaret Magdalen Miller (1897-1938)
- 1900-1957 Olive or Poll
- 1902-1985 Stanley — m — Aline (dvd) — m — Barnie
- 1908-1993 Freda or Bee
- 1909-1918 Muriel — m — Sherard Falkner Allison
- 1912-1994 Ruth

- 1931- Margaret Muriel — m — Robert Bishop
- 1933-2014 John Henry
- 1936- Richard Leslie — m (2008) — Bernice Pickford nee Parkinson

Grandpa Henry Hills

Margaret left and Granny Charlotte Hills

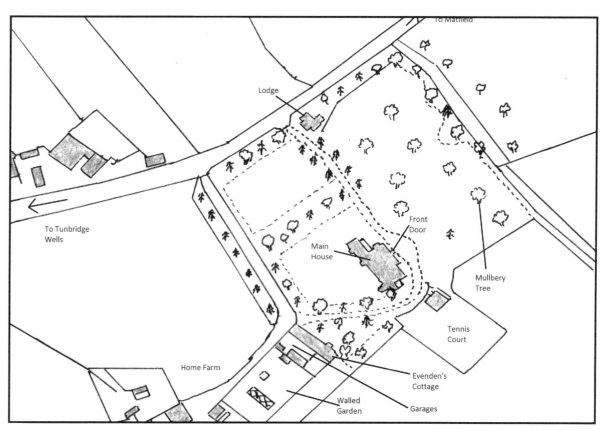

Map of Kingsmead

The drive to the main house

The entrance lodge

View of front of house

late Victorian small country estate, appropriate for the chairman of an important local company. The grounds were entered past the lodge where one of the two gardeners lived.

The rear with the garden

The drawing room

The oak room

At the end of the avenue of sequoiadendron giganteum came the house. Tennis court, stable block, walled vegetable garden and home farm lay beyond. Kingsmead was noted for its fine trees and herbaceous borders. It was kept well supplied with fruit and vegetables and produce from the garden and farm where there were chickens, cows, horses and an Old English sheepdog. Inside the house, Grandpa's study was on the left, the dining room to the right and the main drawing room straight ahead. To the right was a later addition of a single storey billiard room and conservatory. To the left through doors at the end of the passage were the servants' quarters of pantry, kitchen, etc. The upstairs was similarly divided with the bedrooms corresponding roughly to the rooms on the ground floor.

Evenden with Lillian and Ethel

Auntie Poll in her wheelchair with granny and Auntie Kath.

A chauffeur, Evenden, took care of the motor vehicles in the enclosed stable block. These ranged from an Armstrong Siddley saloon to an Austin Seven Ruby saloon. When petrol rationing was introduced, since the Austin Seven was much more economical than the others, it became Grandma's usual car, driven by Evenden in full blue uniform and cap; perhaps the only chauffeur-driven Austin Seven ever.

It was here that Margaret and John returned from their boarding schools for holidays. Margaret went to St. Swithun's, Winchester. John was evacuated from his school in East Kent to one in Worcestershire where he felt utterly miserable and lonely, cut off from family links. However towards the end of the war, this arrangement ceased and they too came to live at Littlehurst.

This was owing to Aunt Poll's deteriorating health. At first she had difficulty managing stairs even with additional handrails and assistance. Soon she needed a wheelchair. Then her bed was brought downstairs into the drawing room. Our grandparents could no longer cope with growing children and their sick daughter. Aunt Poll survived many years in a nursing home in Tunbridge Wells, whether suffering from Parkinson's or multiple sclerosis

I do not know but she was a warning about what might happen to me when I was diagnosed with Parkinson's many years later.

Littlehurst

I was sent to Auntie Kath at Littlehurst, perhaps because she and Uncle Rob never had children of their own. Little did they know what they were getting. Uncle Rob's family

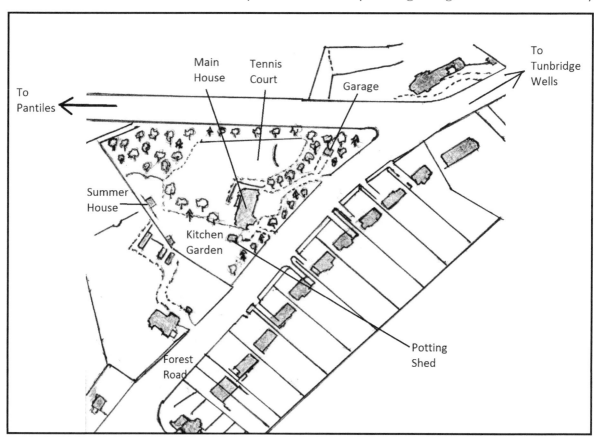

Map of Littlehurst

The rear of Littlehurst from the garden

Auntie Kath

was based at Luton, where he was on the Board and perhaps Chairman of the local gas company. He regularly took the train to London and on to attend meetings. His brother, Maynard, sometimes sent a brace of pheasants he had shot. Once only the label on the necks and heads arrived, the bodies no doubt supplementing some lucky person's meagre meat rations. Uncle Rob was a Scout Commissioner and also an alderman on the Tunbridge Wells Town Council.

Littlehurst was a large Edwardian house set just below Forest Ridge with views to the south over Tunbridge Wells. After entering the hall, straight ahead was the door leading into the patio. To the right was Uncle Rob's study and the much larger drawing room. To the left was a cloak room, a passage to the servants' area and the dining room. The servants' area had a pantry, large kitchen, scullery, larder and sitting room. The accommodation upstairs followed basically the same layout with that room above the kitchen becoming the nursery.

The grounds were much smaller with a 'motor house' down the drive by the front gate. The house looked out over the patio and terrace with rose beds to the large kitchen garden on the left and a herbaceous border stretching down to a summer house overlooking the rockery with its small pond. To the right, obscured by banks of rhododendrons, the ground sloped away to the tennis court, mostly used for croquet, and another rose garden. This side was enclosed by trees growing on the steep slopes that terminated at Warwick Road coming up from the Tunbridge Wells Pantiles. I was used to living in large gardens.

Richard with Uncle Rob on steps below the patio

Tunbridge Wells took its name from the spring in which the water was claimed to have curative powers. The well is still there but I was put off from tasting the water by the noxious smell. There was a tree lined promenade or in wet weather there was the arcade along which the fashionable would stroll in the latter half of the seventeenth century. The Pantiles were called after the fired clay tiles laid down which gave a reasonably clean surface to protect ladies dresses. We used to call this area 'Dust Bins' because at one end was the ladies fashion shop, Dusts, and at the other an excellent cafe, Binns. In between was Judds, the sweet shop, worth a visit if you had any ration coupons or money left. In the tourist shops we admired Tonbridge ware. This was small wooden objects such as snuff boxes ornamented on the outside with coloured slips of wood stuck on in regular patterns or perhaps a picture of a vase of flowers.

Picture of the Pantiles made of Tonbridge Ware

Auntie Bee spotted a rare example of this art in the form of a picture of the Pantiles which she gave to her elder sister and I still treasure. Just across from the Well was the Church of King Charles the Martyr where Uncle Rob and Auntie Kath regularly worshipped in a pew they rented annually, I suppose to support church expenses. It was about a mile down the hill from Littlehurst past the Kent and East Sussex cricket ground.

Growing Up In A War

I have few memories of my very early days at Littlehurst. There was a nanny at first for I slept in a small bed next to her proper bed. A burning nightlight provided some reassurance because its flickerings were fascinating to watch. A little later, I remember Auntie Kath putting me to bed with a cuddle and my playing with her necklace. One was made of red coral. She really became a mother substitute which became a source of friction after father, that strange man in a khaki uniform with Sam Brown belt who appeared occasionally, set up home again at Seal.

Auntie Kath's Armstrong Siddeley, vintage about 1934, was used for visits to Kingsmead. It had pre-selector gear box which made driving easier for her but with interesting results when she had forgotten what gear she was in. She was able to obtain extra petrol coupons to go and look after her elderly parents. Visits to Robson's Orchard were less frequent due to the distance. This involved taking a steam train from Tunbridge Wells West Station to Brighton – a delightful rural line closed in his wisdom by Dr. Beeching – changing to an electric one and getting off at Chichester where at first presumably we were met and taken by car to Robson's Orchard but later we would take the bus. Looking back, I am surprised at the journeys we kids made on our own with no worries. This also applied later when we had bicycles. It was a far safer world then for kids in spite of war. After the war, we frequently made the journey between Littlehurst and Seal with three changes of bus on our own. This period of my life laid foundations which proved useful in so much of my later life. It was learning by observation as well as coping by oneself to solve problems. Resources in the war became stretched so it was often make do and mend or devise some inventive solution. The three houses and gardens themselves provided many resources but first let us think of the effects of war.

Effects of War

All these properties suffered from lack of maintenance during the war years through staff being called up for active service. But this gave greater opportunities for us to become involved. Actual damage through enemy action was minimal. There was the wailing of the sirens to warn about German planes coming. It was spooky going outside at night because there were no street lights and all windows in houses had to have blackout over them. It was once pointed out to Uncle Rob that a light was showing at Littlehurst where a curtain had not been drawn properly. Cars and other vehicles had to have shielded lights so it was dangerous to drive much at night. At Littlehurst, we might be brought down to sleep under the main staircase because that was thought to be the strongest part of the house. We might hear the engines of their bombers and our fighters. There would be the flashing lights of the searchlights seeking the enemy, the noise of the anti-ack-ack guns and sometimes bombs exploding. The all clear siren was eagerly awaited so we could sleep again. After a night raid, we would eagerly search the garden for shrapnel and 'glitter', strips of paper with scraps of metal stuck on and released to upset enemy radar. We might see bomb damage elsewhere where a house had been hit or perhaps a trail of craters across the fields where a German bomber had shed its load to fly quickly home.

Tunbridge Wells lay on one German route to London so during the day we might watch a dog fight between our Spitfires and Hurricanes and German Messerschmitts. Once we saw a Dornier bomber shot down before it reached London. By chance, we happened to see one of our fighters following the first Doodlebugs to be sent over. The British pilot following could not make out what it was as it took no avoiding action but flew straight on. It passed out of our sight still being followed. These were rocket powered pilotless 'flying bombs' which were launched with some fuel towards London. When they ran out of fuel, their noise ceased and they would come down in fifteen seconds and explode. Targets were indiscriminate and so the horror. Attempts were made to protect London with a row of barrage balloons which we were able to count from Littlehurst against the setting sun. As part of his contribution to the war effort, Uncle Rob joined the ARP (Air Raid Precaution) which meant being out at night frequently. War is not pleasant.

Civilian Life

Even without the war, domestic life was so different then with electrical appliances such as fridges and freezers being a rarity. Instead, the larder was on the north side of a house with cold slate shelves. Kitchen food processors, dish washers, washing machines were hardly known. Clothes might be boiled in an electric boiler. The

John on right was very proud of his new tin hat. Uncle Rob in civies at the start of the war

small laundry at Matfield hung out the sheets on the village green. Irons were heated on the gas stove. You spat on it to see if it was hot enough to place in a tin cover before ironing your shirts. Woe betide you if it was too hot and you scorched a white shirt. No television, and radios might need an accumulator that had to be charged up regularly – a job for Evenden. Luckily there were petrol-driven lawn mowers but most garden work such as hedge trimming had to be done by hand.

We were subjected to shortages and rationing. Auntie Kath carefully counted out the 'coupons' in our ration books to see what might be purchased that week. At the grocers, your butter ration was carved from a large block and weighed out for you. The grocer took a sheet of blue sugar paper, twisted it into a cone and filled it with your ration from a large sack. Bacon and dried meats would be sliced on a hand-turned machine that could be set to your desired thickness. For a small boy, it was fascinating to watch the cogs and cranks go round as the slice was peeled off the joint. Biscuits were picked out of large tins and then weighed and wrapped. One tin might contain broken ones at reduced price, a temptation for children.

Sometimes, we might have extra eggs from Kingsmead where a few chickens were kept and their egg ration had been swapped for grain to feed the birds. A few eggs might be preserved for the winter in isinglass, a nasty glutinous substance with dubious results. Of course we were lucky with the kitchen gardens supplementing purchases of vegetables, salads and more particularly soft fruit such as varieties of apples, plums, gooseberries, currants and raspberries. There was a vine at Kingsmead which later suffered from neglect through lack of proper pruning and glass panes bring broken and not replaced. Some fruit was preserved, a rather haphazard operation which involved placing the jars filled with fruit and water in the oven until boiling point had been reached. Then the glass lid with a rubber ring was screwed down with a metal cap, hoping that a proper seal had been made as it cooled. Too often air and bacteria entered so the contents became mouldy. (Freezing is so much easier, quicker and better.) Apples were stored in rows on attic floors while meat might be preserved with salt.

In the midst of all this activity, ordinary life carried on. Breakfast had its own rituals. Lady Miller would enter the dining room, go to the side board where the cooked food was being kept hot and push down the plunger in the coffee percolator. Then we could start eating. At Kingsmead, everybody, staff included, would assemble in the dining room for morning prayers. Granny pushed the floor button at her end of the table and in they came. We knelt at our chairs while Grandpa read a passage of scripture and prayers. Grace was customary at main meals at all houses. On Sunday, attendance at the local church for morning service was observed. This entailed for us younger people a walk along the road (no pavements) to Matfield and back. At Lavant the morning service was usually held in the old East Lavant church where our mother was buried. Another walk, this time over the fields and the cricket pitch, which took us past the Rectory. If you peeped in through the gate, you might be greeted by the hissing and honking of Peter the goose. He was destined for a Christmas dinner but Canon Buckwell did not have the heart to kill him so he survived for many years. I used to watch fascinated as Canon Buckwell preached because he lent right over the edge of the pulpit and I always hoped he might fall out!

Here is the place for a short additional note on Sundays. The domestic staff were allowed one full day off a week and the rest of the day on a Sunday after lunch had been cleared away. They were expected to go to an evening church service. For our evening meal, we adjourned to the kitchen and feasted on bread and dripping. The latter was particularly tasty if it was beef dripping with jelly at the bottom.

Christmas
The tribes would assemble at their respective grandparents for Christmas. Whether we children would go on alternate years to Lavant and Kingsmead I cannot remember. On

the night before Christmas day itself, it was worthwhile hanging a stocking at the end of the bed to encourage Father Christmas. You never knew what you might find because the bedrooms had fireplaces and chimneys. Once when John and I had gone to bed, for we shared a room and should have been asleep, a figure suspiciously like Uncle Rob shrouded in an eiderdown crept in and put some things in our stockings. We of course remained asleep just long enough for the door to shut behind him and...

We celebrated Christmas with traditional lunches. The great cast iron ranges in the kitchens with their large ovens were brought back into use with fires glowing. The pantry would be the scene of hectic activity with the best dinner service being brought out, glasses cleaned and the silver polished. We would have been to church and returned to find a different dining room. That at Robson's Orchard, in spite of only having windows very close to the ceiling through the road outside, was much lighter with its pale green paint compared with the Victorian decoration at Kingsmead. Lady Miller presided. The turkey finished, then came the Christmas pudding, set on fire with some brandy when that was still available at the beginning of the war. Lady Miller thought that Christmas pudding was too rich for young children. (We of course disagreed.) She was also afraid that we might swallow one of the silver three penny pieces concealed in it or worse still one of the charms. She hit upon a brilliant idea. The charms and coins could be put into a jelly where they could be seen and would be safe. But she had not counted on our reactions. The jelly mould was in the shape of a rabbit. On ordinary days, we squabbled enough about who should have the head or who would be relegated to the tail. Now we could see the charms, we all wanted the same one so there was mayhem. Being youngest, I came last to my great chagrin.

After lunch, there would be various card and other games to play before an iced Christmas cake made its appearance together with the silver teapot. In the great billiard room at Kingsmead, the fire was burning brightly with baulks of timber harvested from the surrounding woods. After a time, the soot on the breast of the fireplace would start glowing red. We called this red coat soldiers as they burnt their way across the breast, something not possible with smokeless fuel or gas. The fireplace was set in a large alcove on a low platform which made a good stage for charades or perhaps even a small play. Hide and seek was popular in which certain rooms were declared out of bounds or else the prey might not be found for ages in these large houses. It was surprising in what a small space a child could be concealed.

Learning by Observation

Without realising it, we could be absorbing a lot of knowledge that would prove useful later as we watched the staff at work, played in the gardens, or went out for walks in the adjoining countryside. For example, we learnt the names of trees such as oak, ash, beech and sycamore and their characteristics. At the small pedestrian gate into Littlehurst at the bottom of the garden was a splendid copper beech tree, just right for boys to climb with its smooth bark compared to the rough oak. At first, I had to watch John as I was too small to climb it but later I would cling to a branch and hang over the footpath to scare anyone passing. You treated with respect the hawthorn with its thorns and the holly with its prickles. A hawthorn or privet hedge you could trim with shears but with laurel, you cut off the new shoots with secateurs to avoid cutting the leaves in half so they would die. Particularly memorable was the avenue of immense Wellingtonias leading up the drive to Kingsmead, so aptly named sequoiadendron giganteum, whose soft bark you could punch with impunity. There were the large white flowers of the magnolias or the small ones of the large leafed rare catalpa or Indian bean tree. But you had to be careful when the fruit of the black mulberry ripened not to leave traces of the red juice from its berries from around your lips, or worse still on your clothes, showing what you had been up to.

While Grandpa was tending to his manicured lawn with a jug of poison which he dabbed on weeds, we might be watching a gardener tidy up and weed an herbaceous border. In them was a variety of plants, different sizes, different flowering times, different colours, different heights – all of which knowledge became useful at Seal and later when I set up my own home at Stamford Cottage in Mottram near Manchester. The same applied to the soft fruit. Gooseberries needed regular pruning to produce their best. Red currants flowered best on last year's growth, black currants on this. Last year's raspberry canes were cut down once their fruit had been picked and the new growth tied onto the supporting wires. Testing such fruit to see if it was ripe just had to be done.

The summer house at Littlehurst had some furniture in it including a rug made from a tiger skin with glaring yellow eyes that scared us kids. Outside in the rockery was the pond that was a source of endless fascination. The big floating leaves of the water lily provided refuge for all sorts of creatures. Waterboatmen scurried across the surface. Frogs-spawn could be collected and put into jars to watch for when it hatched into tadpoles. Tadpoles grew into frogs or possibly into newts. When there was sunshine, a lizard might be seen basking on a rock, perhaps minus its tail as it escaped from a predator. But on a really hot summer day, if you approached very quietly, you might be lucky to see a snake slithering away, perhaps a grass snake or more terrifyingly the poisonous adder.

There were various animals to discover, some wild, some domestic. Jack, the Heinz 57 varieties sort of terrier, was the terror of Lavant for he enjoyed a good fight and would come home looking very happy, bleeding, with ears torn. Lady Miller had to placate the owners of his doggy victims. Ferrets were kept at Lavant for catching rabbits which became useful additions to the larder. I had a pet white rabbit at Littlehurst which I am afraid to say was fed more regularly by the kitchen staff than myself. Leaning over the fences bordering our gardens might be horses, sheep and cows asking to be fed. One large pink boar loved to have its back scratched. I never got the hang of sitting on a one legged stool with my head against the cow, trying to milk her. Normally she tried to kick me so I fell off the stool. But I had better luck graduating from tricycle to bicycle. There was very little traffic on the drives around Kingsmead so it was quite safe. Evenden was deputed to walk behind me with a hand on the saddle to keep me upright. Of course I pedalled hard so he had to run. One day, I was aware that the footsteps behind me had ceased, so I looked round to see Evenden a long way behind. I promptly fell off. I was on my own after that, having learnt the sweet taste of independence.

The bicycle reflects a developing interest in science and mechanics. There was Grandpa's weather station where someone took the readings of temperature, rainfall, barometric pressure and 'wet and dry' readings every day. They were forwarded to the Meteorological Office regularly. A reply acknowledged their usefulness even though they could not be entered into the official records through the proximity of trees. I still consult a thermometer, barometer and barograph most days. Meanwhile at Littlehurst, I was exploiting the potential of the nursery. Many of our toys were in store and new ones difficult to purchase so we had to make do and mend. On the floor I made railway layouts with what track we still had. I was puzzled by the trucks coming off a sharp curve especially when I had assembled a special long train. I have retained an interest in railways ever since. The broad nursery window sill with the light streaming in was ideal for taking clocks to pieces and actually reassembling them (sometimes). I had a small model horizontal steam engine, (portent of the future perhaps). I realised that it might develop more power if I screwed down the safety valve. An attempt to cut a Golden Syrup tin in half to make a better one was a failure. Model aeroplanes were constructed from balsa wood spars covered with tissue and doped to waterproof them. I could not afford even a small internal combustion engine so had to make do with winding up

The Grundwell Barometer in my present home at Mottram in Longdendale - to be kept vertical at all times!

elastic bands to turn the propeller. Launched from the top of a suitable bank in the garden, they were too badly constructed to fly any distance. They might have done better if there had been someone around to help me.

Holidays

Auntie Kath and Uncle Rob took us away for holidays in the summer vacation. She would start saving up coupons months before so we would be fed adequately. Their preferred destination was the West Country. The journey would have been a long one in any case but was prolonged due to war-time travel restrictions as we had to cross different zones. Once we stayed overnight at Exeter and looked round the cathedral. We saw the massive organ pipes which it was feared might bring the building down if played. My favourite holidays were at Bude because there was so much 'technology' to see as well as playing on the vast sandy bay. We had to change into the branch line train at Okehampton where the guard checked that each door was properly closed and locked. To open it from inside, the window had to be lowered with its leather strap and you reached out to turn the handle. From the railway station, a short spur for goods trains only led to the canal basin. Our holiday cottage faced the basin on the other side so we had a good view of shunting operations. Here was the blacksmith and we watched him at his forge. A narrow gauge tramway ended here which used to bring sand up from the shore to load it onto standard railway wagons for use as a fertiliser. We would push the small trucks about a bit. An even greater attraction was the canal lock leading out into the sea. It was worth waiting to see a ship pass through particularly in a storm. Then there was the egg packing factory. It had complex rotary machines on which a girl placed one egg at a time into an arm. The machine turned round and tipped off the egg onto an apron at the correct weight for that egg. The egg rolled down the apron to another girl who put it into a box. Surprisingly few eggs were broken (remember it was strict rationing and even broken eggs might have a use). The course of the abandoned canal could be followed into the country. In the other direction, we took our kites onto the cliff top. We found out how to launch them and wrote messages on bits of paper which we would send up the string to the kite. I realised that the tail of my kite was too heavy so I shortened it and it flew better. We must have been to Bude for at least two summers.

Back at Littlehurst, for a short time, the nursery became a sort of kindergarten for a few boys of similar age from neighbouring families. Perhaps these parents felt their offspring would be safer there than chancing being bombed going into the centre of Tunbridge Wells. We had a lady teacher who came, I think, only in the mornings. There were no girls because, as far as I can remember, these families had none. Margaret later appeared much more in the holidays but her friends would be five years older than me which at this

The members of the kindergarten with Richard in the middle

sort of age would be difficult to bridge. She and John were much closer than I and John. I doubt whether he relished the presence of a small younger brother. When he and Margaret squabbled, I soon realised that I should beat a hasty retreat. It was best to observe quietly rather than stoke the fires. All this does suggest that perhaps the large houses and estates in which I first grew up were rather isolated from a wide range of human contacts. Soon the little prince of this fiefdom would be sent out into the wild.

The three siblings with Richard on the left

The Second Age
School Days

Part 1 – Rose Hill School, Tunbridge Wells

Rose Hill School

My first 'magnum opus'

It was most likely in the autumn of 1943 when I was seven that I left the secure boundaries of Littlehurst for Rose Hill School in the centre of Tunbridge Wells as a day boy. It was possible to walk over the fields, preferably by way of the railway bridge on which you could look over the parapet and feel the blast from the steam engine as it flogged its way up to the tunnel through Forest Ridge. The more usual way was to catch the bus from the near-by stop and take it to the Town Hall. A short walk passed the Ritz Cinema and then downhill along Church Road into the back gate of the school. To return home, I would again walk downhill through Lonsdale Gardens to another bus stop outside the Central Station. I was puzzled for a long time why railway buffers should be put in the building called 'Buffer Store' on top of the railway tunnel.

The four-storey school building was set back into the hill. The rarely-used front door was at the bottom with the headmaster's study and one classroom. The more usual entrance for boys was at the rear on the first floor. Here in the old building was the washroom and toilets leading into the changing room. The teachers' room and a small study together with perhaps three more classrooms were at this level. A staircase led down to the kitchen and dining room and up, past another classroom, to the dormitories and matron's surgery. It was all higgledy-piggery. The boarders at least had to be able to use the method of Davey fire escape since there was only one flight of stairs. A fire-proof rope (no doubt covered with asbestos) with a body harness at each end passed through a speed-governing mechanism fixed by a window. On hearing the fire alarm, you put on the harness at the short end of the rope, threw the longer end out of the window to be followed by yourself. You sort of abseiled down as the other end went up to be grabbed by the next boy. Looking out of that top storey window was terrifying. I dread to think what might have happened in a real fire. The school buildings were completed with a much later single storey extension consisting of the gym and two more classrooms.

The wooden ship, 'Scouter'

Rose Hill School had been started in the middle of the nineteenth century. When I went, it had a good reputation under the then head, Mr. Johnson. His was the first close death I knowingly experienced with the consequent bereavement traumas. I do not know whether he was responsible for the school's most noted feature, the S.S. Scouter. This was a full-size mock ship built of wood in the school grounds, complete with central cabin, funnel, bridge, masts, etc. The stern was open, giving access between decks. Lack of maintenance in the war took its toll so it had to be demolished while I was there. In summer evenings, boarders were allowed to play on the grass surrounding it, out of sight from the main house. There were frequent trials of strength. Jones Major learnt how to do the scissors grip with his legs which could be very painful and difficult to escape.

On the starboard side, Scouter was fenced off from a path that continued round the stern. When I first arrived, I was puzzled by boys playing on the far side. I soon found that this path went by the Carpentry Shop where for an additional fee you could learn woodworking skills which I regret we could not afford. Next came the bike shed, a dry retreat from prying eyes of teachers, and then round to a seat at the top of steps leading to the front gate and so to the Common. The seat became our bus terminal. We cut a rectangular window in a small box, inserted two rollers made from pencils top and bottom, round which you stuck the ends of a long length of paper. On this you wrote your destinations and exposed one through the rectangular hole. You set off on your journey proudly showing your destination to the usual entrance by the gym. There was the temptation to have a race round the garden if your competitor had the same destination as you.

The school day started with assembly in the gym for a prayer and sometimes a hymn. Then we dispersed to our classrooms for the three 'Rs', reading, writing and arithmetic. These were taught through Latin, French, history, geography and scripture. For Latin, we followed the suitably annotated 'First Steps in Eating'. Each desk had an inkwell because we had only dip pens, no biros, and fountain pens were an expensive luxury. I carved the face of a rubber into a pattern, spilt a little ink on the desk and proceeded to further embellish the text book. Mr. Grange, then headmaster, did not appreciate my artistic endeavour with the inevitable result. My house was Baden Powell. We were split into 'houses', Baden Powell, McKinnon, etc, to compete in our various activities. In the sixth form, you could earn extra points for your house through adding up 'tots'. These were long columns of pounds, shillings and pence which you 'totted' up between the end of assembly and the start of the lesson. You became adept at converting pennies into shillings, etc., much more interesting than decimal coinage. Of course other imperial measures added more complexity and confusion to our mathematics lessons but later, when immersed in historical research, I was glad of this background. There was also homework to be done after school which, if a day boy, had to be carried to and from home where there were of course lots of counter attractions but Auntie Kath saw that I did mine. Spelling was never my strong point, even today.

From a fairly sheltered existence, it was a shock to be set loose among many much larger boys used to a communal routine. Also when later I became a boarder I felt very abandoned – another sort of bereavement. I and another boy cried our hearts out in the washroom and in our beds at night. I suffered considerable embarrassment when publicly changing into sports gear because we were allocated a locker either in a block or along a wall in full view. It was the same at night when I had to sleep in a dormitory. This was not helped when towards the end of my time at Rose Hill I was taken to the Kent and Sussex Hospital in Tunbridge Wells for an operation on an undescended testis. The scar remained for a long time and I was left wondering what effect it would have later in life. Swimming was another source of embarrassment partly through this operation. The civic baths in Tunbridge Wells where we were taken occasionally were very cold, as was the open air pool at Pembury. At Charterhouse, the pool was down the hill on the far side of the school where nude swimming was the norm so again not very encouraging for me. I wished later that I had become a better swimmer.

I was never any good at ball games. Somehow foot or bat never connected properly with the ball. Bowling at cricket was even worse for I never could throw a ball any distance either so I was normally a fielder in games on the Common. We would be taken to the Kent and East Sussex Cricket Ground to watch these teams play. More interesting was the little printing press underneath one of the stands which printed score cards that had to be kept up to date whenever a wicket fell. We might be permitted to take the latest ones for sale round the ground. My cricketing career progressed to scorer which, while it meant I had to watch the game, it also meant that I went to other schools with our team. It was from the Tunbridge Wells ground that I learnt about the different speeds of sound and light. You could stand high on the top of Forest Ridge, see the batsman hit the ball, but the sound of the impact would follow later.

Boarding School

When I became a boarder, I was more involved with part-time activities at school. After 'prep' had finished, there might be something like the postage stamp club with a visiting speaker or we might turn to model making supervised by Mr. Vaughan, one of the masters, who was setting up an 'OO' gauge railway layout in the cabin of Scouter. There were two different electrical systems, one AC by Trix and the other DC by Hornby. Starting and speed control were simpler with Hornby but, with the more exciting Trix, two locomotives could be run on the same piece of track. To make our models more realistic, we added houses, stations and even rolling stock.

My first certificate

I enjoyed model making and won a small competition by turning the circular metal clip off a paste jar into a waterwheel for a mill. Also I was awarded some certificates for drawing by the Royal Drawing Society. In summer evenings, we might tend to our gardens employing my gardening knowledge. As part of geography, I made a sort of model of a spring of water, showing how rain quickly soaked through chalk but was retained by clay. I lined an enamel pie dish with clay, put a lump of chalk at one end and covered the whole with a thin layer of soil. Grass seed sprouted quickly on the clay part but hardly on the chalk. This revealed where there would have been springs.

On Guy Fawkes night, there would be a bonfire in the yard by the dining room. Perhaps it was lucky that we boys were kept out of harm's way by observing through the windows. We each contributed a few fireworks. One year, Auntie Kath bought me a special box of mixed fireworks. It was placed open by the garage. Unfortunately, a spinning Catherine wheel came adrift and flew straight into her box. Rockets, Roman candles, and other fireworks shot everywhere, spectacular but not what was intended.

On Sunday mornings, we were marched in a crocodile over the Common to the church of King Charles the Martyr. The school sat in the gallery where we could closely observe the extraordinary plaster ceiling with its moustached angel. Also we could watch the organist playing and sometimes were allowed to sit with him. One Sunday after church, we were permitted to wander round a fair set up on the Common. There was a magnificent showman's traction engine with resplendent paintwork and polished brass. It was gently chuffing away, generating electricity. I must confess I found the engine more interesting than the sermon. On Sunday evenings, when we were ready for bed, we would take our blanket (we all had to provide one) down to the large class room and sit in a semicircle in front of the roaring fire. Mr. Grange would read a section of a book to us, perhaps 'King Solomon's Mines'. He would finish at a dramatic point, such as where Gagoole, the old witchdoctor, was about to conduct some nefarious deed, leaving us in suspense for the rest of the week.

Tunbridge Wells Common

The Common might be considered as a sort of park or recreation ground almost in the centre of the town. Rose Hill faced onto it and it was easily reached by going out of the front gate, crossing a service road, some rough grass and a main road. One November I was looking out of a window and saw some veteran cars returning from the Brighton Run going past. I was fascinated by them, shades of what I was to obtain later. Beyond this road was open country with more grass including a football pitch and a cricket pitch you could play on, bushes and thickets you could hide in, paths along which you could lay trails and above all, sandstone rocks you could climb. It was a paradise for all sorts of outdoor activities. Someone found an abandoned nest of a long tailed tit in a gorse bush which we admired for its delicate construction. There were other birds to watch and I am sure I heard a nightingale at night.

Scouting

The Common provided excellent resources for the activities of Rose Hill Wolf Cub Pack and Sea Scout Troop. Lord Baden Powell himself had been a pupil at the school. I expect I was enrolled in the Wolf Cub Pack as soon I was sent to Rose Hill. I soon became a leader of my 'Six'. We learnt how to bandage each other with triangular bandages and other First Aid which was useful when later I became a Mountainwalking Leader. We set trails for others to follow and much more. I still know how to tie a reef knot and a sheep shank. Bowlines were the main knot used later for tying onto the climbing rope. Lashing poles together is resorted to in my present garden. The Sixes took turns to raise and unfurl the Union Jack at the beginning of each meeting which was held in the Gym. Fold and tie the flag too tightly and it might not open while tied too loosely it might unfurl as it was being hoisted. Worse still was when you had raised it upside down so that you lost points. One badge I was awarded was fire lighting with only two matches. I was allocated the fireplace in the headmaster's study. The grate was cleaned, paper found, twigs and sticks broken or cut to size and a fire laid. Would a ten year old boy or girl be allowed to use axe and matches these days? If the fire showed signs of going out, you could stretch a sheet of paper across the front of the fireplace to create a strong draught and divert the air through the fire and up the chimney. You would soon have a blazing fire but you had to watch the paper that it did not suddenly burst into flames as well.

The little prince in his Wolf Cub Pack started at the bottom again when he had to move up to a Sea Scout Watch. The sea was a long way off but in the summer we might be taken to the River Medway at Tonbridge to learn how to row in ordinary boats without sliding seats. One fine weekend, we set off in Scouter on a training voyage. Mr. Grange was Captain and Mr. Vaughan First Mate. The crew of Sea Scouts cleared away some of the trains in the cabin to make space for cooking equipment, food, bedding and so on while charts and navigation instruments were taken up to the bridge. We were split into two watches and kept regular hours with the necessary bells being rung to mark the changes. We had to plot our course and steer with the ship's wheel and give the necessary instructions to the engine room on the telegraph system. Various problems arose during the night with weather deteriorating, other ships in our way and so on. We had to cook our meals on Primus stoves. These had to be filled with paraffin and preheated with methylated spirits. This was liable to overflow the little container and spread flames everywhere. When you thought you had heated the main burner enough, you pressurised the main body containing the paraffin. If it was hot enough, the paraffin vaporised and burnt with a hissing sound. If too cold, hot liquid paraffin spurted everywhere and might catch fire. In workshops, we had blowlamps that worked on the same principle and smaller variants for mountain tents. (Health and safety – modern stoves with gas canisters are so much safer and better.) One boy cooking his breakfast on a Primus cracked his egg on the frying pan only to see it fall outside onto the ground. There were no replacements so he went hungry. Otherwise we survived our voyage successfully and managed to make port.

Positions of Leadership

Back in the dormitory, I was soon selected to be in charge of that room. There were inevitably those who would continue to chatter and not go to sleep or in other ways try to torment me. Sometimes matron had to be fetched to quieten them. Baths were taken on a rota with other boys, feet being washed in the water just vacated by the bather – economical in time of war but perhaps not hygienic. When I became head boy of the school I had the privilege of a separate single room. Amongst other duties was seeing that the later extension of gym and two classrooms had been securely locked up for the night. Mostly this had to be done in the dark. You had to start from the washroom, enter the gym probably inky black with no lights. The light switches were at the far end at the entrance to the first classroom. Your eerie patrol had to be repeated, checking doors and windows were shut to the next set of lights for the second classroom where the entrance door from the garden was at the far end. The great interest in this room, which made it sinister at night, was the collection of African memorabilia of spears, shields and masks probably donated to his old school by Lord Baden Powell. I was always glad when I had returned to the main part of the school and hung the keys up in the headmaster's office. Rose Hill was the first time when I was put in positions of leadership. This would happen in so many different ways for the rest of my life and I have often wondered what those in authority saw in me. But for the next stage in my life, the prince would lose his little fiefdom and move to be bottom again of a much larger one, Charterhouse School.

Seal Near Sevenoaks, Kent

While I was at Rose Hill School, the fortunes of the family changed through father accepting the living of St. Peter and St. Paul at Seal, Sevenoaks, Kent, and soon marrying Audrey Mann.

Audrey Mann, 1904 – 2003

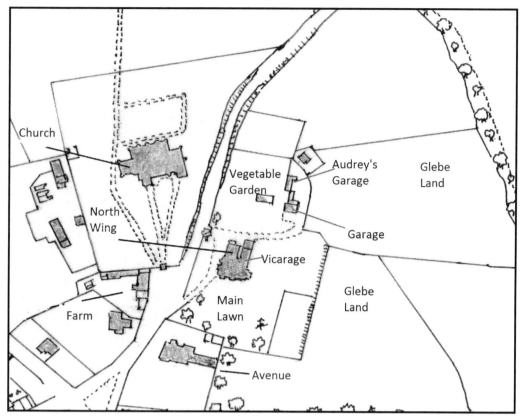

Map of Seal

This parish had been carved out from one of the ancient strips of land that lay side by side from the North Downs to the Weald. It originally began at Kemsing at the foot of the chalk Downs but Seal parish started midway across the valley at the headwaters of the River Darenth.

Seal Church viewed from the south, on a 1953 painting

Seal Church viewed from the north

It faced north across fields where the greensand ridge emerges. The quiet of this rural valley is now blasted by the roar of traffic on the M26 motorway. The A25 ran through the village from east to west where it met the road from Kemsing in the village centre. The village had many shops such as the sweet shop of Mrs. Morgan who sang in the church choir on Sunday evenings. The bread shop was up the A25 towards Maidstone with the garage father used opposite. I say up because Seal lay at the foot of a steep hill down which lorries sometimes came too fast and crashed into a building at the bottom. In the centre of the village was a cabinet maker, the telephone exchange, a general store, an inn, another garage, the blacksmith, a butcher, the village hall and the volunteer fire station. The village was a self-contained community with frequent bus services to Sevenoaks and elsewhere. I gather few of these amenities remain now. Moving south, you crossed the golf course which was part of the Wilderness estate with its up-market houses for London commuters. The large house later became a school for the blind. Just before entering the small hamlet of Godden Green, you passed a house used as a holiday home for members of the Time and Talents Club in Bermondsey. By the Green were riding stables and another pub. Continuing south would take you to the top of the wooded escarpment overlooking the Weald.

The Vicarage

The vicarage faced west on the opposite side of the road to Kemsing from the church. The road dropped steeply down through a cutting with stone walls which gave us a good vantage point to watch the traffic. The eighteenth century house was originally weather-boarded on a timber frame. While most of the weather-boarding had been removed, the wood-worm that remained found our furniture delicious. The front was clad with a rare type of yellow tiles from Chevening. These were brick-shaped facing tiles, pointed between each to look like a brick wall. They were scarce and very difficult to replace. To the right of the front door was the dining room with a window that had been blocked up because a large bay

The vicarage viewed from the church tower

window had been added at the side looking out on a lawn. The vicarage had no central heating but in cold weather we were allowed to light a paraffin stove in this room half an hour before mealtimes. John had the room above with similar windows. Behind the dining room was one we children had for ourselves until father remarried when we had to vacate it for Audrey and move up to an attic.

To the left of the front door (which incidentally had only one key) was the study with Margaret's room above and, beyond, the main stairs and passages to the kitchen and servants' rooms. Below the three main rooms were large cellars for storing food. In the far corner of one was the single electrical fuse for the whole house. The building had been modernised in the early 1920s for lighting only with no power circuits. When a light went out in the evening, you first opened the wooden shutters in the study (they kept in the warmth more efficiently than double glazing) to see if the village was in darkness. If so, it was a power cut and you lit candles. If the lights were on, you took your torch or candle with you into the cellar to repair the fuse. Wisely the servants had left gas lighting in the kitchen where we joined them in power cuts. A Courtier slow-burning coke stove heated the study.

The vicarage seen from the road, with the north wing to the left

A north wing had been added to the left of the front door consisting of two rooms up and down. At the far end of the upper floor was a toilet where the pipes always froze with any frost. In the furthest corner in the adjoining room was the bath. The boiler was way off in the kitchen so hot water from it never reached so remote a spot, and the room was bitterly cold as well. If you wanted a hot bath, you took a couple of jugs or kettles full of boiling water with you and did not stay long. Father later had this wing converted into a separate residence perhaps for a retired clergyman who might help in the parish. Our bedrooms had no heating so you took a hot water bottle to bed. Only when you were very ill might a fire be lit. One advantage was seeing the delicate frost patterns on the windows which is impossible with double glazing.

A large drawing room had been added to the rear. It looked out east towards what had once been a tennis court and the glebe land beyond. It had three large drop-sash windows, one with a low sill. All sorts of meetings and parties were held in it. One summer afternoon, the tea trolley was left there with a large chocolate cake ready for the guests while the meeting was held on the lawn opposite the dining room. Audrey's elderly cocker spaniel, Wendy, appeared looking rather pleased and contented, perhaps a little drowsy. When the guests adjourned to the drawing room for tea, the cake had disappeared. Wendy had climbed in and out of the window. Should you want a fire in the winter, that was easy. You went into the glebe land, dragged home a few branches and cut them up with saw and axe. I discovered it was possible to use the large two-man saw by myself if you kept the far end running down-hill. Half an hour's hard work was usually sufficient for a fire in an evening if the wood had been already dragged in from the field. Father and Audrey's bedroom was over this drawing room on the first floor which you approached by a short flight of stairs. My room had a narrow flight of steps and through a door into their bedroom (useful as a bookcase) or through the opposite wall by a door into John's room. Presumably these allowed the chamber maid to bring water and other necessities into these rooms unobserved. Shut off by a door were the domestics' stairs down to the staff areas and up to three attic rooms for the staff. While the stairs for the master of the house were broad and shallow, those up to the attics were steep, twisting and narrow which made it difficult to carry heavy pieces of engines up to the attic where I made a workshop. There I mounted an old metal-turning lathe which I had been given on a chest of drawers. I arranged for it to be driven by an electric fridge motor. I turned up a steel pulley to fit on the motor which drove a large aluminium disc round the circumference of which I turned a groove for a belt. This was fixed on the end of the countershaft for which I turned a three-stepped pulley to match that on the lathe. This arrangement worked very well and was very useful. At the top of the stairs, a door opened onto flat roofs, ideal places for the young to sunbathe.

The Grounds

Looking across the lawn to the vicarage

The grounds consisted of a large area around the house with lawns, orchards and kitchen gardens together with about three acres of open grass glebe. The previous incumbent had concentrated his pastoral activities more on his herd of bullocks than on his human flock so the gardens were seriously neglected. This was quite a change from the previous three which had full-time gardeners. Father and the one day a week gardener, Godden, struggled to maintain what they could. My gardening skills were stretched to their utmost but it was frustrating to see, after a lot of effort, our hard work reverting to nature again while I was away at boarding school. Godden would arrive with a sack over his shoulder that had suspicious lumps in it. He would appear at the back door; 'Mrs. So and So has a glut of lettuces so I thought you could do with one rather than throw them away'. The sack returned to his home later that day with different lumps in it. We didn't enquire into the ethics of this sort of bartering.

To approach the front door of the house, you drove up the curving drive with a lawn on your left and an overgrown holly hedge on the right under some tall acacia trees. You could carry on, turn left and descend back to the main road at the back gate where two large horse chestnut trees stood sentinel. Turn right, you passed the back entrance to the coal shed and kitchen. Further on, you came to the coach house and stable for two horses. The coach house became father's garage. The stable was Godden's lair with the garden tools. There were still objects left from the coaching days such as harness and lamps which I renovated for the front porch of the house. A track past the garage led to corrugated iron structures for the wood store, a semi-derelict shack, the cattle shed and hen coop. Out in the open was a rather fine four-wheeled farmer's hay wagon which sadly gradually rotted away so it became unsafe for us to play on.

There was a large lawn on the south side of the house which continued on the east with rose beds in it. Slashing back the drive holly bush revealed a path which continued round the south side of the lawn. The rockery in the corner contained a pond full of leaves and sludge. When cleared out, the concrete lining had cracked so it would not hold water. A kind parishioner had donated an avenue of lime trees along which the priest could promenade, meditating on his sermon. Our thoughts when clearing up the autumn leaves were not sermon material. However the limes provided suitable sticks for supporting peas and other plants. In the paddock here were mature fruit trees. We learnt how to recognise the early ripening Red Worcester which did not keep well and the small Cox's Orange Pipin which might last until March. The large green Bramleys were excellent cooking apples and could be an additional source of pocket money if three large similar ones could be entered into the autumn village show and won first prize. I was able to grow some mistletoe on one tree. The orchard was separated from what had been the tennis court by a fence smothered in blackberry brambles – the fruit being very tasty when cooked with those Bramleys. Between the lawn and this orchard was a magnificent mature Cedar of Lebanon. Storms blew off some of its spreading branches which burnt with an aromatic smell on our fires.

It was father who normally mowed the front and back lawns with a heavy cylinder type motor mower. He brought back after a trip to Switzerland a light scythe, on which I learnt a little of the skill so that I used one on the Welsh Highland Railway into the twenty first century. While I avoided cutting my feet, or anyone else's, with the scythe, I luckily avoided badly gouging a big toe with a fly-mow. Good leather shoes saved the day. However there was a sequel because while on a family holiday at Brightlingsea, I had an allergic reaction to the penicillin the hospital had pumped into me and nearly fell out of

Using a scythe at Dinas on the Welsh Highland Railway

the bathroom window in the middle of the night. The sound of the falling glass woke the others who may have been relieved that it was only me and not a burglar.

Between the lawn and the drive to the garage lay the herbaceous borders. A helping hand to keep them tidy was always welcome. The upper path to the garage circumnavigated a large holly which, to our surprise when cut back, revealed a garden seat. Near here was a tap and old bath used as a cattle drinking trough. The former filled our watering cans for the garden while the latter filled whatever livestock was grazing on the glebe. It also provided a useful meeting point for man and beast but you had to watch out for the cleggs or horseflies with their vicious bites.

Our neighbours were generally black and white Friesian heifers belonging to the farmer across the road from the vicarage. They were growing up where he could keep an eye on them. They were very friendly and inquisitive, sniffing and licking us. We had to learn the different ways of feeding a cow and a horse or fingers would be nipped. One horse became a long-term resident. Some gipsies could not pay a debt so the farmer took Peter, a massive cart horse, instead. Peter had never been broken in so was useless for hauling any cart, let alone the heavy ones full of harvest produce, to the farmer's annoyance. But he did not have the heart to dispose of Peter, in spite of Peter falling into the cess pit and having to be hauled out, a smelly operation. Peter would break out of most fields but was quite happy in our glebe, perhaps because we fed him apples. If he saw us at the garage, he would come thundering over for his titbit. I was relieved there was a strong gate between us. Equally he would come charging to us if he saw us in another part of the glebe, mane flying, hooves clumping. It was not so funny when there was no fence between you and him (he was so strong that a fence would have given little protection).

Beyond the drive was the large kitchen garden with the greenhouse. For water you could manually operate a cast iron pump. Asparagus was one treat to furnish our plates in the Easter holidays. Rhubarb, raspberries, red and black currants, bushes of gooseberries, provided soft fruit while among the apple and pear trees were a yellow and Victoria plum. I have missed these now living in the Manchester area. This garden had been extended into the glebe with more fruit trees. Other than picking the fruit, we did not try to cultivate this further part and it became the garden for the tenants of the north wing.

The glebe consisted of about three acres in two fields. There was a row of trees at the southern highest end and hedges and a copse along the east. A valley opened out towards the north where there was a gate into the Kemsing road. In the winter snow, this valley became full of village people and their sledges. We inherited from Kingsmead a heavy toboggan built by Uncle Stan with two sets of runners, the front one pivoting. Ideally a regular covering of snow had fallen sufficient to smooth out the grass. The sun would have melted the top layer. A sharp frost would follow at night leaving an icy surface. Set off at the top of the valley and you would shoot down the hill, steer through the gate in the fence, out into the second field and as far across that as your momentum would carry you. But you had to drag that heavy sledge all the way back up.

The glebe always remained pasture. It was a source of dung for the garden, wood for the fires, large horse mushrooms and blackberries for cooking, rabbits and woodpigeons for the pot. Father had a double-barrelled shot gun which I came across in the attic with some cartridges. When old enough, I would go out in the evening when the rabbits came out to eat the lush grass in the bottom of the valley. I would carefully work my way round by the top of the field to the bramble bushes at the bottom where I would lie in wait until a rabbit came within range. Audrey taught me how to skin a rabbit without bursting the guts (a dreadful mess) and pluck a woodpigeon or other birds. Susie, Wendy's successor, quickly associated gun with rabbit and howled with disappointment when she was not allowed to accompany me. One day I risked taking her. All went well and we waited at the bottom behind the brambles. A rabbit came near enough. I fired. I am sure she would have overtaken the pellets from the gun, such was the speed at which she fled back up the hill. My shooting days might have ended when I returned to school having forgotten to clean the gun. Father was so angry that Audrey escaped to the pub for lunch.

Outside the Home

While all these gardens could have kept us well and truly occupied in playing and helping, they were all situated beside or near to open country filled with further learning potential. Walking in the lanes close to Littlehurst or Kingsmead was much safer than it would be today because there were few cars on the road due to petrol rationing and they were much slower. There were lanes that you could follow between our two houses and watch gipsies making clothes pegs or little baskets for the primroses they had dug up to sell. At Kingsmead we saw hops being dried in an oast house. The hops were spread out on hessian trays through which the heat from the fire below would be drawn up by the draught caused by the tall conical 'chimney'. The fire was charcoal which did not pollute the hops like smoke from coal. When dry, the hops were compressed into the 'pocket', a long thin sack, for transport to the London market. From Littlehurst, we might catch a bus to Frant and walk over Ashdown Forest, a stretch of open moorland. While we might have a map, we did not have all the equipment such as emergency First Aid which we would carry today.

The country at Lavant was very different. We followed the Lavant stream up its valley towards its source near Midhurst. The railway line to Lavant station was on the far side, giving the additional bonus of watching an engine shunting goods wagons. I could not understand why there were passenger trains at Chichester where our line started and passenger trains at Midhurst where it ended but none at Lavant. Later the line was totally closed after a locomotive fell into a collapsed culvert and embankment. We might be taken up to see the empty stands of Goodwood Racecourse where we would wander freely over the short downland turf, pretending to be horses. A little further away was the brick tower of the disused Halnaker windmill with its fascinating mechanisms. It has since been restored. Perhaps the highlight of our visits here was catching the double-decker bus to the sea at the Witterings. Front seats on the upper deck were most sought after but it was a bit terrifying climbing the staircase which was open at the rear. Only if it was high tide might we be able to paddle in the sea because scaffolding and barbed wire had been erected there as at many other costal places to prevent a German invasion. Little did I think that I would be teaching here one day.

Of course Robson's Orchard was sold in 1948 when Lady Miller died. Sandy and Evelyn moved to a cottage on Hayling Island. To get there, we had to change trains at Havant onto the Hayling Island branch. We might be lucky to see our connection for the Island drawing into the bay platform. The engine, an elderly little Brighton Terrier, would be

An imaginative painting of the Hayling Island 'Terrier' tank engine

uncoupled and shunt round to the other end of the single carriage. I had my first footplate ride on one of these engines.

We pulled out of Havant, round the curve down to the level crossing beyond which were the two bridges onto the island, one for rail and the other for road, both owned by the railway. The railway charged a toll on the road bridge which, later when petrol rationing had ceased, might cause the trains to stop through the long queue of cars on a summer weekend waiting to pay their due and blocking the level crossing. Both bridges were constructed of wood which gradually deteriorated so that severe weight restrictions were imposed necessitating the use of these delightful little Terrier engines. Bus passengers were turned off and had to walk over. I always received a warm welcome from Sandy and Evelyn as well as from their golden Labrador, 'Gelert', who was pleased to see someone who would take him for walks on the salt marshes. We looked towards the mainland at some weird box-like concrete structures moored in the creeks. Their sudden disappearance coincided with the D day landings and later we realised that we had been looking at sections of the Mulberry harbour. This charming line was closed later, perhaps due to old age on the part of the Terriers.

The area around Seal village was completely new territory to us so we explored it on foot and on bike. For example, we would walk across the golf links to Godden Green past the manual telephone exchange. If he had a crucial meeting or knew he would be out, father asked the operator not to put any calls through. In addition, if the operator saw father driving past in his car, she might suggest that the caller tried later – a useful service but I suspect that calls were 'tapped'. Provided that we did not interfere with the golfers, we could walk on the grass and not the tarmac of the road.

At Godden Green were riding stables. Lady Miller thought young gentlemen should be able to ride a horse so she supported our lessons financially. We had to inspect our allocated pony for any injuries. Its shoes might have become loose so you picked up a hoof. The pony quickly recognised a novice and would put its full weight on that leg. Or, when saddling up, it would inflate its tummy. You would be sure you had tightened the girths but when you had mounted, the pony would relax so the saddle became loose and might rotate and you fell off. When sitting on the horse, you seemed very exposed with little to hang onto except the mane. The steering mechanism did not always point you in the right direction while the brake was quite useless. I did learn how to jog and gallop but the money probably ran out before I could master jumping.

Sometimes we went into the woods beyond Godden Green and saw the charcoal burners with their blackened faces. Our more usual destination was the Time and Talents holiday home cottage where we met people with a very different social background to us. Father did seem to spend more time there than on some of his other pastoral visits. In my innocence, it came as a shock to be told when I was at school, that he had married the manageress. Audrey Mann and father married on 7 June 1949.

Her father had been one of the founders of the coach-building firm of Mann Edgerton in Norwich. Her widowed mother still lived at 126 Newmarket Road, Norwich, a semi-detached house which we got to know quite well. During the war, Audrey had worked in the Land Army as well as in the Time and Talents Club in Bermondsey in the East End of London before moving to Godden Green. She replaced Miss Gorham, father's housekeeper, and certainly livened up the cooking.

Audrey and Father

Wendy, her cocker spaniel, came with her. This was the first time we had any pet living in the house with us, and we knew she was there especially when in the kitchen at night she would try to catch a mouse, upsetting all the pots and pans etc. Audrey was a great help to father in the parish, organising many meetings, Sunday school and the like. I got on well with her and welcomed the youth parties which she instigated so that for the first time I really met girls. This meant learning how to dance when the carpet would be rolled back in the drawing room to clear a space. I preferred country or Scottish dancing to waltzes, perhaps through my Miller ancestry. The more practical Audrey was a very different mother from the ultra neat and tidy Auntie Kath who placed a fan of Vogues or other glossy women's magazines on the coffee table beside your armchair so neatly that you did not dare look at them.

It was at Seal that our bikes rally came into their own. I splashed out twelve pounds on a new one with three-speed gears. It was so easy to jump on a bike and nip round to see a friend in the village. Except for one steep hill, it was easier to go into Sevenoaks on the bike than on the bus (and cheaper; quite a consideration). Sevenoaks had a strange road layout with its two main roads forming a letter A, joining at the southern end of the town. This A had two cross-bars which formed a one-way system. I had returned from Charterhouse for the holidays and turned right along the second which would give the one-way system a clockwise direction, quite logical. Nearing the end, I saw a policeman standing and realised my mistake. 'Do you realise you have cycled the wrong way up a one-way street?' 'Yes Sir.' 'How long have you lived here?' 'Five years, Sir.' 'Well don't do it again.' Perhaps I looked like the fool I felt.

Bicycles broadened the area we could cover. We explored the ancient burial chamber of Kits Cotty with its massive slabs for walls and roof. When excavated in the nineteenth century, the skeleton was taken probably to Maidstone Museum. The incumbent asked that the bones of his most ancient parishioner should be returned for a decent burial. They were but the skull was placed in a glass cabinet where you could see it, sending shivers down our spines. Another expedition was following the track of the Pilgrims' Way to a friend of Audrey who had a cherry tree at Wrotham. We were shown how to lean ladders against the tree to pick the fruit. We loaded our bags but I hit a pothole and fell off my bike, spilling cherries. We refilled the bag – what the eye does not see... Stoning cherries to turn them into jam is a tedious task. Audrey borrowed a machine from a friend. The jam would not set properly but it was poured into jars and sealed. When cooled, it was found to be a very sticky sort of jelly. Water was added and it was boiled again with better results.

Through Audrey, we made other contacts. Margaret Brownlow at the Herb Farm was a world authority. We occasionally helped her with her garden maintenance and, perhaps in return, she presented Audrey with a copy of her book, *Herbs and the Fragrant Garden*. She prepared all the coloured illustrations herself and it became a classic. I still have a copy from which I have just learnt that there are around thirty different types of lavender.

The dust jacket of Margaret Brownlow's book

Thinking of classics and types, there was old Mrs. Alexander, known as Mrs. A. who lived on her own in an extensive garden with many plant varieties. She was a blue stocking, and was an early female undergraduates at Oxford. She fell in love while there and announced not only her engagement but that she was going to marry. A married female undergraduate was contrary to regulations and was told she would be sent down and expelled if she did. She said this was ridiculous, stood her ground and was the first female to be expelled. She was always very generous to us.

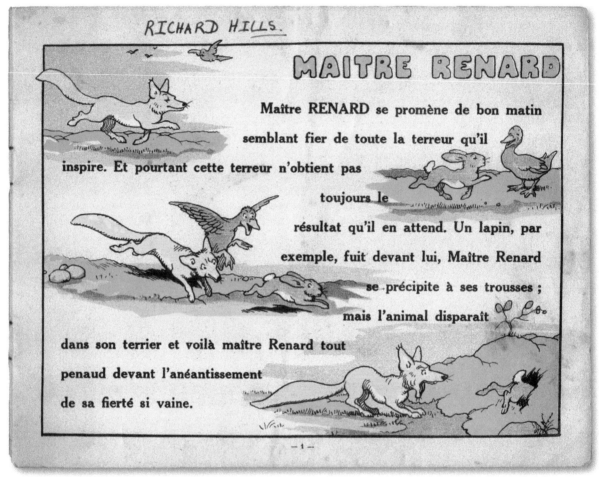

Richard tries to learn French

School Days

Part 2 – Charterhouse School, Godalming

Robinites House

In the autumn of 1950, the little prince fell off his perch again and landed with a bump in the much larger school of Charterhouse. In 1611, Thomas Sutton, described as 'England's wealthiest commoner', purchased what remained of the Carthusian monastery in London from the Crown. He established a foundation for impoverished gentlemen and a school for forty poor boys. While the almshouses remain, in 1872 the school with one Robert Baden Powell was moved out of its confined premises in the polluted atmosphere of London to the spacious countryside and pure air above Godalming, Surrey. 'Mens sano in corpore sano', a healthy mind in a healthy body, something which has stood me in good stead many a time later. It flourished, so that when I went there to join brother John, there were eleven houses containing 50 to 60 boarders each. John was well ensconced at Robinites. I do not know what he felt about having his pesky brother

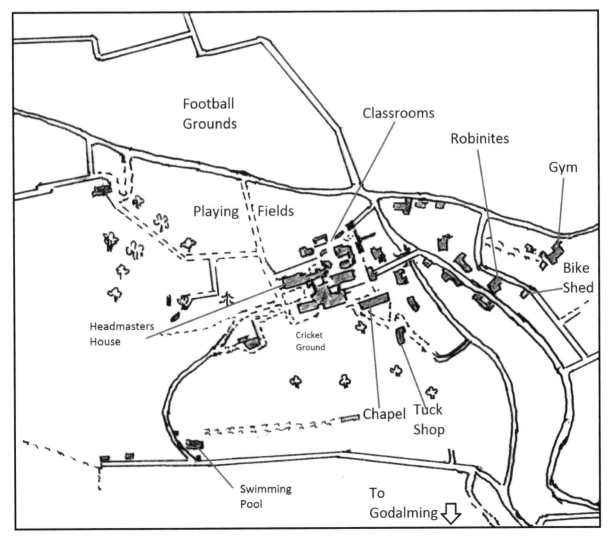

Map of Charterhouse

arriving but there was quite a gap in seniority so we rarely clashed. It was rumoured that Charterhouse offered a two-for-one bargain - or at least a reduction - for the second sibling. There were of course no girls.

Robinites was one of the further houses from the centre of the school so we had plenty of fresh air walking to and fro to lessons, carrying our books under our left arm. Our house was fortunate in that it backed onto a rough field, called I think Doddites, where we had our Physical Exercise sessions and in spare moments could play about with a football. I discovered that, if you kicked the ball hard and straight at your opponent, either he got out of the way and you ran past, or the ball bounced back and you had another go. Unfortunately a better footballer than I sussed out my tactics and started beating me. On the further side of the field were a gym and a shed where the sailing dinghies were maintained.

Fond parents (or perhaps relieved parents) would deliver their little darlings to the front door of the appropriate house to be greeted by the housemaster, in my case W.O. Dickens so nicknamed WOD from his signature. Housemasters had their separate apartments in a house, probably originating from the time when they owned the house and took in paying pupils. The new boy would be slightly apprehensive and self-conscious in his new uniform which hung limply being either a cast-off from elder brother or, if it had been purchased, was a few sizes too large to allow for growth. Rose Hill shorts had been changed into grey flannel trousers. The new white flannel shirts with their thin blue stripes had no collars. Starched white collars were fitted onto the shirts with studs. While smart, they were tricky to fix and tie but at least you had two clean collars a week to go with the single shirt. Ties were black with coloured stripes across showing to which house you belonged. The jacket was special browny-white best quality long-lasting tweed. Its disadvantage was being instantly recognised if you had strayed beyond the school boundaries into the flesh pots of Godalming or Guildford (or even a public house). Much of this special clothing could be purchased from Bentalls, a sort of department store which had a shop in the school grounds where stationary and other essentials for class work could be purchased as well as some confectionary. We pupils always suspected them of exploiting their monopolistic position.

On first arrival, you were allocated another junior boy who looked after you. He showed you round your house and school grounds as well as teaching you the school slang, its history and some of its famous people. After a few weeks, you were examined by a house prefect and woe-betide you if you failed. You became a 'fag', who might be called by a prefect to deliver a message to another house or a personal fag who took your prefect's books back to his study, cleaned his shoes and his study one day a week. You might get a small remuneration or gift at the end of term. You would be called upon to look after any boy who arrived subsequently. The school motto, 'Deo Dante Dedi', - to the god who gives I give – was something we remembered whether god was spelt with a lower case or a capital. Certainly I found that giving something back was something I learnt to do.

The newcomer at Robinites would be allocated a locker and place at the bottom of a long table in the main common room. As senior boys left, he would progress to a 'carrel' at the side of the room. Each consisted of a vertical board about five feet high fitted with a horizontal board to act as a desk. Seating was a hard wooden bench. You soon acquired cushions and a reading lamp to add comfort. I took advantage of this little bit of privacy by rigging up a crystal set I had been given and listening to the radio through an earphone concealed in my cupped hand. From the main common room you progressed through shared studies to, in my case, the large single study on the first floor for the head of house where you could hold small meetings. On this floor and the next were also the dormitories where most of the rooms were partitioned into cubicles with a bed, chair and a wash-stand. There was no plumbing in these cubicles so you had to go and fetch your own water. Here could also be found Matron, her surgery and her flat.

Underneath the main common room was a large cellar with two coke-fired boilers, an upright one for hot water and a larger horizontal one for the central heating. It was the duty of the senior boys to tend to the fires in the evening and at weekends. Sometimes we forgot, the fires went out and we had to relight them. One boy decided to speed up proceedings by pouring thinners into the vertical boiler with spectacular results. One evening I had forgotten it was my turn. The central heating boiler was cold. The grate was cleaned out and hot coals taken from the vertical boiler to start the fire again. A little later, bubbling in the heating pipes in my study reminded me about the boiler. I rushed down to see a white hot fire glowing in the boiler, the boiler furiously boiling with air rushing in through the partly opened fire door. The noise was terrific. Luckily there was no damage.

Meals were provided at each house. Their quality depended greatly upon the skill or interest of the housemaster's wife. Rationing of some things was still in force so we were all given an allowance of a quarter of a pound of butter each week to enjoy at our tea. Mrs. Dickens replaced it with a larger block of margarine at which some of the senior boys protested and we all returned the marg. This became known as the great Robinites butter strike. There was a small pantry with a gas ring where we were permitted to do a little cooking. Someone heated a tin of soup without piercing it first, with spectacular results to the decoration of the room when he opened it.

Opportunities At Charterhouse

Moving to the much larger Charterhouse opened up many more possibilities. There was of course one's own growth with a larger stronger body. Teaching covered an advanced curriculum with many more choices such as French and German or physics and chemistry. After a couple of years and when 'O' level exams had been passed, there would be specialisation in subjects in preparation for 'A' Levels. The sixth forms were split into different disciplines. Out of formal school hours, the choice was yours. As well as a variety of sporting activities, there was the art studio tempting you with oil and watercolour painting as well as pottery. The carpenters' shop had a small metal-working section. The library had two roaring fires in the centre of the room, tempting in cold weather. The chimney passed down between the pair of fires, under the floor and up the side of the building to the open air. Then there would be special lectures with visiting speakers and drama productions such as Shakespeare's plays.

The daily routine was basically the same for both winter 'quarters' or terms but in summer there was an early morning class before breakfast, leaving the afternoons free. After breakfast you went to the morning service in the large chapel. You should have taken your books into the classroom of the teacher of your first lesson. Each master or 'beak' had his own room. Because this could mean a long extra walk causing you to be late, there was a temptation to leave your books outside the chapel on the path, only to find they had mysteriously disappeared when you came out.

Christian Background

The chapel was an impressively tall narrow building that could be seen from Godalming and much further. The pews were arranged in choir formation facing each other on either side. You were allocated your own seat and gradually moved up the chapel towards the altar as the years progressed. The end seat of each row in each block had a small pad of paper on which it was noted if you were absent. The headmaster was the last person to enter, after which the doors were shut and you were reprimanded if you failed to make chapel in time. In the centre were the chaplains' seats, the choir stalls and the pulpit. Boys whose voices had not broken were much sought after for the choir. I was not one. It was not easy to preach from the pulpit with boys to the left of you and boys to the right of you and no amplification. Prefects read the lesson from the lectern at the end by the altar. This I found terrifying; not only facing 500 or 600 boys but also the headmaster sitting at the further end of the chapel. He would summon us to a practice first, very necessary for someone like myself with a quiet voice.

I was confirmed at Charterhouse so becoming a full member of the Church of England. I was prepared by Henry Bettinson, one of the chaplains, who I learnt afterwards was a noted New Testament scholar and had translated some of the later epistles that were not included in the Canon. I am afraid that we failed to recognise his great learning and found it more interesting to run a sweep-stake on the number of matches he used to light his pipe during a class. Before our actual Confirmation, the candidates were taken to Farnham Castle, seat of the Bishops of Guildford, for a day of quiet and meditation which was helpful. One Advent Sunday morning, the sun was streaming through the window onto where the Bishop of Guildford was laying his hands on us. I knelt before him and was disappointed not to feel any tongues of fire.

These were still the days when we had Scripture, not Religious Instruction lessons. I kept my Exercise Book for many years and found the contents applicable not only when studying for my Lay Reader qualifications but even for my priestly ordination. Another custom which I started about this time was reading a passage of the Bible daily when saying my prayers. We could buy Bible readings and short notes about them from the Bible Reading Fellowship. An evangelical group met for prayer on a Sunday afternoon in a near-by private house but my upbringing was more 'Liberal' so I did not go regularly. This group was linked to the Varsity and Public School Camps which offered holidays out of school term but I went to the Public and Preparatory School (PPS) Camps which I will describe later.

Practical Christianity in The Community

Dr. Iliff, a medical doctor whom I knew a little through PPS Camp, gave a talk to the school about his work at The Church Missionary Society hospital in Peshawar, Pakistan. We asked whether we could help? He replied, 'Did we have any surplus sporting equipment especially cricket gear?' I obtained permission to circulate an appeal to all the houses with a date to meet Dr. Iliff's deadline for transporting anything to Pakistan. Two days before that deadline, we had virtually nothing. Then came the deluge. Another sort of 'work in the community' was cycling over to Guildford Cathedral on some summer afternoons. The Cathedral was still being constructed. We were positioned at the exit beside a pile of bricks. The visitor could buy a brick, write their name on it and have it built into the structure. I have wondered since how much our Charterhouse uniform and our straw boaters boosted sales.

One memorable preacher at Sunday chapel was the elderly Brother Douglas of the Anglican Society of St. Francis. A group was organised to visit the Society's mother house at Cerne Abbas near Sherborne in Dorset. We went by train and were met by Brother Peter who told us we could look round Sherborne, where the bus left and at what time. One person nearly missed the bus, much to the amusement of Brother Peter who had not told us it was the last bus until a week later. The Cerne Abbas giant impressed us but this was not true of all the brothers' services in which we joined, particularly the one at some dreadfully early hour in the morning. This was not repeated back at Charterhouse but we did try their way of singing psalms antiphonally.

Another eye opener was staying for brief weekends at Charterhouse in Southwark. This was another form of outreach to help those less fortunate than ourselves. There was a hostel for assistants as well as the main club building with a church on the ground floor with clubroom on the first and a flat roof covered in a wire cage for football and other sports. In the afternoon, we might assist with the sports while in the evening we fraternised with the youth club – fraternise because at least in the building itself there was little contact between the sexes. We would attend the Sunday morning service in the church. Meeting very high church practice for the first time with coloured vestments, incense being puffed everywhere and much bowing and scraping was a new experience.

Uncle Sandy and Aunt Evelyn with Gelert on Hayling Island

Charterhouse in Southwark ran a summer camp at Bembridge in the Isle of Wight. A few of the senior boys went to help. I decided to cycle there and save the fare. It didn't look far from Godalming on the map and I could call on Evelyn and Uncle Sandy on Hayling Island.

I was an already very tired boy who arrived at their house. After suitable sustenance, one reason for going that way, Uncle Sandy helped me to the ferry for Portsmouth by slowly driving his car while I on my bike hung on. Our activities at the camp mostly were playing football. Luckily one of the Charterhouse party was Don Cupitt who played in the first eleven. He later became more noted for his outspoken theological convictions

Education

But it is time to turn to the real purpose of my going to Charterhouse, education. I was not an outstanding scholar to say the least. I struggled with calculus but passed 'O' level Additional Maths. Ironically in view of later achievements, I failed history, partly because I did not like that master. General Science was different but I took a long time to find out the difference why the basic unit in biology was the cell and in chemistry the atom. Of course, it eventually dawned on me that cells are made of atoms. Simple! It was fun in chemistry chasing drops of mercury over the bench as well as heating glass capillary tubes to blow bulbs for thermometers. Filling them with alcohol and sealing the end might, if mistimed, result in a flame of alcohol spurting out. Physics was more my line and I helped demonstrate during a special 'Conversazione' the power that could be developed from the ordinary water mains to break small pieces of wood.

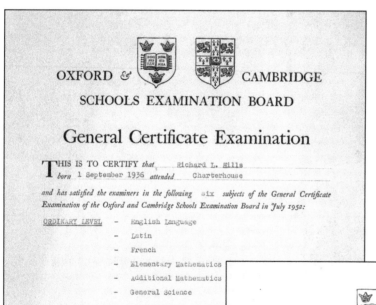

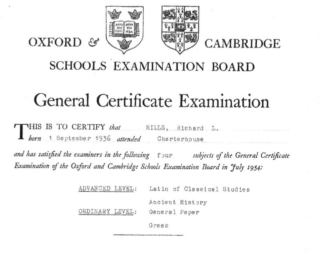

Oxford and Cambridge Certificates of 'O' Level and 'A' Level passes

Probably I should have taken the more intensive Chemistry and Physics course for 'O' level but through W.O. Dickens, himself a classicist, and my father who still held ambitions for me to go into the Church, it was Latin and Greek. I struggled. I did make the Classical Sixth. One evening, I was due to take some composition I had finished to the house of V.S.H. 'Sniffy' Russell. He was playing the piano so beautifully that I did not have the heart to disturb him for some time. When he had stopped, I ventured in with some trepidation. He scribbled his adverse comments all over my studiously prepared masterpiece. His views were seconded by R.L. Arrowsmith. After I had tried my best to translate a passage in one lesson, he said, 'Hills, I had remembered that you could not translate Latin prose but I had forgotten you could not translate Greek prose either. Next'.

I had great respect for our headmasters. John was there under Frank Fletcher who was famous and still sometimes appeared in Chapel as a very old man. His son was housemaster of Hodgsonites and later accepted me to teach at Worcester College for the Blind where he had become head. In 1946, George Turner was appointed headmaster for a term of five years, a man short in stature but full of personality. One master had his classroom on the path leading from the Headmaster's house into the rest of the school. I suppose we had been taking advantage of this master's inability to control a form of boisterous boys. The door opened slowly. Hush descended. 'I am sorry I have interrupted. I thought there was no master here.' We were better behaved in that class for a little while.

Brian Young at the youthful age of only thirty followed Turner in 1952. He was an impressive figure, tall, dark hair with dark eyebrows, striding across to Chapel in his dark suit and black academic gown. He had a full teaching role in the Classical Sixth. For a weekly task, he set a series of questions to which we had to find the answers. This involved researching various dictionaries and so on – no internet in those days so good practise for my later career. For senior boys, and when I was head of Robinites, he entertained some of us at his house for an evening. One game was 'Are You There, Moriarty?' Two blindfolded volunteers lay head to head on the floor holding left hands. In their right, they had a wad of rolled-up newspaper. After the question, 'Are You There, Moriarty?' You could take a swipe at the other who tried to move out of the way. Brain would sometimes join in. He had to retire soon after I left through severe migraine but went on to be knighted for his work at the BBC setting up Channel Four as well as much work for Christian organisations.

Broader Education

Our education at Charterhouse stretched beyond the classroom. Tuesday afternoons were reserved for the Combined Cadet Force, the Scouts and perhaps the farm. I was sorry that a choice had to be made and, in view of impending National Service, opted for the CCF. Most of the time, this covered the usual syllabus of drill, rifle practice, navigation, attacking the enemy and so on. There was an annual camp, one of which was near Aldershot. We slept in tents and had to fill our palliasses with straw. I had been warned not to overfill mine but one boy came into our tent triumphantly carrying a fat sausage he had stuffed tightly. Of course he rolled off when he tried to sleep on it. One exercise was being dropped off at an unknown point and finding our way back to camp. My map showed the route of the Basingstoke Canal which I and my partner followed. There was a night exercise with blank rounds for our rifles, flares and other fireworks. The event did not go quite as planned. On return, we were assembled in the Armoury and the Major in charge prepared to harangue us. Unfortunately for him, as he was jumping onto a table to stand in a more commanding position, he hit his head on a beam, knocking off his hat – not quite the impression he wanted to give. During my last summer term, I was in charge of the Robinite platoon entry for the Arthur Webster Competition. This involved inspection of turnout, drill and similar activities. After much polishing of boots and burnishing of brasses, I was pleased that we came second.

The other afternoons when there were no lessons were theoretically free and we were left to our own devices. However participation in some major sport such as football, hockey, cricket or athletics was expected. I enjoyed hockey but never achieved any school eleven. Running, including cross-country, and jumping were more my forte. A bicycle presented much broader opportunities because the school regulations stated that you should not cross any railway lines. It was possible to obtain a 'chit' from your housemaster which admitted me to the public library in Godalming. Here I discovered books such as Hughes', *Immortal Sails*, on the sailing ships of North Wales, describing the small ships built mainly in Porth Madog to carry the slate across the world. Guildford could be reached by following a path over a tunnel so, fortunately, not seeing the railway! The lure here was A.J. Reeves, suppliers of model engineering equipment, at the top of the cobbled High Street. In the other direction, it was possible to cycle for many miles, perhaps westwards along the Hog's Back towards Farnham or towards the south and the Devil's Punch Bowl at Haselmere. All this gave us plenty of scope for exploration, particularly in the summer but I expect that today such roads are highly dangerous with the increase in traffic.

Soon after arriving at Charterhouse, I found my way to the Art Studio where I discovered the joys of oil painting. A wide range of colours could be mixed from the small range of blobs of paint on our palette. It was easier to paint over mistakes than with watercolours. I tried my hand at pottery. 'Wedging' the clay to prepare it for the potter's wheel was hard work but I managed to 'throw' for Audrey some clay lamps similar to ones used at Bethlehem at the time of Jesus. In later life, I did some paintings with oils but this sort of artistic skill has been overtaken by the need to produce maps, diagrams and art work for my various historical publications.

Model Engineering

At Charterhouse, soon art was forsaken for model engineering. It may have been another Robinite who was making a small petrol engine to power his bicycle, or it may have been the possibility of making small parts for OO gauge model trains which some of us were building in the evenings or wet afternoons that introduced me to the machine shop at Charterhouse. I built for myself a small layout in an alcove in an attic at Seal but money was lacking to purchase proper transformers and controllers so it was never a great success. At Charterhouse, the carpenters' shop had a small corner set aside for metal working. I wonder what that says about the attitude of public schools to industry. There were a couple of foot treadle lathes, a Boxford 4 ½ ins. screw cutting lathe, a pillar drill, grindstone and

The unfinished model of Invicta

The inclined cylinders will be fitted on the outside of the framing close by the tall chimney. The connecting rod drove the rear wheel. Boiler fittings have yet to be made.

hearth. I was taught how to use a foot lathe and succeeded in finishing some small brass buffers for railway wagons.

Then a major project attracted my attention. The Model Engineer was running a series by 'LBSC' (London Brighton and South Coast Railway) on how to build a 3 ½ ins. gauge live steam model of 'Invicta'. This engine was supplied in 1830 by Robert Stephenson & Co. to haul passenger carriages on part of the Canterbury and Whitstable Railway, so a suitable project for a Kentish Man. It had only four coupled wheels and a small tender and seemed within the realms of possibility. I knew WOD thought I was spending too much time on it instead of my classics. Father probably didn't know too much about it. We had to write home every Sunday to describe our activities. I quickly learnt that if the return letter came addressed in a hand-written envelope, that was alright. However if the envelope was typed, I had done something wrong. So the obvious thing was to tell him as little as possible. Sadly I could not complete this model while at Charterhouse. While I have tried many times to work on it, it is still unfinished although the wheels can be rotated by compressed air. Perhaps one day... What it did was to teach me the rudiments of mechanical engineering, turning, milling, soldering, brazing, and much more. All this has been excellent value in later life, particularly for the Museum in Manchester.

Railway Interests

My interest in railways resulted not only in my running the Railway Club but in other adventures. An early one was the closure of the Kent and East Sussex Railway, one of Col. Stephens unprofitable lines with antiquated rolling stock. It ran from Robertsbridge through Tenterden to Headcorn. While it was taken over by British Railways, it did not survive even into the Beeching era. I heard about its closure and realised that I could visit it on the final day as part of a visit to Auntie Poll in her nursing home at Tunbridge

Wells. So I left there, set off to Robertsbridge and caught a train to Tenterden, knowing I could return the same way to Sevenoaks. At Robertsbridge, I heard that the final train that evening would carry on to Headcorn and connect with the mainline postal train to Tonbridge and Sevenoaks. That was it. I joined in the 'funeral' service with band and fireworks, etc. The walk home from Sevenoaks station to Seal past midnight was worth it. Many years later, I was showing my photo album to Robert Manders, my Deputy in the Museum in Manchester. He gasped - we had been standing side by side that day on the platform at Tenterden.

As part of the Charterhouse Railway Club, we attended the closure of the line from Pulborough through Midhurst to Petersfield.

March, 1955   THE CARTHUSIAN   333

A FUNERAL

THE British Transport Commission had decided it was no longer an economic proposition to continue running the Petersfield—Midhurst—Pulborough branch line. (There had only been a small deficit the previous year—£31,000.) So on Saturday, February 5th, the last passenger train was to run after a life of nearly a hundred years. A small band of Carthusians decided to attend the funeral.

Midhurst had been a very important place with two railway stations and three railway lines worked by two companies; one to Petersfield and its rival to Pulborough (hence the two stations) and a third line to Chichester passing near Goodwood Racecourse. On racing days long trains of horse-boxes and spectators would pass through and the railway staff had to work hard to keep the time-table. Now we were about to embark on a huge train of three coaches. We wanted to go to a small station just beyond Midhurst but the staff in the booking office at Petersfield had never heard of the place and we nearly missed the train while they found out, which shows how much the line was used.

We travelled with the guard in his van who showed us the place where an engine had come off the lines 'when they were not so well laid.' Our train was too long to fit on the platforms of the small halts but that did not matter as nobody wanted to get off. At the large station of Midhurst (three platforms), we passed the other train and went on to Selham Halt. Here the 'man-of-all-jobs' porter, ticket-collector, etc., told us that earlier the same day a white horse had got on to the line just before the train was due. At Midhurst all the press photographers were waiting for the train when out of the tunnel trotted the white horse, followed soon after by the train.

At Midhurst somebody provided flags and bunting with which to decorate the engine. The Carthusians gladly assisted while one tried to take a photo of the train with a Heath Robinson flashlight. The town band arrived and played some discordant music, climbed into the train and we set off for Pulborough. I wonder what the people in the main-line trains thought as they saw the crowd on the platform, top hats, black armbands, people dressed as old countrymen, and engine festooned in bunting and a small band trying to get a tune out of its cold instruments.

It was a perfect night as we set off on that last journey, the full moon shining, a cloudless sky and the threat of frost in the air. Somebody had placed a whole barrage of fog signals on the line which exploded as the train went over them. We slowed down to collect the staff for the single line and then away on a journey never to be repeated. How can one describe the wind howling through the tall funnel or the quick pants of a steam-engine at full speed, or the clickity-click of the wheels and the swaying of the coach! Stations lit by oil lamps were left behind as we puffed through the night. At Midhurst the town band left us, playing a last farewell. The other train was late so we had to wait. At last it arrived and we were able to proceed. Petersfield was reached nearly half an hour late but nobody grumbled: for the railway was no more.

R.L.H.

An early effort bursting into print in The Carthusian

A photo of our group appeared in a local paper and an account I wrote entitled 'A Funeral' was published in the March 1955 edition of *The Carthusian*, one of my first literary endeavours. Film evenings with British Transport Commission films shown in one of the larger lecture rooms were always popular. A small entry charge more than covered their cost. Visits were organised to locomotive depots, signal boxes and the like. But one stands out when a music master took three of us in his car to the Dorking Greystone Lime Quarry where three elderly Fletcher Jennings engines were still at work. Baxter, a standard gauge

0-4-0, struggled to haul one wagon at a time from the main line for loading at the quarry. Inside the quarry were two narrow gauge engines chuffing round with the odd gauge of 3ft. 2 ¼ inch. All these three have been preserved since.

Public and Preparatory School Camps

The Public and Preparatory School Camps were run by Basil Clarkson from his home in Bedford. Therefore he was conveniently situated mid-way between Oxford and Cambridge from where he drew most of his officers. He organised some activity in each of the school holidays. At Easter, there were three one week cruises on the Norfolk Broads. During the summer, there were three two week camps in North Wales. While at Cambridge, I helped on a short-lived pony-treking venture in Northumberland so becoming a rare 'fourther'. After Christmas, you could be invited to a house party at a Christian Conference Centre perhaps in the New Forest or at Capernwray Hall near Carnforth, Lancashire. I have to admit that I saw the possibility that going on one of the summer camps might introduce me not only to the mountains of North Wales but also to the numerous narrow gauge railway systems, many of which still existed in the 1950s. I had a copy of Whitehead's slim volume, *Narrow Gauge Railways of Britain* which became a sort of Bible and guide. Interest was further stimulated by L.T.C. Rolt, *Railway Adventure*, and J.I.C. Boyd's numerous volumes on the lines in North Wales such as *Narrow Gauge Rails to Portmadoc*.

The Norfolk Broads

However it was to the Broads that I went first in the spring of 1953, following the example of John. Basil hired the Leading Lady and Perfect Lady boats from Herbert Woods at Potter Heigham. The Leading Lady was a little larger having an extra bunk in the bows as well as four berths. Basil might add a couple of mattresses in the main cabins and even one in the well. To save a little on hire charges, the engines were not fitted after the winter overhaul so the boats had to be worked manually. Chemical closets also came later, which meant that we had to make a trip to a near-by reed bed with trowel and paper.

After breakfast, while the officers had a prayer meeting when instructions for the day's sailing were given out, the crew prepared the boat for inspection. Then each boat was free to make its own way to the designated mooring for that night. When I had become a Skipper, we were tacking towards Horning. We made the most of the width of the river, going about close to each bank. We were turning on one tack when the boat shuddered and continued to swing round. The rudder had hit a tree root concealed beneath the water. The boat broke free but would not straighten up. We were towed to Horning. A spare rudder was brought from Potter to replace ours in a very efficient operation. Obviously we were not the first to have such an accident. Sailing up the narrow twisting River Ant in such large boats was very difficult because there was little room to tack. That meant bow-hauling and quanting. After holding a race with the other boats on Horsey Mere came the return to Potter. This presented a tempting challenge. You had to lower sails and mast to go under Potter railway bridge. Then you should have continued to quant through the next bridge and so into Woods' basin. But the more adventurous upped mast and sails, sailed the very short stretch to the narrow arch of the road bridge, down with sails and mast, quant under the bridge, up with sails and mast again to sail the short stretch and take them down again to go into Wood's basin. The skipper was not very popular with Woods' men if you tried this because a mistake could bring disaster. I never tried.

Basil resided in a motor cabin cruiser with all the stocks of food etc. He went ahead to the selected mooring place causing merriment to other passing boats when they saw the rows of loaves of bread on his cabin top. After mooring, we had to furl the sails, put up awnings over the well and bows, and prepare the evening meal from the rations we had collected from Basil. A knowledgeable skipper took an extra potato peeler with him. Cooking facilities provided on board were two gas rings supplemented with Primus stoves. With the awning up, lighting in the cooking area relied on a single 12 volt bulb. One evening, the person preparing bed-time cocoa mixed it with Persil washing up powder instead of sugar, not recommended. Ever since I have followed Basil's instructions for cooking kippers. He always supplied Manx kippers which he thought were the best and was furious if you spoilt them. 'Fry Them Dry' was his instruction – and it works.

In the evenings on my early cruises, the crews assembled in a pair of launches moored together. Hissing Tilley lamps gave a soft light. Any important notices would be given and then a boat might contribute a 'log' of the day's adventures. These were humorous accounts of imaginative events. I wrote quite a few which were generally well received. The launches were replaced by 'Moby Dick'. This was an inflatable marquee designed by Basil. It worked on the principle of later 'Bouncy Castles' with ribs that were inflated by battery-driven electric fans. The theory was great but in practice the edifice tended to deflate. Basil had special expansion tubes fitted but even so those who slept in it overnight might find it had deflated on top of them. After the informal proceedings, there followed prayers, Bible reading and a short talk. I had returned to my boat one evening when an excited officer came in and said to the skipper, 'The Lord has come to my brother tonight'. I puzzled over what he meant for some years.

North Wales

The daily routine at both camps and house parties roughly followed that on the Broads except that cooking was done by proper staff. For the camps, Basil would welcome parents and boys at Paddington Station in his trilby hat. Luggage and bikes might be put in a special luggage van and sometimes there might be a special reserved carriage for us boys. These involved much blowing of whistles and puffing of steam at Ruabon to attach them to the branch line train to Pwllheli. It was a slow journey through the Welsh countryside to Barmouth and then along past Porthmadog and eventually Pwllheli. Boredom might be alleviated by opening the window and watching the changing of single line tokens without stopping – never mind the smuts in your eyes. At the end of camp, we would change from the Great Western lines at Afon Wen onto the London Midland and Scottish to return by Bangor and Crewe.

The camp site was near Morfa Nefyn. Coaches could not go along the farm track so we walked past Porth Dinllaen Farm and suddenly came to the top of a rim of a bowl or basin with the camp site laid out below. On the far side a small stream ran past the camp down to a rocky valley and the sea. The track curved round and steeply down to a grassy conical mound called the Tump. On top was a large meeting marquee and, in a circle around it, the bell tents which would be our home. I went the first year Basil moved onto this site so the bell tents were erected on the slope of the Tump. When asleep at night, you were liable to find yourself rolling across the tent and perhaps even outside. There was another large marquee for dining, temporary buildings for kitchen, storehouse, toilets as well as a row of small square tents where Basil slept and there was a surgery and other facilities. A little way off was a separate row of tents for the lady volunteer domestic staff. It required a large organisation in the background because all this equipment had to be erected and taken into store each year. I later helped to do this. Gradually the site was improved with level areas dug out for the tents, water pipes installed and so on.

Ball games might be organised on the camp site while the Lleyn Peninsular could be explored along the cliff tops to the west. In the other direction, across the golf links there was swimming at the Porth Dinllaen hamlet off the lifeboat jetty as well as the Ty Coch pub. I was sitting on a bench in the pub when I heard a clicking noise. I jumped up quickly because there was a large lobster approaching me. The Welsh fisherman grinned and pulled it away. The camp had two sailing boats in the bay which always sailed together in case of emergency. The Bay Tree cafe in Morfa Nefyn was another local attraction. A bike ride away was the mountain Yr Eifel, the Rivals so called from the distinctive three peaks visible from a great distance. Below it down a steep track was the deserted village, once occupied by men working in the local quarries. Only one cottage was inhabited in the 1950s but later the village was restored as a sort of memorial to the workers. There were other walks in the countryside. We climbed Snowdon by the Miners' Track.

Narrow Gauge Railways

While all these opportunities kept most boys entertained, I had gone to North Wales in the hope of seeing narrow gauge railways. By good luck, this was fulfilled. Basil organised a special whole-day excursion for all the camp to some normally less easily accessible destination. Joy, oh Joy! In my first year it was the narrow gauge Talyllyn Railway, the site of Rolt's *Railway Adventure*. The slate quarries at Abergernolwyn had been virtually abandoned but Sir Hayden Jones kept open the little railway to take the villagers from there and other isolated farms to market at Tywyn on the coast. It was still using, just, its original locomotives and carriages from 1864. Heading the train to take us from Pwllheli was an antiquated 4-4-0 Duke Dog that just managed to haul our mainline train up some of the gradients. I do not remember that trip along the Talyllyn but would help there a little during National Service.

Another of Basil's excursions was to the Llechwedd Slate Quarries at Blaenau Ffestiniog still in full production. We descended long ladders to the vast caverns to see where the slate was extracted, followed to where the large blocks were taken on narrow gauge railway trucks to the saw benches for trimming to a specific size and then being split by hand into roofing slates. We watched loaded trucks careering down inclines so the slates could be loaded onto standard gauge wagons for despatch. Today production has finished and this is a major visitor attraction. Yet another of Basil's mammoth excursions was by coach to Llandudno where we boarded a Yellow Funnel steamer bound for the Isle of Man. We had about two hours to look round Douglas, perhaps buy a kipper to post home and then sail back to Llandudno. Luckily on this the first of many later visits to that island, the sea was calm.

Porthmadog was within cycling distance from camp and so a 'must'. We looked sorrowfully at the rows of rusting slate wagons and the rotting guards van with elegant double curved roof in the harbour station of the Ffestiniog Railway. We proceeded across the Cob to Boston Lodge and found a way into the deserted Works. A piece of metal remained in the lathe chuck, and the spanner was still there on the cylinder cover of an engine awaiting the return of the fitters laid off at the end of the war. Out in the yard, the rear end of Moel Tryfan could be discovered in the mass of brambles that had grown over it while the engine shed sheltered that engine's boiler mounted on its driving wheels. It was a sad scene of dereliction but surely one of promise. We were lucky not to be caught for trespassing. When we went again in the following year, a preservation society had been formed. The little World War I Simplex petrol engine was hauling a passenger carriage between Boston Lodge and Porthmadog. We helped a little to clear the line towards Minffordd of saplings and brambles.

A small group took the train to Bangor and walked over to Port Penryn where we watched one of the 'main line' engines bringing a train of loaded slate wagons down from the quarries at Bethesda into the yard. The quays were a hive of activity with slates being transferred from the 2 ft. gauge wagons either into piles for stock, lorries or ships. We were glad to make use of the famous round structure on the quay which was flushed twice a day by the tides. Alas there are no more slates to be seen there now. Later I was able to further develop this interest in the North Wales slate industry into lectures for Industrial Archaeology and also assist with the restoration of both the Ffestiniog and Welsh Highland Railways. But we must return to Charterhouse to look at another line of my development that would become very important in my life.

Wilfrid Noyce

Wilfrid Noyce and I must have arrived at Charterhouse in the autumn of 1950, he to teach French and myself to do what? He was already famous for his mountaineering expertise and authorship so that John Hunt, later Sir John, invited him to join the expedition that was being planned to try and conquer Everest in 1953. Wilf was granted leave of absence from his teaching duties. 1953 was of course the year of the Coronation of our present Queen Elizabeth II. In those days, televisions were scarce. Those lucky enough to have one with a small black and white screen offered to share viewing with their neighbours. We must have been given a holiday from school so that I was at Seal with Margaret. As neither of us had received an invitation to watch a television, we decided to go to London and see the procession. Hearing on the previous evening that crowds were already massing along the route, we caught the last train from Kemsing to Victoria. We found a front-line pitch near Wellington Arch and tried to rest. At 3 am, newspaper sellers came round announcing, 'Everest Conquered'. While it was not Wilf who reached the summit, he certainly was welcomed back to Charterhouse as a hero when he returned there in 1954 after various lecture tours. Meanwhile Margaret and I braved the rain and watched the Queen of Tonga getting soaked in her open carriage and our Queen waving from the comfort of her golden coach.

I do not remember how I became acquainted with Wilf. It certainly was not through his French classes. He may have heard about my interest in the Welsh mountains. He invited me to join the parties of boys he took to Stone Farm Rocks and Harrison's Rocks near Tunbridge Wells where we could learn some rock climbing techniques and rope work. I remember sweating as I struggled up one climb feeling very insecure. Wilf was in charge of my rope which continually went slack in spite of my shouting, 'Take in'. When eventually I surmounted the climb, there was Wilf reading a book, casually taking in my rope and putting his foot on it.

34 Charterhouse Climbing Meet, Cwm Glas, April 1955, l. to r.: John Hansbury, David Cox, Dick Marsh, Alistair Gourlay, the author, Roy Davey, Peter Norton, Jon Moore, Richard Hills, Donald Percival.

Group photograph of the Charterhouse meet in Llanberis, April 1950. I am second from right

In April 1955, Wilf organised the first of a series of school mountaineering meets. We took over the Climbers' Club hut, Cwm Glas Mawr, in the Llanberis Pass.

He arranged for several experienced climbers to 'tutor' us. The weather was fine and some of us progressed to climbing 'Very Severe'. Wilf, David Cox and myself set off at 3.30 am to climb Central Wall in Cwm Glas because the sun was shining on it. David was leading me. He later became President of the Climbers' Club and climbed in old-fashioned boots nailed with vicious saw-toothed tricounies around the edge so he clanked his way up a climb. He smoked a pipe like a chimney and I wrote later, 'It was easy to follow him because at every belay there was a pile of ash and matches and the smell of tobacco told us where he had gone.'

Wilf was editing a new guide book for the Moel Hebog area and took me with him to check some of the climbs. He was leading, leaving me securely belayed. Soon there came rattling down lumps of rock, clumps of heather and grass as Wilf did some 'gardening'. I cowered against the rock face and luckily was not hit as we had no safety helmets in those days. Encouraged by the success of this meet, on returning to Charterhouse, Wilf called a meeting of boys who might be interested in mountaineering. About forty attended so on 11 May 1955, the 'Charterhouse Mountaineering Club' was founded with Mr. Noyce as President and R.L. Hills and S.J. Hawkins as joint Secretaries. Mountaineering would play a crucial role later in my life. I had found something in which I could excel and loved doing. Perhaps I had inadvertently stumbled on what Kurt Hann described as a 'Grande Passion' that helped to guide me through my teenage years. But, having ascended the mountainous heights of Charterhouse to become one of the top school prefects, how great was the fall into National Service.

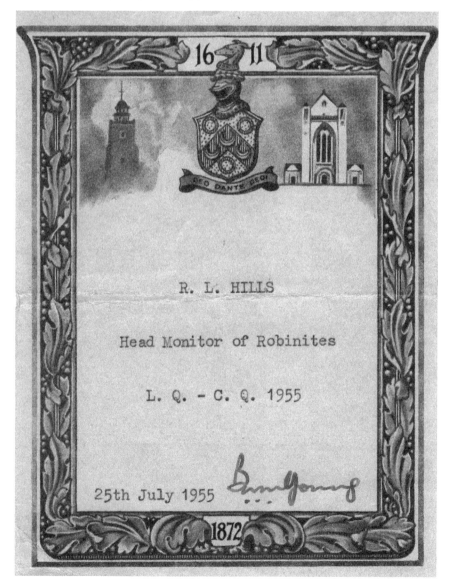

The final gift from Charterhouse

R. L. HILLS

Head Monitor of Robinites

L. Q. - C. Q. 1955

25th July 1955

The Third Age
National Service

Part 1 – Basic Training

Park Hall Camp, Oswestry

Next, '23179358 Gunner 'ills' the sergeant shouted. I stepped forward to have my photo taken for my army identity card. That number was displayed across my chest and had to be stamped on all the kit I was about to receive as a new recruit. I still have the shoe brushes marked thus with which I polish my shoes, a reminder of the present Her Majesty gave me when I entered her service. I was in the reception area of the Royal Artillery Basic Training Unit at Park Hall Camp, Oswestry, in early September 1955. I had opted for the Royal Artillery following the examples of my father and brother John and was due to start my two year period of National Service. I had to strip off my civilian clothes which would not be needed for some weeks and join the queue of other naked youths waiting for our medical inspection. I passed. We had been reduced as it were to the lowest common denominator.

Kitting out followed. For most items, the army dictum of 'one size fits all' was applied. One short person tried on his pyjama bottoms. He hoisted them up under his armpits and found that the legs reached well beyond his toes while the jacket could have done duty as an overcoat. At least there was some attempt to fit our battledress with the services of a tailor. Army jungle underpants were best forgotten as were puttees, presumably left over from World War I. We were issued with boots that had not been nailed, a job for us which had to be done in a particular pattern.

In our barrack room, we were allocated a bed and a tall wardrobe. For morning inspection our kit had to be laid out in a certain way, folded into nine inch squares. You soon learnt that it was easier to keep one set folded neatly all the time while the rest in use was concealed as well as possible. Blankets and sheets had to be folded in a particular way round the pillow. Boots and brasses had to be polished, something we learnt in the CCF at Charterhouse. Rooms, washrooms had to be cleaned, not forgetting the area outside our barrack room. Coal was reputed to have to be whitewashed and the grass cut with nail scissors but we were spared such excesses. There would be a Lance Bombardier (Lance Corporal) in charge of our room who would march us off for our meals and for our lectures or drill sessions.

Basic training at Oswestry consisted mostly of learning how to use a rifle, parade ground drill and physical education. I was fairly fit but found I had muscles that I did not know existed when hanging on the wall bars with my feet straight out in front. 'Keep 'em up', the sergeant shouted. That September was hot. When lying on the gym floor struggling with some exercise or other, I looked at the puddle of sweat running off my face. It was certainly an advantage on the parade ground to have already learnt the basic drill especially with rifles. Our parade ground backed onto the Great Western Railway main line between Wolverhampton and Birkenhead so it was a great temptation to turn my head and look at the locomotives so different from the Southern ones to which I was accustomed. We must have been allowed a little free time because I went out for a walk to where a small stream had been culverted to pass under the railway in an inverted siphon. A local person baited a hook on the end of a fishing line and dropped it into the siphon. He hauled out quite a few reasonably sized fish which would have made us a much better meal than army provisions.

Tywyn

After the first two weeks, there followed another eight of more specialised training. This is where I learnt something about the army – never anticipate what may happen. If I had had a choice about my future career, I am sure I would have put down the field artillery after father's example. Where was I posted? To some remote location in the middle of Wales on the coast which most of the lads had never heard of – a ray of hope, Tywyn!

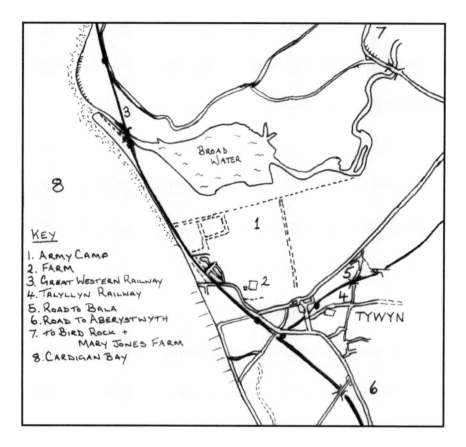

Map of Tywyn. The camp was to the north. The Talyllyn Railway is at the bottom right.

I have no idea how we were transferred, whether by train or by 3 ton lorry. Looking back now I rather suspect the latter which would have given door to door transport. Tywyn-By-The-Sea was the major artillery training centre for the Anti-Aircraft (Ack Ack) with both light and heavy 3.7 guns. The firing range stretched out into Cardigan Bay. A light aircraft would fly parallel to the coast but out at sea towing a target behind. The radar units would locate the target and an order sent to the guns how and when to fire. Safety officers had to be positioned behind the guns to ensure there was no danger of their hitting the plane as sometimes the radar would creep along the towing wire and fix onto the plane. All these guns and radar units were situated along the shore line at the far side of the railway line to the camp itself. The area was patrolled by some fearsome Alsatians.

Our new barrack room differed little from the first with its standard army furniture. One bright senior officer decided that the decor could be improved if the floor was creosoted. This was brushed onto wooden floors that had been wax treated so it never properly dried with the resultant mess getting everywhere. This time our bombardier was not so co-operative. It was rumoured that he had failed his WOSB (War Office Selection Board) and so had not been selected for officer training. Perhaps he was trying to get his own back, taking it out on our draft of mainly public and grammar school boys. Some of the lads felt that he might be missing female company in that remote part of wild Wales so caught one of the sheep that roamed the camp and put it in his bunk room. He was not pleased.

In the middle of each barrack room was a cast iron coke burning stove with a backing of an asbestos panel to protect the chimney. To smarten up our beds for morning inspection, we placed strips of card around the edges of the mattress to square the corners and then covered them with the blanket. Some enterprising lads in another hut discovered a stack of asbestos panels in the engineers' workshop just the right size for a bed. Some mysteriously found their way to that hut. Then the rumour spread that their loss had been discovered and there would be an inspection with severe disciplinary action taken if the thieves were caught. It so happened that a new draft arrived who were only too delighted with the generous offer of flat asbestos panels to square up their beds. Since the newcomers arrived only after the loss had been discovered, obviously they were not the culprits and no official action was taken.

Those barrack room stoves were the only means of heating our billets. We were given a weekly coke ration which became less and less adequate as winter closed in. There was sufficient fuel for either a blazing fire one night and then nothing or a faint glimmer every night. Our hut was closest to the coke dump. A high wire mesh fence topped with coils of barbed wire prevented entry and it was rumoured that it was patrolled by the fierce Alsatians of the radar park. But a small stream ran under the fence in a concrete culvert where the wire had been bent back. We would take a receptacle and crawl through the culvert into the coke compound. It is surprising the noise that pieces of coke make when rumbling down a stack. One dark night we were filling our receptacle when a dog started barking. We rapidly escaped through the culvert, taking no chances with Alsatians, but it was probably only the sheepdog in the adjoining farm.

There must have been a set time for lights out and I was grateful for the support of those who showed their Christian commitment by saying their evening prayers kneeling at their beds. I suppose that because we were all at the lowest common denominator there was little mocking or bullying. I felt sorry for 'Scottie' from the Gorbals in Glasgow. He was on his own and had a very broad accent which we southerners found hard to understand. When he spoke, someone would shout, 'Translate'. We quickly came to recognise the reply, 'Ach Ye Bloody Sassenachs'. In the morning, we were woken by the Reveille. Woe betide anyone who thought they could indulge in a lie-in because, when the duty sergeant came round, he might try the toothpaste tube method to get you out of bed. With his stick, he would beat across the bottom of the bed, close to your feet. If you failed to move, blow two would strike your feet so you moved them up the bed, and so on until you wriggled out of bed like toothpaste coming out of its tube.

There were the usual drill parades, lectures and being shown the guns and radar equipment. The area round Tywyn gave quieter roads for route marches. Just occasionally we all got in step so the road resounded with the noise of our nailed boots. We were told that we would have thirty-six hours off with no duties one week end. Where to go? The snag was that on Saturday morning we were paraded for the Medical Orderlies to give us some jabs in case we were sent overseas. One jab in each arm. One or two lads fainted even before they were given their jabs. The remainder needed those thirty-six hours to recover. At least this prevented us being allocated cookhouse duties such as peeling potatoes and clearing up after meals. An evening duty there had some advantages because slices of bread and blocks of butter could be concealed in the fronts of our loose denims to be taken back to our huts to supplement our not too generous rations.

The camp had a NAAFI that sold some food and confectionary but above all Wills' Woodbines cigarettes. Our pay was little over one pound a week. Most of that was retained to start a savings account to give a lump sum on finishing training. The payment of this at the end of basic training was one of the few times in my life that I received the old Bank of England white five pound note, an absolute fortune! Smokers spent the rest on cigarettes. Those Woodbines were the cheapest available but, even so, on the days preceding pay day, there was a great trade among smokers desperate for a drag. These cigarettes had no filters so some lads resorted to sticking a pin in the last short quarter inch stub and holding the pin for a last final drag. A nasty trick was to pierce a virgin cigarette with a few pin holes so it did not draw properly.

Being a non-smoker, I put some of my savings into an electric flat iron for pressing my clothes. Thermostatically controlled irons were more than I could afford so I learnt how to heat it up, switch off when hot, do some ironing, switch it on and so on. One trick for sharp creases in battledress was to damp some brown paper with your shaving brush, (no electric razors) and iron that over the place where the crease was needed. I heard that you could toast bread with an iron. So I put a slice of bread on something flat and proceeded to iron it. The result was a sort of thin tough biscuit. What I should have done was to support the iron with its flat face uppermost and put the bread on the flat face. That result was quite tasty.

We were given some leave after Basic Training and I remember that first journey after ten weeks isolation when the only female we saw regularly was the Commanding Officer's daughter going to the little camp halt to catch the train to school in Tywyn – and of course the sheep. Starved of greater variety, it was a pleasant shock to see real ladies on station platforms. The return to camp involved taking a late train to Crewe and catching the night Post Office one into Wales. Trains in those days had proper carriages with blinds on both the outside windows and also those on the corridor. You found an empty compartment, pulled down the blinds and shut the door, hoping no one else would disturb your privacy. You spread out over one side of the seats. You would be lulled to sleep by the gentle clicking of the wheels over the rail joints and the swaying of the carriage. There was the puffing of the engine as it struggled up an incline and followed by rushing down to the next station where it would stop with squealing brakes. The noise and clatter of mail bags being loaded and unloaded in the dim light of dawn and the shouting of the station master warned us where to get off.

I had always known that if I were to be commissioned, further selection and training would be necessary. I do not know when I went to the WOSB. Before leaving Charterhouse, I was sent to see a retired Colonel who gave me a reference, I suppose in glowing terms, so that I was selected to go to one of the Boards. We were in groups of half a dozen to whom we had to give a talk. There were tests of our ingenuity and resourcefulness, such as how to get my troop across a swift flowing river full of hungry crocodiles with perhaps a pole that was too short to reach from bank to bank, a rope of similar length, and if you were lucky, a short plank. I passed.

While waiting to be called for my officer training, I took the opportunity explore the vicinity of Tywyn. Some officers had formed a sort of walking group. We went to Bird Rock where sea birds still nested miles inland even though the estuary had long since silted up. Close by was (and still is) the farmhouse where Mary Jones worked and from where she walked bare-foot across the hills to Dolgellau to buy a Welsh Bible with the few pennies she had saved in her domestic service. She was disappointed. There were none for sale. The priest was so impressed with her earnestness that he founded the Bible Society which today publishes Bibles in many different languages. We turned more westwards and caught the train back from Fairbourne. What a relief to climb into a nice warm steam-heated carriage.

One weekend, advantage was taken of army recreation transport to Aberystwyth. I wandered round and found the terminus of the Vale of Rheidol Railway. No trains were running since it was winter but the engine shed door was open and I was able to inspect the narrow gauge locomotives. Years later I travelled on the line and watched the engine snake its way along the track as the steam drove one cylinder after the other. Then there was the Talyllyn Railway on the camp doorstep. I volunteered to help with the permanent way maintenance. Among one party was the author, J.I.C. Boyd himself. We had to replace some of the sleepers on a section that could not have been touched since the line was laid in 1864. Two rusty red lines in the grass showed where the rails were. We removed the turf and dug down to try and find a sleeper. They had almost completely rotted away and were quite useless. We dug a trench, slid a new sleeper under the rails, packed it up and drove in spikes to hold the rails to the correct gauge. We carefully replaced the turf because it was only that which was stopping the rails from spreading and derailing the train. That railway certainly had a guardian angel.

Officer Training, Aldershot

It must have been into the New Year of 1956 that I was posted to Aldershot for training as an Officer Cadet. Any thoughts that we were superior beings were quickly knocked out of us by the stricter attitude of the instructors. The Sergeant Major reminded us, 'I call you Sir and you call me Sir. The difference is you mean it'. One morning a sergeant came up behind one cadet and shouted, 'One step forward, Quick March'. The cadet obeyed. 'Did that hurt?' 'No Sarg.' 'Next time get your hair cut. What is inside the beret is yours.

What is outside is mine. Get it cut'. This particular lad was very proud of his hair. We had to line up with the tallest on the right and the shortest on the left. One of the sergeants might look along the front of the line to see it was straight. We had the classic example with one stout cadet. 'Move back, number 5'. Then the sergeant looked along the back, 'Move forwards, number 5'.

We were introduced to our proper guns – 25 pounder Field Artillery. Ack ack and radar were forgotten. These guns consisted of two parts, the gun itself mounted on two wheels and a two wheeled trailer in which the ammunition was stored. Both had to be manhandled into their correct positions. The gun had to be raised onto its stand so it could be turned and accurately aimed. The crew each had his allotted position and function. The breech block had to be opened. The shell came in two parts. There was the actual missile which had to be checked for correct type; anti-tank, high explosive or what. This was rammed into the breech and, if not shoved in hard enough, might slide back. The propellant came in coloured bags which had to be selected, checked, put into the brass container or cartridge and shoved into the breech. Meanwhile, the layer was turning the gun both horizontally and vertically to aim it correctly. We had to learn how to do all this and much more to work as a team quickly and efficiently. Between these bouts of activity, there would be periods of calm. One important subject was map reading. This was vital for locating our guns, estimating the distance away of the target and the type of terrain between. That winter turned severe. We heard later that parts of the camp at Tywyn had frozen up so that hot water for shaving had to be fetched from the cookhouse. Aldershot was also freezing. Denims did not give much protection so I resorted to lining my legs with newspapers.

Some of our duties were night patrols round the camp. There would be an evening parade and inspection of those detailed before manning the Guard Room where we slept waiting our turns. I put a bar of chocolate in my top battledress pocket and slept on it, to find next morning that it had melted and caused a stain which luckily was not noticed. We patrolled with our rifles, not loaded I am sure. One night was cold and misty. We were of course on parade the following morning and, having cleaned everything the night before, I just did a quick going over. On parade we had to show our rifles to the Officer by holding it at an angle, opening the bolt and putting our thumb across the bottom of the bore to reflect light up it. The Officer looked down mine, 'Sergeant Major, I have never seen so much filth. When did you last clean it?' 'I thought this morning, Sir'. 'You are on a charge. Off to the Guard Room with him'. The mist of the previous night had caused the bore to rust. That was extra drill on the Saturday afternoon so no going home for me that weekend.

On those weekends when I remained in camp, I would go to the Garrison Church. The main altar was placed in a semi-circular chancel at one end of the rectangular building. This left spaces either side for a vestry and another room. I commented that the altar was on a set of rails and was told that originally there had been two altars, one for Church of England worshippers and another for Roman Catholics. The appropriate one would be pushed out for that service. My usual weekend procedure was to dash back to the billet as soon as official duties had finished, change into civies and race to Ash station which was closer than Aldershot. This meant I might catch an earlier train to Waterloo. There I would charge up the ramp to the high level platforms and jump on a Charing Cross to

Sevenoaks train. I became adept at waking up at the correct station. This was re-enacted in reverse on the Sunday evening.

Our training climaxed in a shooting camp at Sennybridge near Brecon in South Wales. In those days, the valley branch lines were still functioning and our little tank engine struggled along with its couple of carriages. We were not allowed to drive the gun towing tractors, Quads, with their crash gearboxes and none too good brakes on the steep narrow twisting roads leading to the ranges. Once there, we took it in turns to man all the functions of placing the guns, plotting where to aim and firing them. The four guns of a troop would be given a common feature to align them. I looked at the summit of the Brecon Beacons and decided it was not prominent enough. My inspecting officer decided otherwise. I took *War and Peace* to relieve the boredom between shoots. We were lucky with reasonable weather and I had done sufficiently well to have passed.

Back at Aldershot, there was the usual Passing Out Parade with the whole battalion lined up on the parade ground. For one practice in the cold of winter, we had to wear our army greatcoats. Our tall right marker, incidentally the son of the then Speaker of the House of Commons, had been issued with one from the Canadian army that was a slightly different colour from ours. The Sergeant Major looked him up and down. I sensed trouble. The Sergeant Major did not want that greatcoat in such a prominent position spoiling his parade. He found no fault and passed on. He returned up the middle row, looked at that greatcoat again, opened the flap at the back and spied the small Canadian army buttons. 'Here Sergeant – look at this – improperly dressed – Take him to the Guard Room'; and woosh, left right, left right. The cadets in the front row shuffled up to fill the gap.

Our Adjutant had the task of ordering the salute on proper Passing Out Parades. He looked resplendent in full red uniform on his horse but he did not have a strong voice to give the commands. Now Farnborough aerodrome was close by where jet engines were often tested at full throttle. Once this coincided with a Passing Out Parade. The adjutant gave the order for the battalion to march forward and give the salute. A jet engine started at the same time. Those nearest to him heard the order and started moving but those further away did not through the noise of the jet. Some saw the centre of the line moving and started. Then those further away followed suit. The result was our nice straight line ended in a chaotic bow.

I suppose that before our final passing out parade we were still gunners but afterwards I was Second Lieutenant Richard Hills. To celebrate, there was a formal dinner at Woolwich Arsenal, the Head Quarters of the Royal Artillery. We had little time before that event so my new pips were stuck onto my battledress with Copydex. We were shown the secure room with its magnificent array of silver objects of all sorts, collected from various officers' messes of various units as they were closed down or amalgamated. Some centre pieces with guns and horses were outstanding and a few were placed on the lengthy mahogany table in the hall where we were to dine. Along each side of the table, there was a strip of spotless white linen with our places laid on it in full glory. When we had finished eating and our places cleared, a person stood at each end. At a given signal, the cloth was rolled into a long tube and the two men at the end nearest the kitchens dashed off, dragging the cloth so it was whipped away from in front of us. Luckily I had been warned so kept my hands well clear.

448298 Second Lieutenant Richard L. Hills

This time, no photographs were taken with my new number. We had become real people. While there was still a high mountain to climb, both physically and metaphorically, from now on I would be much more responsible for my own life although still under orders in the army. We were sent home on stand-by to await our posting, partly because officers were needed to help run the CCF school camps in the summer holidays. This was great because it gave me the chance to return to Charterhouse to see the Masque which had been postponed for a year to celebrate the 350th Anniversary. But I was summoned to Woolwich to take a draft over to Germany so feared I might miss the Masque. We crossed on the ferry from Harwich to the Hook where I nearly had to sign for the train. While I would have loved to have owned a train, I was relieved that I was not responsible for any breakages, etc. At my destination, everyone was away on manoeuvres and the officers' mess was shut up. However I was given a meal and a bed and caught the next train back to the Hook. At Harwich, the Customs' Officer gave me a thorough search because he could not believe I had no cigarettes or alcohol. All this haste was in vain because the Masque I had hoped to see was cancelled due to the death of 'Sniffy' Russell while acting during a performance.

In July, I was posted to a camp on the Norfolk coast near Wells-Next-The-Sea where we had to plan exercises for the CCF camps such as a patrol coming under attack and how to wipe out the enemy. The sea was close by and tempting with broad stretches of sand but care had to be taken to avoid being cut off by the incoming tide. This pleasant way of life was cut short by Col. Nasser seizing the Suez Canal. I had to report to the 26 Field Regiment, Royal Artillery, at Shorncliffe Barracks near Folkestone. Chaos reigned everywhere with reservists being called up and equipment taken out of store. All vehicles and guns had to be painted desert yellow with the secret white 'H' on the side to show they were part of the allied forces. When some of our troops reached Suez, what did they see? Egyptian army vehicles painted desert yellow with a white 'H'. I was sent to Ashchurch near Tewksbury to collect some Karrier 3 ton lorries. They had crash gearboxes, permanent four-wheel drive and steering that was not self-centring. I nearly crashed one into a telegraph pole when it did not straighten up and I was struggling with the gearbox. Much later when I was driving a modern Bedford 3 tonner, I commented to the usual driver that I seemed to have conquered the crash gearbox. He pointed out that this vehicle had synchromesh. Before National Service, I had passed my ordinary driving test on Audrey's Ford Popular, only once bending a mudguard when I was backing it out of the cowshed garage at Seal and caught a fencing post. Driving these three tonners enabled me to pass my test for heavy vehicles and at the other extreme I passed my motor bike test as well.

We practised with our small arms, rifles and revolvers on a range near Folkestone. We were allowed all of ten rounds for our revolvers. Our troop commander failed to hit the target at about ten yards away. I did little better which confirmed my belief that it would have been more effective to throw the revolver at the enemy. At least it might have scored a hit. To show how prepared we were, a massed artillery shoot was organised on the ranges at Lark Hill near Salisbury. One Saturday, I was responsible for the recreational transport into that city so I had to wear uniform. I spent some time sketching the outside of the cathedral before sampling a meal in the Cathedral Hotel. The Dover sole filled one plate, the chips another and the bones a third. One of our tracked Bren gun carriers must have broken down there for, after we had returned to Shorncliffe, the driver was sent to collect it. The radiator in the centre of the vehicle needed a strong fan to keep it cool but the fan-driving belts had been wrongly fitted so it was not working properly. Coming back to Shorncliffe, the engine blew up, showering green antifreeze everywhere which had no means of draining away. The situation was made more embarrassing because the driver had left the proper route to see his girlfriend. I was sent to sort out the mess. Later I was able to drive one of these Bren gun carriers. Each side track was driven through a clutch. To turn, you declutched the track on the side to which you wanted to turn and put power onto the other side. If you were not careful, you would spin round and round. I regretted I did not have enough lessons to pass my tracked vehicle test.

The only part of our regiment that reached Suez was the Scammell heavy duty recovery vehicle which was found on the quay there. Once the Six Day War had been stopped, life settled down to a regular routine of giving the vehicles their normal 406 monthly inspection even though they had not moved. On pay days, an officer would be sent to the bank in Folkestone to collect the money which had been carefully sorted into the correct amounts for the respective units and put in blue canvas bags. The driver parked the open sided 'Champ' by the bank. The officer and one of the Army Pay Corps clerks walked into the bank, collected the bags and went out into the street to the waiting 'Champ'. I could not imagine that being done today. If the paying-out officer found he did not have enough to pay the last person, he must have made a mistake and had to make up the deficit. But if there was some money left over, that had to be handed back. Once I was very nearly pounds out when I mixed up the bags for the different units. Luckily the Sergeant Major spotted the error and helped to sort it out.

Hoping to save the time and cost of going home at weekends by train, I looked round for a suitable motorbike that would be cheaper to run than a car. Father arranged for me to buy one from a parishioner, a 98cc. Excelsior two stroke. Petrol was rationed and this machine was very economical. Returning to barracks at night, there were no motorways in those days and the roads were clear, so I could open the throttle and cruise at its top speed of I suppose 45 m.p.h. I was a little more careful going through Maidstone. I fitted it with a Perspex windshield to give some comfort. One stormy day, I was going into Folkestone when a gust of wind roared through the gap between two hotels and sent me flying across the road only to be forced back again by the wind hitting the buildings on the other side – quite terrifying. I realised that through this weekend commuting I was not joining either community, home or work, so I resolved that in the future I would try to put roots down in one or other place.

This little Excelsior introduced me to the Royal Electrical and Mechanical Engineer artificer because it inevitably needed repairs. Watching his skill with hand tools taught me a lot. Engine, clutch and gearbox were stripped down and given a thorough overhaul.

This improved performance considerably. I asked him if he would finish the boiler for my Invicta because, although I had been making parts on my small lathe, I did not have the heating capacity for silver-soldering the boiler outside flanges and stays. I did not realise that he did not know how to silver-solder so he ruined it by brazing it. Even so, Invicta was 'highly commended' when displayed at the Army Art and Crafts Exhibition at Eltham Palace in 1957.

I found my way to the Education Department where I attempted to explain fractions and decimals to some 'other ranks'. I was asked to invigilate a maths examination. The candidate was an Irish substantive sergeant who had never been able to pass that exam but was vital for running the stores for one of our companies. If he failed this time, he would revert to Bombardier with loss of pay and might well leave. When I entered the room, I was surprised to see another sergeant sitting beside him. In his rich Irish brogue he said, 'Begorrah, its all in me mind but I cannot put it down on paper'. He started dictating with the other sergeant writing. A little later I looked to see progress. I checked over the supposedly dictated answers and reckoned that, if I did not stop the other sergeant, the one who had failed so often would get 100%. Luckily for me, the results were not queried.

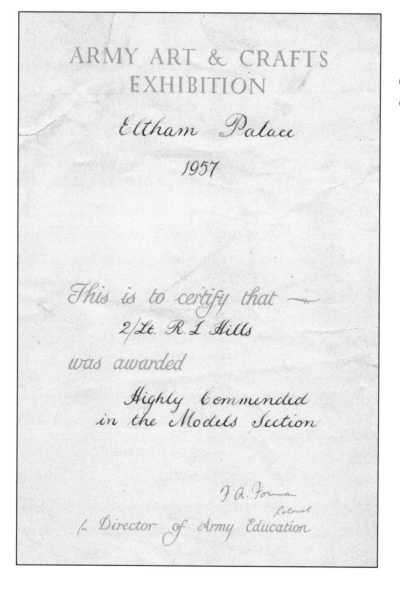

Certificate awarded for the model of Invicta

National Service

Part 2 – Commissioned Officer.

The Army Mountaineering Association

National Service surprisingly gave me the opportunity to climb higher mountains than I had ever done before. But it is first necessary to return to the summer of 1955 after that successful meet in North Wales with Wilfrid Noyce and leaving Charterhouse. I was hanging around waiting for my call-up papers so I was able to go to Switzerland with father, Audrey and Margaret for a holiday at Evolene above the Rhone valley and Sion.

My first passport photo

I did a little walking in the Val d'Herens but the climax of that week was hiring a guide to climb the Pigne d'Arolla. Great excitement for we stayed the night in a genuine Alpine Club hut and made a successful ascent up what was really an easy climb. This my first true snow and ice Alpine climb was exhilarating. Down to earth back in the valley I watched the smiths forging climbing equipment such as crampons. I still proudly display the ice axe I purchased made by P. Bovier, Evolene, a treasured possession.

My ice axe

Somehow I found two kindred spirits in the camp at Folkestone who joined me in obtaining permission to form a 26 Field Regiment Royal Artillery expedition to Ben Nevis in February 1957. The train journey across Rannoch Moor in the teeth of a blizzard was spectacular with the engine belching out smoke and steam as it battled against the elements in that bleak landscape. We felt sorry for the kids waiting on the platform at Carrour for the train to take them to school. That blizzard deposited so much snow on the peaks that we realised it was unsafe to climb them. We had been issued with army compo rations – mutton Scotch style; open the tin to be greeted by a layer of fat on removing which you might find a couple of nondescript brown lumps of supposedly meat and the rest swede. You had to be hungry to eat it. We stayed at the Youth Hostel and transported some of our supplies to the Charles Inglis Clark Scottish Mountaineering Club hut at the foot of the crags below the north face of Ben Nevis. One route passed the Glen Nevis distillery with its distinctive aroma encouraging you up the path. We cached our stocks in the box containing the rescue stretcher outside the hut. I had obtained permission to use the hut on the strength of my being a candidate for election to the Climbers' Club. But what to do next?

Fortuitously we met an RAF rescue unit that was going south who agreed to take us to Glencoe and bring us back three or four days later. We were deposited at that Youth Hostel. During our time there, we climbed peaks along the south side such as Bidean Nam Bian and Buchaille Etive Beag. We cut through the cornice and descended into the 'Hidden Valley' where the villagers had driven their cattle to protect them from being stolen. I looked back up at the ridge to see the setting sun glowing through the hole we had made, colouring the snow with a startling blue and white tinge. We celebrated at the local pub in a special bar for climbers. On our request for beer, the landlady attached a rubber pipe to the cock on top of a barrel and started to pressurise the barrel by means of a car foot pump. After much effort, she turned on the tap and a thin trickle of beer emerged, slowly filling the mugs with mostly froth.

Next day, we took the bus up the valley to tackle the famous Aonach Eagach ridge. Snow and ice conditions were ideal. Many years later in September 1991, I booked on an HF Holidays Ridges and Scrambles week at Ballachulish to see what that organisation was like and whether I should help them as a leader. We were tackling the Aonach Eagach ridge and, as I was plodding up to the start in my steady Alpine fashion, one of the younger members asked my age. 'Fifty seven', I replied. His response was, 'I hope I am as fit as you when I reach that age'. That day, we were caught on the ridge by deteriorating weather conditions with gusting wind and dashing rain. I was faced with a problem – being short-sighted, I could not see clearly where to place my feet without glasses but neither could I see clearly with rain pouring down my spectacles.

Returning to our army expedition, we decided to tackle the Buchaille Etive Mor and afterwards to go to the King's House hotel for a venison dinner and return on the bus. We glissaded down so quickly that we arrived far too early and decided to walk back to the Youth Hostel for a more meagre repast. The RAF folk were due to pick us up the next morning but they forgot and we heard their lorry passing by on the main road. We resorted to walking to Ballachulish ferry and bus from there to Fort William.

Once more at the CIC hut we found other occupants who admitted they would have eaten our cache of food had they known about it. Snow conditions had improved. One classic route we tackled was Tower Ridge. The face of the Tower itself was well glazed over so it had to be tackled by a delicate traverse around the side. We achieved the summit of the highest mountain in Britain to find the concrete trig point covered in a mass of delicate featherlike snow crystals, pretty but deadly if built up on ones clothing. The compass bearing from the summit to the Col was accurate so we descended safely to the hut. Other climbs on the ridges and summits around the Ben were conquered to complete my successful first serious winter mountaineering expedition.

I do not know how I heard about the Army Mountaineering Association but in May 1957 I had leave of absence to join their meet at Helyg in North Wales. There to my surprise I met cousin Maj. Hugh Robertson, one of its leading lights. It had been formed only recently and this could have been its inaugural meet. We went walking in the Carneddau and rock climbing on Tryfan and in particular Craig yr Ysfa at the head of Cwm Eigiau.

Possibly because I was so close to ending my National Service that August, I was given further leave of absence to participate

My Father's prismatic compass, which I also used in my mountaineering

in the Army Mountaineering Association meet at Zermatt, their first Alpine adventure. Hugh was there as well. The only way to reach that town was by railway up from Visp. The train had to struggle up lengthy rack sections to gain height. No cars were allowed. Benjamin Edgerton, the mountaineering equipment manufacturers, asked us to try out an ultra lightweight high altitude tent. Some new manmade fibre formed the main cover. It was sewn onto the groundsheet which reached a little way up the sides to make it draught-proof. There was no flysheet. It snowed at our high level while we were away climbing to find that back in Zermatt it had rained. The rain came through the thin material but, from the way the groundsheet had been sewn on, it could not drain away so much of our equipment was soaked. Luckily the August sun in Zermatt soon dried everything out.

A guide was hired to instruct us in snow and ice techniques as well as lead some routes. I followed often leading another rope. Many of the notable peaks around Zermatt such as the Allalinhorn, the Alphubel, and the Taschorn were tackled but not the Matterhorn. The guide wanted us to conquer the Dom, the highest mountain entirely in Switzerland. We took the train a little way down the valley to Tasch where we began the ascent. Two quite strenuous days were needed to cover the total height so we spent one night in a hut. There was the usual Alpine start well before dawn when the condition of the snow would be better. On the summit, the guide produced a hip flask. It contained the banned substance Absinthe but we all had a sip to toast the Swiss. While descending, I found a patch of edelweiss. I picked a flower and put it in the back of my little travelling Bible where it still resides.

My final climb was the Zinal Rothorn on which I was pleased to have been the rope leader as there were some difficult parts. I had to return to England so I could arrange to be demobbed while some of the party stayed on to climb the Dente Blanche. One subaltern leading the descent slipped and pulled off his leader behind so they both fell down the mountain side. A tragedy was nearly avoided because the rope passed over a rocky buttress with one sliding down either side. This ought to have stopped them but the rope broke and their descent continued. The subaltern survived but the older man died in hospital. This occurred just when the older types of rope made from natural fibres were being superseded by nylon so perhaps if it had been nylon, it might have held. I heard about this accident only after I was back in Folkestone but it did not deter my enthusiasm for mountaineering. I had learnt a great deal about snow conditions, glaciers, crevasses and the like as well as climbed some high mountains.

The Lydd Army Camp

Lydd is situated well out on the flat Romney Marsh where the more fertile ground gives way to shingle. The army camp consisted of three sections. First were the barracks and accommodation for the regular army. Frequently this was occupied by a unit of one of the Guards' Regiments. In 1957, this was the Scots' Guards. When one of their officers was asked, 'Wasn't it rather remote from life in London?' 'Oh no', he replied, 'We can just nip round to Lydd airport, put the car on a plane and be in Paris in no time'. Then there were the Lydd ranges principally used for anti-tank shooting practice. These were maintained mostly by civilians. Finally the third section was temporary accommodation for Territorial Regiments and others using the ranges. This was the section for which I was put in charge.

My detachment had a sergeant and six to eight men. We were responsible for seeing the incoming unit had the equipment they needed and tidying up after they had left. Most of those who came were T.A. units for weekends. A quartermaster appeared from time to time to see all was in order. He knew some of his colleagues who worked in a shared office elsewhere. When he was discussing a difficult problem with one of them and heard the click of a telephone receiver being picked up, he would ask, 'Now are you both listening? I will repeat what I have just said so you both know'.

I was given a room in one of the huts used by visiting officers. It backed onto the small parade ground where the Guards pipers practised. Often there would be four at once trying to learn different new tunes. The noise was a bit much even for me with my considerable Scots ancestry. A special arrangement was made for me to have meals in the Scots' Guards mess. Even their National Service subalterns were expected to have a private income so their normal charges were reduced for me. Breakfast was a quiet affair with peaked hats worn and heads hidden behind newspapers. Everywhere was cleaned up and people on their best behaviour for a visit by the Duke of Gloucester. I was introduced and remember his startling blue eyes. He had made an earlier visit probably during the war when he inspected a specially cleaned Ack Ack gun as he was coming out of Rye. There happen to be two routes from Rye to Lydd. One was by the sea through Camber and the other a more circuitous route inland. The gun quickly upped itself and went by Camber to take up position near Lydd station. It was duly inspected by the Duke who went on into the camp. Lydd has two routes to the camp from the land side so while the Duke inspected the Ranges, the gun upped itself again to be inspected for the third time. It was not worthwhile polishing up three guns even for a Duke.

I attended few of the formal Officers' Mess dinners because they were very expensive but I took care to go to what would be my final one. I was warned that towards the end, a piper would march round playing appropriate tunes. Guests might be asked to suggest one. The youngest subaltern had to remember these, go out and tell the piper. Older officers would choose the most obscure reels and woe betide the subaltern if he got one wrong. The Colonel turned to me and asked what I would like. All I could remember was 'Auld Lang Syne'. Luckily I had a sudden flash of inspiration. I apologised that I could not suggest one as I was a 'Kentish Man' which went down very well.

Out on the ranges, the guns were positioned facing towards the sea with a limited arc of fire. The targets were mock tanks cut out from plywood. They were mounted on 2 ft. gauge four-wheeled railway bogies powered by twin 'V' cylinder internal combustion engines. The bogies ran on tracks concealed from the guns by mounds of shingle which had been dug out from the route of the track to lower it so that the track itself and the bogies would not be hit by the gunfire. The track was laid out in various routes. Some went across the

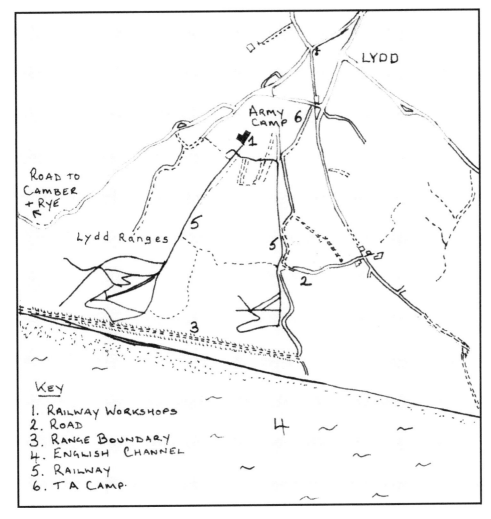

Map of the Lydd Ranges

firing line of the guns at right angles set at parallel distances from the guns. Others were aligned diagonally so that the tank could approach or go away from the guns. The speed of these plywood tanks was controlled by 'trips' between the rails. On nearing a corner, a trip would operate a brake on the bogie and slow it down. Once round the curve, another would reset the throttle to speed it up again. Today, these mechanical devices would be replaced by electronic.

These railways were maintained with the help of at least a couple of Ruston two cylinder diesel locomotives. I happened to enter the workshop when one was being tested after an overhaul. One man stood on the engine where he could reach the compression cocks. A massive crank handle which turned a heavy flywheel protruded from the side. Two men started cranking with great effort. When they thought they had achieved sufficient speed, the man on the engine flicked the compression taps shut – 'bump'. The crank stopped dead without the engine firing.

I became acquainted with the civilian Range Manager who invited me to see the model railway, either 'O' gauge or gauge 1, I forget which, that he had built in a barn behind his house. Through Lydd's exposed position way out in the marshes, there is always a wind blowing either up or down the Channel. This carried some salt which tarnished the rails on his track so unless he cleaned them every time he wanted to run a train, he could not have electrically driven models. He devised a layout in the shape of a capital 'E' laid flat. There was a terminus at the top and bottom arms while in the middle was the signal box controlling the layout. A person sat in the box. The trains were set out in a predetermined order. The first train was attached to one end of a piece of string which passed round pulleys to the other terminus and back to the signal box. The operator pulled the string and the train set off to its destination. I know there were cable-operated tram systems but I have never heard of a model railway worked by this means.

One group came for a longer stay at the Lydd camp, not for shooting on the ranges but because they were 'extras' being shot while acting in the film 'Dunkirk'. The advertisements for the film stated it was 'Shot on the beaches'. This was quiet correct but the beaches were those of Camber Sands. While the film stars stayed in the luxury of the Mermaid Inn at Rye, the ordinary soldiers were played by a platoon of the Argyll and Sutherland Highlanders who were billeted in my part of the camp. They had to stand for hours in the sea while the pictures were taken with clouds of black smoke billowing behind them. But they were a tough lot. Their officer told me they were one of the first units to land at Suez. Their landing craft approached the shore, let down its front ramps to be confronted by the barrel of a tank gun pointing straight at them. Nevertheless they scrambled out and ran up the shore. They banged on the side of the tank, the hatch opened, the Egyptians climbed out and ran away.

After their ordeal at sea on the Camber Sands, these regulars needed their usual evening entertainment of downing a few beers and a wee dram. Lydd had three pubs and two beer houses. Generally they could estimate demand fairly well but they had an unofficial agreement that one would hold an extra stock for that week on which the others could draw. On more than one occasion, the barman was seen carrying back a large jug full of a brownish liquid. The Argyll and Sutherland Highlanders soon drank Lydd dry and went further afield. To return late at night, they would 'borrow' a car. Car security was minimal at that time. On many a morning, I had to deal with the police and an irate owner come to collect his car.

Possibly because there was little activity as the Suez crisis faded away, some of the National Service subalterns acquired what euphemistically were called second-hand cars; old bangers would be a better name. Maintaining these was certainly instructive. Luckily the MOT test was still well in the future. One car broke down at night close to the camp and would have to be towed back. Was it just coincidence that an army one tonner happened to be passing? We attached a rope to a convenient bar across the front of the radiator that carried the headlights. Unfortunately the bar was in fact a tube not strong enough to take the towing strain. It bent so that the headlamps pointed outwards and part of the front wings became detached, flapping rather like those of a bird. Its owner was not amused.

I fell for an Avon Standard Special which had been damaged in some accident so the rear body and seating was a write-off. The men at Lydd Ranges built an open body from scrap plywood off the tank targets. We painted it bright red. However running it was another steep learning curve. It had cable operated Bendix front brakes which were very difficult to adjust. Once coming round a sharp corner, I stopped just in time to avoid a large tanker.

26 Field Regiment Royal Artillery, officers' Mess Ball, Summer 1957. Shirely Sennett on left then myself

The water pump did not work properly so it had a tendency to overheat and spew water out of the radiator cap onto the occupants.

I did use it a little and it was certainly preferable to the little Excelsior motorbike for trips between Lydd, Folkestone and Seal. One of these was to take my current girlfriend Shirley Sennett from Seal and back afterwards to the Regimental Officers' Mess ball near the end of my time at Folkestone. She appears in the photograph with me and another subaltern loading up our plates. Luckily the following morning was dry and bright for our drive back as the car had no hood.

Eventually a big-end bearing failed. I took the engine to pieces at Seal and tried to fit bearings out of a similar engine found in a scrap yard. I had neither the skill nor the equipment for such a task at this time and the car was scrapped.

Conclusion

I completed all the formalities to finish National Service at the end of August and was looking forward to Cambridge and Queens' College. Theoretically we were retained for a couple of years in the reserve. One report summed this up, 'This officer has not reported for annual training'. This is not quite the end of the Lydd story because while I was there in the army, I got to know the lady who ran the antique shop. Her husband was A.J. Bird the author of *The Veteran Car* and owned a very early Lanchester. When later I was searching for a vintage car, I was in Lydd and called to see her. She suggested that I tried an architect friend, Roger Castiglioni, who she thought was selling his Lancia Lambda. That story forms another chapter.

The little prince had grown up. He had lived with people from many different walks of life. He had had to lead them both up physical mountains as well as sort out so many other metaphysical ones. He had been entrusted with his own quasi-independent command. But one never knows what may happen as this final story from National Service days will show. I shared a room at Folkestone with another subaltern who had completed his university degree before his National Service so tended to tease us public school boys. He felt I ought to see how the other half lived so invited me for a long weekend to his home in Oldham. While I was fascinated by the new electric trains snaking their down the Woodhead valley which we watched from our vantage point on one of the rocky crags we were climbing, I was not impressed by the mile after mile of rows of red brick cottages with their slate roofs and the vast grim cotton mills. 'I hope I never work here' I thought...

The Fourth Age
Cambridge Undergraduate

Part 1 – Life at Queens'

The Family Background

It is time to catch up on what had been happening to other members of the family. Uncle Stanley Hills was working for the Sheikh of Bahrain as a civil engineer in charge of the Public Works Department.

Uncle Stan with the Sheikh of Bahrain

He built a new hospital and a new palace. This had a demountable copper dome that was turned green by spraying it with sulphuric acid in England because Bahrain had so little rain. It was taken to pieces and reassembled out there. Owing to the heat, he found he needed at least two clean shirts a day. To have a cold bath, he would fill one at the beginning of the day and allow it to cool by evaporation. He married Barnie and they invited Margaret to stay with them for a little while. Margaret flew home on the newest jet aircraft, the Comet, and luckily was on the last flight before the one that crashed in the Mediterranean through faulty window design. I think she never flew again but started training to be an Occupational Therapist with the result that we shall see in a moment.

Partly through Uncle Stan's suggestion and help from a Seal parishioner, John joined a shipping agent in Basra as a clerk. He spent many years in the Persian Gulf before a spell in Nigeria. He went to Isfahan in Iran to work in the Church Missionary Society hostel for boys and was lucky to escape when the Shah fell. Auntie Kath and Uncle Rob also accepted an invitation from Uncle Stan to visit Bahrain. A typical Arab feast was laid on in their honour. She was the special guest so was offered the choicest part of the roast sheep, the eye. She turned down this treat by suggesting that there must be someone more worthy. Around 1958, Auntie Kath and Uncle Rob moved out of Littlehurst with its large house and garden to a slightly smaller one at Westerham.

Family group possibly at the christening of Rosamund c. 1944.
Back row, Leslie Hills, Robert Tomson, Freda Hills, Stanley Hills, Alina Hills (Aunt), Falkner Allison; Middle Row, Kath Tomson, Olive Hills, John Hills, Henry Hills (grandfather), Charlotte Hills (grandmother), Ruth Allison, Richard Hills; Front, Margaret Bishop

Auntie Ruth, the youngest of that generation Hills, married the Rev. Faulkner Allison. He had three brothers, all ordained. The eldest, Roger, became a Canon at the Anglican Cathedral in Jerusalem. Oliver became Bishop of the Sudan where he is credited with helping to maintain peace in that unhappy country. He was always good company. Gordon remained in England. Some have called him the real saint because he kept house for their mother into her old age, freeing the other three for their seemingly more glamorous careers. Faulkner had a parish at Erith, North Kent, where we paid the occasional visit. They had three children, Sherard a little younger than myself, Anthony and Rosamund. In 1945, he was appointed Principal of Ridley Hall, Cambridge, one of the Church of England theological

*Ruth and Rosamund on
Littlehurst steps*

colleges for training ordinands. I stayed there when I must have been about twelve and was invited to join the Ridley team and play cricket against Queens'. I cannot think we did very well.

Alas that family suffered a tragedy there. Anthony, a bright mischievous boy, had been warned not to play on the large wooden gates at the entrance to Ridley Hall. Faulkner had repeatedly asked that the gates should be repaired, to no avail. Of course Anthony climbed on one and pulled it onto himself. Faulkner and Ruth decided to try for another child who was Phillipa, a bit of a tom boy.

Years later, I went into the Principal's house again and hardly recognised the interior, the once magnificent sweeping staircase had shrunk dramatically. Faulkner was offered the See of Chelmsford where the Bishop's Palace was next door to the

*Richard, Rosamund, Ruth, Sherard
and Phillipa at Littlehurst*

Uncle Faulkner outside Ridley Hall with his A40

vicarage of the priest of that parish – his brother Gordon. Ruth and Faulkner purchased a small fisherman's cottage in Aldeburgh where they could escape from their onerous church ties. As part of his duties, Faulkner sometimes had to attend on the Queen. He had no chauffeur so had to follow in his own Austin A 40. This was alright in urban areas but when they were out in the country, he had great difficulty in keeping up with her large powerful Daimlers.

Aunt Evelyn and Uncle Sandy Miller first moved to Hayling Island but decided to

Family group at the seaside, most likely at West Runton

Sherard and Richard sailing in a dingy

emigrate to Calgary in Canada to be near their daughter and that family. They could not adapt to a strange country, especially the cold winters, so returned to Chiddingfold, south of Godalming. Of the Robertsons, Elspeth became Elspeth Quayle through marrying a Manx architect. She had Nicholas and Cornelia. Pru became a Sykes and lived at Lydham Manor in Shropshire. I had warned her that I might call on my way back from a Public and Preparatory School (PPS) Camp. On nearing her home, I smelt a very familiar smell and could not think what it was until I caught up with a tractor and trailer full of HOPS! Pru was out when we called. We explained to the person in the kitchen that Pru was expecting us and that we had just come from Wales. 'That must be a terrible long journey'. The border was less than two miles away. We saw a newly baked fruit cake and thought our waiting for her justified trying it. But we had to leave before she appeared. She wondered what had happened to her cake, having forgotten all about us. She may have blamed her brother Hugh because he frequently called there in his Morgan Plus Four sports car on his way to and from North Wales.

A Changing World

For myself, Cambridge presented new possibilities but we did not realise how much the world would change after the debacle of Suez. World War II had been won not only with the help of the United States of America but with the armed forces from so many countries of the British Empire – that Empire on which the sun never set. The advance at Suez was stopped by the intervention of the United States. Great Britain's pride had been severely dented and her commanding position in world affairs challenged. With his background of so many members working overseas, it was natural that the onetime head of Rose Hill School, head of Robinites, 2nd. Lieutenant Royal Artillery, should consider a career in some part of the Empire. But India, once the jewel in the crown, had experienced vicious riots that resulted in its partition into India, Pakistan and Bangladesh. Parts of Africa were chaffing under colonial rule such as Kenya and the Mau Mau. It became clear during my time as an undergraduate that the possibility of a career in the Colonial Service would be less and less viable. Sir Alfred Lyall had started his service in India just before the Indian Mutiny. Now one hundred years later, this possibility was closed to his great-great grandson.

Christianity also was undergoing many changes with its dominant position as the Church of England being challenged. When new National Service recruits were first registering upon joining up, they would be asked, 'What is your religion?' Most looked bewildered so the clerk entered 'C. of E.' Adherence to Christianity was minimal. For most it was irrelevant. Many long established theological certainties were being questioned. New translations of the Bible such as the New English Bible and later the Good News Bible presented different meanings from the Authorised Version of King James. Indeed was the Bible the inerrant Word of God? Then the book, *Honest to God* by John Robinson openly expressed the doubts that many people felt about Christian doctrines – and that coming from a bishop. What should one believe? Yet in the midst of so much uncertainty so often the way ahead opened up. Sometimes it seemed that I had reached a sort of fork in the road when either way might be the right one. Ordination or teaching presented themselves as possibilities.

Queens' College, Cambridge

I must have gone to Queens' College in December 1954 while still at Charterhouse to be interviewed for acceptance as an undergraduate. I think I took the scholarship examination but with no success in being awarded a grant. I was interviewed by the Senior Tutor, Arthur Armitage, with his imposing thick eyebrows. I do not remember any conditions being put on my acceptance such as a certain number of 'A' Levels and it was agreed that I would first finish my National Service before joining Queens'. I still think that it may have helped my case following in father's footsteps. A couple of years later it would have been much more difficult to gain a place because by then the termination of National Service had been announced so that demand for places was tremendous.

And so I arrived in Cambridge, another learning curve starting at the bottom again. No sooner had I arrived than I

Dean Henry Hart's Bookmark with College shield

Portrait of myself at Queens'

had to go my Tutor, Peter Mathias, to ask for an 'exeat' or time away to be an usher at Margaret's wedding to Robert (Bob) Bishop.

Bob Bishop and baby Stephen

Bob was studying for his doctorate in some form of astronomy at Oxford. Margaret was there, learning the craft skills then taught as Occupational Therapy. She made her own wedding dress and cake. The marriage service was held in Seal church followed by the reception in the vicarage garden. Luckily it was fine. The top two layers of the cake were too heavy and started sinking into the icing of the bottom one. A guest asked, 'Am I drunk or is the cake really leaning?' Bob was offered a job at GCHQ in Cheltenham where they moved and set up house. Their eldest child, Stephen, was born the following June so they purchased the Old Malthouse in Brimpsfield where they lived until 2016.

It was Queens' policy to put first year undergraduates in digs with the following two years in College. My digs were out beyond Coe Fen towards Grantchester. Unfortunately my landlady decided she did not like me and resented my having friends back for tea or coffee. One afternoon I went out to play hockey wearing a brand new pair of rubber-soled boots. She was not pleased thinking they must have nailed studs. I asked for a transfer and was lucky that the Head Porter was taking students again following the death of his wife.

Being out of college necessitated a bicycle and padlock. I fitted mine with a ladies shopping basket on the front handlebars for carrying gowns, books etc. While the rear lamp was fixed, the front one had a sliding bracket so could be 'borrowed' easily. I purchased a small lamp that fitted into a pocket. It gave a legal but poor light. One night as I was cycling back across Coe Fen, I saw a large black object on the path. My brakes squealed and I just avoided running into a cow. I am not certain which was more surprised, me or the cow. I was tempted to see what would happen if I tried what one student is said to have replied when stopped at night by a policeman for riding the wrong way up a one way street. The officer pointed out that he had no rear light. 'But I don't need one, do I'. A Queens' engineering student in my year was stopped and charged by the police for faulty brakes.

Unfortunately it was Arthur Armitage sitting on the bench that day who showed no mercy. 'You of all people should have known better'.

For my second year, Humphrey Nye, who had been on PPS Camps and Broads with me, agreed to share a room, or rather a bedroom and a sitting room. The one we were allocated was in Essex Court. That part of Queens' must have been built in the 1750s. While the best rooms fronted the Cam, ours looked into a small courtyard and never saw the sun but was large enough to hold meetings for small groups. This was long before the days of en suite washing facilities but we were graciously allowed the use of a bathroom up two flights of stairs. I suspect that Henry Hart, the Dean, fared better in his larger suite immediately above ours. In the third year, I shared rooms with Laurie Hubbard in Walnut Tree Court. This time we were on the first floor with a pleasant view out with the Library and Old Chapel on the left and the new Chapel to the right. Growing in the grass between them was a large walnut tree, reputed to be the second. The reason for the demise of the first was attributed to the toilet facilities. For the nearest, it was necessary to go into Old Court and down the stairs by the Porters' Lodge. Or if you wanted a bath, you had to go right round the new Chapel and down the stairs of the Dockett Building. At least gyp rooms with water and basins were provided on each floor.

Daily Life

We paid a single fee to the College which covered everything, tutorials, lectures, accommodation, meals, etc. You could opt out of breakfast and lunch and receive a refund. This was a cause of many complaints because the refund was less than what we had to pay. This was justified by the catering manager on the grounds that he had to provide the service whether you were there or not. In fact, it was discovered that he was providing more lunches than there were Queens' students. Our College was situated conveniently close to a main lecture block in Mill Lane so students from other colleges were coming for a free meal. You could not claim a refund for missing dinner or 'Hall' in the evening. This was meant to be compulsory and you had to wear a gown.

Mornings were set aside for lectures which would be recommended by your Tutor or Director of Studies. Libraries would be open all day so that reading could be done in the afternoon if not playing a sport. The evenings would be the time to attend special interest societies such as the Railway Club or the Cambridge University Mountaineering Club, drama or singing groups. Black gowns were normal evening wear. On a Sunday, you could find a meeting at some type of church virtually all day. There would be a college Holy Communion at 8 am. Great St. Mary's University Church and other parish churches like Holy Trinity would have a morning service; after a break for lunch, there might be the University Sermon at 3 pm. in Great St. Mary's. You might go to the vicarage of Holy Trinity for a Pastorate meeting over tea. College chapels had evensong with a sermon and to finish the day there might be discussions or talks in the evening. You could choose from the very high church of Little St. Mary's to the low Round Church. As if that was not enough, there might be mid-week discussions and meetings for the Cambridge Intervarsity Christian Union or the Students' Christian Movement perhaps over breakfast where obviously the thick chunky marmalade was for the CICU or the thin jelly Golden Shred for the SCM (or vice versa depending on your views).

Academic Studies

I had to decide what to read. My academic career so far was not outstanding. Having read Classics at Charterhouse, I did not have the necessary background for engineering, physics or mathematics. My attainments in Latin and Greek meant that classics would be a desperate struggle. Theology seemed to limit the choice of a later career. This really left history to build on my Ancient History. My Director of Studies (and Tutor) was Peter Mathias, a fellow of Queens'. He was already noted in the realm of Economic History for his study of the brewing industry and in particular Whitbreads. He showed this Company that they had not been founded in the year they thought but earlier and so had missed their 300 anniversary celebrations. It is said that his completed history of brewing was too massive to be accepted for a doctoral thesis.

We were expected to attend recommended lectures and write an essay once a week on a subject set by our tutors. I went to G.R. Elton's fiery lectures on the Tudors and Stuarts. Earlier writers on this subject were wrong so he said we had to buy his books (groans!). For Economic History, there was Prof. John Saltmarsh, Vice Provost of Kings'. One highlight of his course was his demonstration of fulling stocks, one of the very few teaching aids other than chalk and talk in any of our lectures. What was really memorable was the tour he led round Kings' Chapel. He took us up into the space above the fan vaulting and under the lead covered roof with its massive beams. Holes in the stone vaulting enabled us to appreciate (or otherwise) the drop to the floor below. Back at ground level, John showed us how Henry VIII had altered the original design of his father for the sake of Anne Boleyn. The pillars supporting the roof had been modified from an earlier Gothic style to support the fan vaulting. As he was explaining this, John gently caressed the stonework showing his affection for the fabulous building.

In order to catch up on my knowledge of these new subjects, I was allowed to borrow some books from Queens' Library and take them home during the vacation. On returning through Liverpool Street Station, I needed the toilet so added my heavy case to a pile of others and nipped downstairs. Coming up again, my case had vanished, never to be traced. After that, Humphrey Nye's parents generously allowed me to stay in their Edwardian house in Dulwich Village because I had obtained a Reader's Ticket for the British Museum which proved very useful later. I commented on the single step down to the back bedroom and was told that the first two houses built in their row had this room on the same level as the rest of that floor. They could not be sold because the maid was on the same level as the master and mistress! Humphrey's father loved trifle. One evening some had been left over. At breakfast next morning, his mother suggested he might like to eat it then. He looked sheepish and confessed he had already eaten it with his early morning cup of tea.

Another tutor was blind Miss Woodleigh. I had to read out my essay while she took notes. One of her more famous pupils was David Shepherd. She said he sometimes apologised for the inadequacy of his essay owing to his cricketing commitments. He would later be Bishop of Liverpool. Miss Woodleigh was partly instrumental in founding the Anglican Society to promote the Liberal cause in the Church. One speaker was the Rev. John Habgood, then Vice Principal of Westcott House, a leader at PPS Camps and later Archbishop of York. He covered his subject so fully and succinctly that nobody could ask any questions afterwards. I enjoyed Economic History with, for example, Carus Wilson promulgating an Industrial Revolution in the 13th. century due to the employment of water-powered fulling stocks and helve hammers. I began to realise that the Second Industrial Revolution of the eighteenth and nineteenth centuries was an important British contribution to world civilization. This topic was not an option in my third year so I turned to Economics which I found rather 'lies, damn'd lies and statistics'. However I managed to scrape through with a third class degree which gained me acceptance to take the Diploma of Education course the following year.

Other Activities Connected with Queens'

Our rooms were heated with gas fires which were useful for toasting bread or even, if lucky, crumpets. Most rooms were provided with a gas ring in the hearth on which a kettle could be boiled. After Hall, we gathered in groups for coffee in our rooms. Ours was quite varied with historians, theologians, natural scientists and others. One member of our group would put the coffee grounds in a saucepan on the ring and light it, only to find the kettle was empty. He made a quick dash to the gyp room. By this time, the roasting coffee filled the room with a delightful aroma. On returning, he tipped the water into the pan which splattered everywhere in clouds of steam. Spectacular but the taste of the coffee did not come up to expectation.

Out of this group was formed an 'Eight' to row in the May 'Bumps' on the Cam. We called ourselves the 'Queens' Beasts' and were allocated the eighth boat. Needless to say we did not succeed in winning our oars. After practice, we would adjourn to an Indian restaurant. Usually each person would order a separate curry dish such as mild, vegetable, prawn, Madras, etc. and we would mix them all together. One evening, someone decided he wanted his own mild curry and wasn't going to share it round. Needless to say, he had the very hot Madras curry. He did eat it!

There were various clubs for Queens' members such as Henry Hart's reading group where each person read a poem or a passage from some book he had read. The Queens' drama group, the 'Bats', performed their major Shakespearean play in summer against the background of the black and white Elizabethan Long Gallery of the President's Lodge. Their name was taken from the bats that flew around there. One evening when I was standing as umpteenth soldier waiting to go on stage, I felt something warm and furry on my lantern. It was a BAT!

More strange creatures came swarming from places like Girton, Newnham and New Hall. They might take appropriate parts in a choral performance by the St. Margaret's Society in Chapel. They might be invited for a trip in a punt either along the Backs past the colleges or upstream towards Grantchester for a picnic. Henry Hart taught us how to use the pole correctly and steer with it. Also we judged how to avoid getting the pole caught under bridges. One fine evening, we joined a punt to return it to its moorings. The pubs around the Mill Pond were full and people were sitting on the grassy banks. In the middle of the pond, our punter got his pole stick in the mud. He dived off the punt fully clothed to retrieve it. Cheers all round. The crowd was unaware he had already fallen in once.

There were other opportunities for socialising with the opposite sex. One was through the Pastorate. This was a middle of the road Christian organisation based on Holy Trinity Church. On a Sunday, the vicar, Cyril Tucker, would hold open house for afternoon tea to discuss that morning's sermon. Friendships were made especially through a mission to the Sussex port of Newhaven one summer vacation. Here we had to defend our Christianity against Communist dockers. The Pastorate was closely linked to the Church Missionary Society prayer group which met at lunch time in Clare College. I became Secretary and had an interesting time meeting various missionaries who came to speak. Then there was the Student Christian Movement which held a conference in Edinburgh with internationally known speakers. This was my first visit to Edinburgh, a city that impressed me. The SCM also organised a major event at Great St. Mary's with notable speakers in the evenings. Where could they be offered hospitality and a meal before their presentation? Queens' allowed us to use our room in Walnut Tree Court to host dinners for them. Meeting some famous people was memorable.

The highlight of an undergraduate's time at Cambridge must be regarded as the May Ball. We organised a group of our Queens' friends and lady acquaintances. Luckily the night was fine so a good time was had by all. There was a marquee in which bands played. Hall was laid out for a splendid feast. One speciality of Queens' besides the boar's head was a meringue basket filled with mixed fruits. There was punting on the Cam past the colleges as dawn broke after which we went our separate ways to start new careers.

Other Cambridge Activities

There were innumerable clubs and societies in Cambridge all touting for business. One such was the Railway Club offering lectures and visits. Through it I met kindred spirits who were passionate about the narrow gauge railways of North Wales. Any self-respecting club had to have an annual dinner which for the Railway Club took a rather unusual form. Those in the know caught the Cambridge Buffet Express to King's Cross on which the chef would serve at lunch a curry not on the official menu. The party for dinner assembled in a special restaurant car attached to one train. Dinner would be served on the train while it was moving. Then at Hitchin, the restaurant car would be uncoupled and shunted into a siding so that the speeches could be heard in relative quietness. An hour later, the restaurant car would be re-attached onto the next train to Cambridge. I doubt if this would happen today. Some of my adventures with the Cambridge University Mountaineering Club will be described later.

There was a Cambridge motor car club whose members were mostly interested in racing which was not my line. After car-ownership in National Service, it was only natural that I should aspire to one through the greater mobility it would give. A faithful member of Seal congregation was 'peg leg' Gordon who had lost a leg in the First World War. He would arrive in his Vintage 12/50 Alvis, an object of great interest. To supplement his income he cultivated a small market garden and transported its produce in what remained of the dicky seat. He had kept the car because the accelerator pedal was centrally placed between those of clutch and brake. By dextrous use of his right foot, Gordon could operate either brake and accelerator or accelerator and clutch. This was a trick I was to find useful later. In fact, once the car was moving, and you knew your crash gearbox, the clutch was rarely used.

Gordon had never maintained his car, except possibly topping up the radiator with water and the engine with oil. The wooden frame surrounding the dicky had mostly rotted away. The time came when he had to dispose of it. 'Would I like it?' 'Yes please'. So it arrived at Seal vicarage. I checked it over. I took out the plug in the sump and a sort of tarry black liquid dripped out. The engine oil had never been changed for years. Putting in clean oil dropped the pressure considerably. The engine was not running properly so I took off the rocker box cover. It had overhead valves worked by pushrods. When I turned the engine over with the crank handle, I saw that two valves barely opened. Luckily they were inlet valves. I found that the hollow pushrods of each had broken and the broken parts worked into each other. I made adjustments on the tappets and, after a general clean, the engine ran a little better.

Auntie Kath had agreed that I could put the Alvis in one side of her large garage at Westerham. The steering wheel had nine inches of play around the rim so it was a matter of having to steer the car along a straight road. I had to judge which way the car might turn due to bumps etc in the road, flick the wheel round to stop the turn, watch for the next bump and flick the wheel round to correct that. Brakes were operative after adjustment so I did get the car into her garage. I started totting up the cost of rebuilding the engine, other mechanical parts, the woodwork, toneau cover and hood and realised that the amount would far exceed what the car would be worth. So it was taken away by a person who specialised in repairing Alvises. Its fate would have been a different proposition today. I had learnt a lot that would be useful later.

The Lancia

The Lancia after restoration in 1962. The photos are put here at the beginning of this story for ease of reference.

Having heard about a 1924 Lancia Lambda for sale through my contact in Lydd, I started to read about this marque and was impressed. I was more impressed when I went to East Grinstead and saw the car cowering under an open-sided lean to alongside Roger Castiglioni's garage. I was besotted (perhaps the appropriate word) by the elegant fine lines, with the long sweeping front mudguards and large Zeiss front headlights. The wheels were the thin beaded-edge type which added to the impression of lightness. I noticed that the clock was missing in the dashboard and that there was some rust on the side of the body above the running board. Even so I decided to cash in most of my National Savings and purchase her for a small fortune in those days of £75.

Friends agreed to help tow her back to Cambridge where we could give her a thorough inspection. We left early on the day of the Brighton emancipation run in November 1958. We decided to watch the start in Hyde Park. No convenient toilet could be found. I was surprised at the sound of using a drain outside the Albert Hall. Of course it was raining when we set off again for East Grinstead. We hitched a tow rope onto the front framing of the Lancia, and turned towards Cambridge. I quickly learnt the power of those front brakes when I applied them and the rope broke in the middle of a large puddle. I had to clamber along the front wing to re-attach it. After that, we reached Cambridge safely and left the car in a public car park near the Fitzwilliam Museum. There were few restrictions in those days on undergraduates having cars in Cambridge and no vandalism either.

After making the car roadworthy, it was necessary to insure the beast. Peter S. Taylor offered the Vintage Sports Car Club a very good insurance package providing the car had been passed by one of their assessors. Off we went to Terry Breen in North London. All was well and we pointed for home. A hitch-hiker thumbed a lift so we put him in the rear seat. We did not have the hood erected or a tonneau to cover him. After we had parked again in the car park, the hitch-hiker gave us no thanks as he stumbled away, blue with cold.

To finish the saga of the missing clock, I was returning from a meeting late one night from the west of Cambridge. The lights flickered on and off and I noticed through the hole in the dash that something was shorting out. As we drew into Royston, I decided to pull onto the grass verge beneath a street lamp to look under the bonnet. At that instant, the street light went out and the near side of the car sunk into a ditch. We were stuck. Another car stopped and the occupants of that and some others lifted the Lancia back onto the road. We were soon on our way again. The fault was caused by the main lead from the battery to the starter motor shorting on the exhaust pipe. A little later, when driving up the Great North Road in the days before Grantham was by-passed, a car caught us up and started flashing its lights and gesticulating. I was used to children shouting and waving. This driver was more persistent so I stopped. It turned out he was the owner of the missing clock which he generously gave to me.

I do not know how I was introduced to the Kennys, Andre and Leslie. He had read classics at Trinity and had owned many different Lagonda cars over the years. He had been running a garage at Fulborn on the outskirts of Cambridge where he maintained not only his own splendid cars but helped impecunious undergraduates with theirs. He had moved to Alpheton Mill near Long Melford, a little water powered corn mill, no longer in use, with various barns and buildings suitable for conversion into engineering workshops. The reason for our meeting was the discovery that the rust I had seen on the body of my Lancia had worked through the thin metal skin not from the outside as I had thought but from the inside. And so began the start of my battle against rust that lasted for the next fifty years.

The Lancia was one of the first cars constructed on the unitary principle where the main chassis was the shape of the whole body. It was made from pressed steel parts welded together. The outside was covered with thin steel sheeting. Damp and condensation had penetrated behind the leather-covered plywood panelling causing rusting to the main frame and the outer skin. The Lancia was driven over to Long Melford where the wings and rear mudguards were removed. The long front wings went to the room I shared with Humphrey Nye in Essex Court for rust removal and repainting. He referred to them as mummy cases. It was lucky for me that we had a large room. The car was driven to a coach builder in Norwich where the offending side panels were plated over. Some other rusty parts were treated and the outside repainted. The car was reassembled but no mechanical work was attempted.

The Lancia proved to be a remarkable car. It could turn in a very small circle and its front wheel brakes were better than on many later cars. To put on full lock from one side to the other required only one and a quarter turns of the steering wheel. Both these features were excellent on narrow twisting mountain roads. It had excellent cornering characteristics. Once when driving through the Fens, a French car drove up behind and started making rude gestures about old cars. The road took a sharp left bend with a ditch or drain on the far side. I drove on at the same speed. The French car tried to follow but nearly went into the drain. They had more respect for the Lancia after that! Or again, in the Isle of Man, Ken Barlow, my Keeper of Industry in Manchester, also happened to be over with a German friend from Volkswagen. He was driving a brand new Passat. We had arranged to have dinner in the north of the Island. We set off from Douglas with me leading in the Lancia. We decided to follow the TT Course round the west side. I set off at normal Lancia speed and, after a few bends, was aware that the Passat was not following. The German was furious that the latest Volkswagen could not keep up with the Lancia cornering.

With the outside of the Lancia restored, attention turned to the interior. There was a vehicle trimmer and upholsterer in a shed on Magdalene quay. He not only made a new tonneau which covered all the seats but also renewed the squabs of the four passenger seats. These squabs were designed to be easily removable because they covered wells where tools and other essential supplies could be hidden. Underneath the driver's squab was a tray with a complete set of special tools for maintaining the sliding pillar front suspension as well as the crucial crank handle for starting the engine. Later I made two more trays to fit under the front passenger seat with slots to fit an array of spanners. These tools spared the necessity of carrying a tool box all the time.

A Trip to the Continent

With such a fine touring car, and the long summer vacation of 1959 approaching, thoughts turned to a Continental expedition. It so happened that General Franco was easing his grip

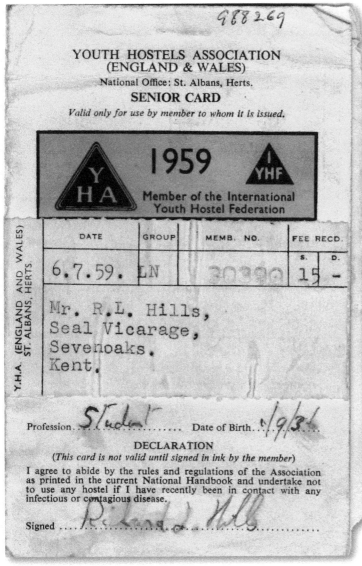

My Youth Hostel card

on Spain and opened a few youth hostels which were adapted from those of the Falange youth movement. One of my Queens' friends, Peter Calvert, wanted to go to Spain to see what was happening through his interest in political history. A like-minded friend of his, Jonathan Tinker, also decided to come. We were joined by a Queens' theology student, Edward Clark from Jamaica, who wanted to see more of Europe. Tragically, Edward was drowned a year later when swimming early one morning in the Cam below Queens'. He caught cramp and could not climb the brick walls to get out. His shouts for help were not heard until it was too late to save him.

We agreed to go away for a month at the end of July when I had finished as Temporary Instructor on an Outward Bound Course at Ullswater. I may have gone to that course straight from climbing with the CUMC at Langdale, along with the Lancia. I was driving back to Langdale from Windermere when I felt an ominous bumping from the rear axle. I was at a 'T' junction where a policeman was standing. In order to avoid blocking the road, I pulled round the corner to see a rear tyre roll across the pavement and stop at the policeman's feet. He did not blink an eyelid as an embarrassed undergraduate grovelled to retrieve the tyre. The wheel was soon changed as the Lancia carried two spare wheels and the necessary jacks, hammers, spanners, etc.

Somewhere between there and Seal vicarage which was to be our rendezvous for the Continent, a second tyre blew. Even then, beaded edge tyres and inner tubes to fit the Lancia's 765 x 105 wheels were scarce. Going abroad with no spare seemed very risky. In the end after much searching, the AA was approached and two inner tubes were located but would not reach us in time for our departure. The AA arranged for them to be air-freighted to Bordeaux in about ten day's time. The irony of this little escapade was that, in France, a garage lent us a spare, we collected the two in Bordeaux, and the Lancia never had another roadside puncture during the fifty years I owned her!

With all the bravado of youth, we decided to set off for Dover. I was the only person with a continental driving licence so I had to remember the prioritie à droite and going the correct way round roundabouts. We passed over to Boulogne and decided to take our time to reach Bordeaux. We stayed at Rouen the night of 23 July. We looked at the cathedral there and the one at Chartres with their magnificent stained glass windows. One or two of the chateaux on the Loire were visited but, being bereft of furniture, I found them rather cold compared with English country houses. We passed through Blois to reach a camp site at Cap Ferret on the sea close to Bordeaux by 26 July.

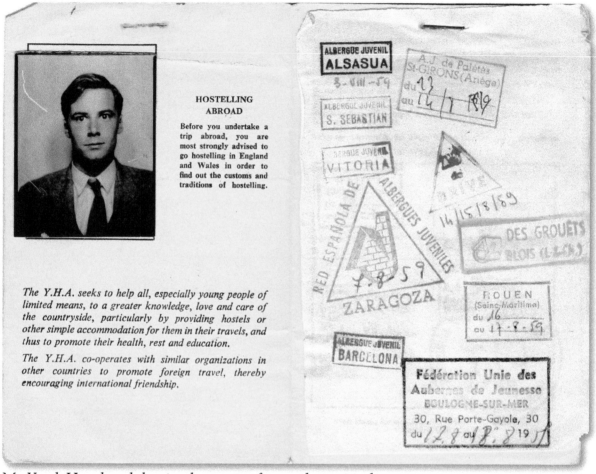

My Youth Hostel card showing the stamps of some places visited

However around this time, another near disaster struck. The dynamo to supply the electric current for the starter motor, the lights and to recharge the battery was combined in the same Marelli unit as the magneto which provided the high tension electricity for the sparking plugs. The interior coupling linking these broke down. Luckily an engineering workshop was found that could take out the armature of the dynamo and replace it with a shaft to connect the magneto with the original drive from the engine. While the engine ran perfectly with the magneto, the battery could not be recharged. For the rest of that trip, the engine had to be started with the crank handle and the lights used as little as possible.

We collected our new inner tubes from the airport and decided to enter Spain by one of the high passes in the middle of the Pyrenees. To secure beds at French Youth Hostels, we would arrive in good time and so prepare an early evening meal. Then we started the climb up to the Col with the Lancia feeling the weight of four passengers in the rarefied air. After passing through French and Spanish checkpoints, we decided to go for a walk in the high meadows. On our return, we saw Spanish soldiers surrounding the Lancia. We should have descended straight away to be checked in at the border control in the village. The local inn could put us up for the night and we settled in. 'When was dinner?' 'It will be ready in about half an hour' so we ordered a bottle of wine. I am not certain how many half hours and bottles of wine followed. We had forgotten about the Spanish habit of eating very late in the evening.

For a couple of days we explored the Pyrenean foothills. Our route to the Spanish National Park went through a tunnel. Trying to drive through it without headlamps in order to save the battery was hazardous. Traffic was sparse but I managed on sidelights. At Canfranc Estacion, the French standard gauge electric trains met the Spanish broad gauge steam-hauled trains where all through traffic had to change. The steam engine had struggled up from Jaca where we saw more elderly British-built steam locomotives. We descended to the coast at San Sebastian in order to say we had crossed the whole of the Spanish Peninsula to Barcelona. This was the Basque region and every few miles along the main roads soldiers were stationed.

We stayed in Vitoria so we could watch a bull fight in Pamplona. Our seats were on the sunny cheap side of the arena. Students came round with large demijohns of wine. One student held either side and between them they poured the wine straight into your mouth – no glasses. Stopping them pouring was difficult. While I admired the horsemanship of the mounted matador fighting the bull, I would not hurry to see this spectacle again. Then on to Zaragoza. Wine here was cheap, 10 old pennies per bottle if you had remembered to take your bottle. We stayed at some of the Falange hostels and our budding politicians watched the morning parades of the youth lined up and praising Franco with great interest.

Next came Barcelona which we reached on 8 August. After seeing the unfinished cathedral, some museums, getting caught in four rush-hours a day, enjoying the afternoon siesta and the evening promenade, we set off for the free state of Andorra. A catastrophe was narrowly averted. Somehow I felt that the Lancia was performing peculiarly. On examination, I found that the front bracket of the rear offside spring had almost torn out of the steel chassis. It was only just hanging on. Luckily it was welded on securely again. After another walk in the mountains, we left for home.

At the border control, we just waved our British passports and went straight through. After about an hour's drive into France, there was another checkpoint to catch those French who had purchased duty-free goods in Andorra and not declared them. 17 August saw us back in Rouen for the final drive to Boulogne where we caught the ferry on the following day. All the British customs officer was interested in was looking under the bonnet of the Lancia. So concluded what must be regarded as a successful expedition which had cost a little over £30 for each member for everything. However it had become obvious that the Lancia required mechanical attention.

The Lancia ready to leave for the Continent

Queens' coat of arms

Cambridge Undergraduate
Part 2 – Mountaineering Activities

Helping at PPS Camps

I had enjoyed mountaineering at Charterhouse and my experiences in National Service did nothing to deter me. Also I enjoyed the PPS Camps at Morfa Nefyn where I had made many friends. The one in July was only for Preparatory School boys while the last towards the end of August and into September was for older boys. For this third camp, a new activity had been introduced. A couple of officers would take away a group into the Welsh mountains for two days and nights walking and camping with mountain tents. I felt here was something where I could contribute. In fact it was partly this which induced me to offer my services as an officer.

There was also another sphere in which I thought I might be able to help. While the firm from which Basil Clarkson hired the marquees and ordinary tents erected them, volunteers were needed to assemble the temporary buildings for the kitchen, storerooms, toilets, etc. as well as dismantle them later after the last camp. Basil hired lock-up garages in Morfa Nefyn where all this equipment was stored during the winter. He somehow acquired a new army 1 ton lorry with four-wheel drive that was capable of hauling a trailer filled with the heavy loads of roofing slabs, kitchen equipment and everything else up and down the steep track to the camp site. The attraction of helping these advance and rear parties was free board and lodging but the problem was how to get there in the days before I had the Lancia.

One year, I accepted a lift from Basil in his lorry. It was a long journey from Bedford in a vehicle that was not the quickest on the road. Later, I made two memorable journeys by rail. One was in 1958 when I heard that lesser used passenger services to Wales were being cut. I wanted to see the scenic line from Bala up to the Ffestiniogs. I enquired at Sevenoaks station whether the early morning train would be running and was assured that it was, waving the Great Western Railway time table at me. In spite of being a bit doubtful, I set off to Paddington and took the night mail to Ruabon. There I enquired of the station master about the connecting train to Ffestiniog. 'No, I am sorry it no longer runs'. 'But I have arranged to meet friends there who will be worried if I do not arrive.' 'Well, don't say anything yet but get on the branch train to Bala and remain sitting on it at Bala Town until the Station Master comes along. A goods train used to follow the passenger up the line and he might allow you to travel on that'. At Bala Junction, I climbed into the single carriage with a pannier tank engine waiting to take us to Bala Town where I remained seated. The door opened and more gold braid appeared. 'Where are you going, Sir?' 'To Ffestiniog', I replied. 'But this train doesn't go there any more'. 'Oh dear. What am I to do? I am meeting friends there who will be very worried if I do not appear', says I looking very distressed. 'Well Sir, if you really don't mind, you could travel in the guard's van of the goods train'. I hope I didn't show my enthusiasm when I accepted the offer.

Another pannier tank engine appeared with a couple of goods trucks and a guard's van with an open veranda facing towards the engine. There was a nice hot stove burning away inside. After a short fairly level stretch, the pannier tank began the long struggle up the 1 in 40 gradients if not steeper in places to Arenig. I had a grandstand view of the engine puffing and panting up to the stone quarries where we did a little shunting. Part of this section now lies under a reservoir. As we breasted the summit, we hit the full force of a south westerly gale and I retired inside, grateful for the heat of the stove. We rattled away down through spectacular scenery along a shelf cut high on the mountain side to Trawsfynydd where the atomic power station was built later. At Ffestiniog, I caught a bus bound for Pwllheli and then the camp.

The other journey was when I heard that the line from Llandudno to Blaenau Ffestiniog was being operated by the newly-introduced diesel railcars. I knew there was a good bus service from Blaenau to Pwllheli so I decided to take the night train from Euston to Llandudno Junction and catch the early morning quarrymen's train to Blaenau and the bus on to Pwllheli. After much squealing from the wheels as the railcars climbed the sharp curves from Bettws y Coed, we entered the blackness of the long tunnel under the Crimea Pass to emerge at around 5.30 am in Blaenau with its grim slate tips. There was no bus until after 10 o'clock.

This was when the Ffestiniog Railway was still in dispute with the Central Electricity Generating Board over the railway being flooded by the Ffestiniog pump storage scheme so there were no Ffestiniog Railway trains. I decided it would be as quick to walk down the railway to Tan y Bwlch as it would be to wait for the bus. The weather was fine so off I set. I had to climb over a fence or two and came to where the line was going to be flooded. Rails still ran into the Moelwyn tunnel mouth. It looked very black inside but it was worth trying to walk through to save time. I soon found that I had to retreat out again because I had no torch and was afraid that I would trip over the rails and sleepers with my heavy rucksack. I found a route over the top and rejoined the railway just beyond the southern mouth of the tunnel. By this time, I suppose it was around 10 o'clock and I surprised a permanent way gang working at Tan y Bwlch station to prepare it for the opening of that section of the line to passenger traffic. After a welcome warm drink and ascertaining that there was no train scheduled, I staggered on to Penrhyndeudraeth station. I went into the centre of the village and caught my bus there. Neither of these journeys would be possible today for one reason or another.

When we arrived at the camp site to prepare it, there was only a bare field. Therefore our meals were provided by Mrs. Williams, the farmer's wife, and we ate in her kitchen (and did the washing up after). The farm had no mains electricity. You switched on a light and nothing happened for a few seconds. Then you heard the sound of a diesel engine starting and the light bulb began to glow. On the camp site there was originally no piped water supply or sewage disposal. New water pipes were installed to service all the main requirements of kitchen, wash tents, etc. Basil solved the problem of sewage disposal through a chemical system similar to the Elsan principle. He had a pair of large steel enclosed cylinders sunk above a little gully close to the stream flowing down to the sea. Into the top of each cylinder were cut I think four manholes. Over each manhole was secured a toilet seat that emptied into the cylinder. At suitable periods, the now inert effluent would be flushed out to sea down the stream and more chemical added. A toilet block with roof, walls and partitions was erected above the seating. At the end of one season, the structure had been taken down, leaving the seats exposed. A photo was taken of the Rear Party members sitting on them. Basil was not amused.

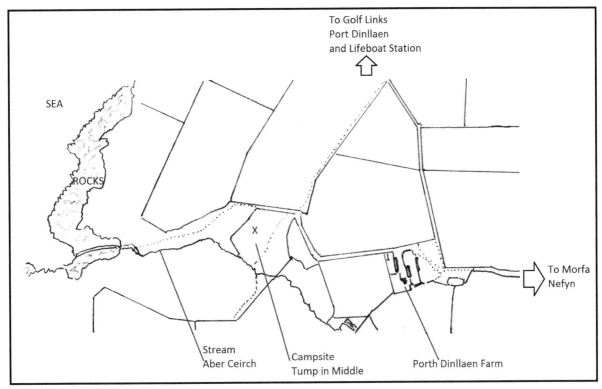

Map of PPS Camp

For our mountaineering expeditions, we chose areas away from the popular tourist routes and the main central Snowdon massif. We also tried to find camp sites close to where it would be possible to be dropped off to avoid walking far with heavy rucksacks carrying tents, sleeping bags, cooking utensils, etc. In addition, a supply of fresh water was also essential. The mountains surrounding the Pennant Valley to the West of Snowdonia were one such place. A track out of the Nantlle Valley going south was passable by car close to Cwm Silyn on the northern side of the hills. Not only was there the Llyn Cwm Silyn suitable for swimming but a circuitous route could be followed to Y Garn (633m., 2080ft.) with a view across to Snowdon. The spectacular Nantlle Ridge with its bilberries in season took us westwards to the top of Mynydd Tal y Mignedd (853m., 2329ft.) and so back to the campsite.

A favourite place was up Cwm Ystradllyn following one branch of the abandoned narrow gauge quarry railway until we came to the former manager's house of the Groseddau slate quarry. A key to it could be borrowed since it was used by the Youth Hostel Association as an unmanned hostel until it was vandalised. The entrance to the quarry passed under an impressive overarching stone wall to protect the route from falling boulders. Behind the house, the boys could be set a task of mapping the abandoned quarrymen's houses. One fine walk from here was to follow another branch of the railway north up the Pennant Valley to the Prince of Wales Quarry at the head of the valley below the Nantlle Ridge. Tracing dams and watercourses for waterwheels in the quarry was another activity. The way back was over Moel Lefn (638m., 2092ft.) and Moel Hebog (782m., 2566ft.). A visit to the impressive churchlike remains of the slate dressing mill further down the valley was worthwhile for its Industrial Archaeology to determine how it worked. Cwm Ystradllyn has since been dammed to create a reservoir to supply drinking water to the Lleyn Peninsular.

Another suitable area was to the east of Snowdon where a long ridge extended from the north at Moel Siabod (872m., 2860ft.) to the south at Cnicht (689m., 2265ft.), called the Matterhorn of North Wales through its shape when viewed from Portmadog. From a camp here, we descended into the Gwynant Valley and climbed Snowdon by the Watkin path past the rock where William Gladstone addressed thousands of miners, now deserted. The Roman Steps and up Rhinog Fawr (720m., 2433ft.) behind Harlech was a good area but a little too far to drive from Morfa Nefyn.

One really hard expedition was tackling all the Welsh mountains over three thousand feet high in a day. In July 1959, I was a Temporary Instructor at the Ullswater Outward Bound School. I was given a couple of days leave to join Henry Hart in his annual walk round the fifteen three thousand foot peaks in the Lake District. That September, I decided to do the same in Wales where there were about fifteen. I took a group of strong lads from camp and we pitched our tents behind the Pen y Gwryd Hotel by Llyn Cwm Ffynnon. We set off early. The round Welsh trip has two problems. One is that there are a couple of 'outliers' from the main circuit. On the Carneddau, there is Foel Fras (941m., 3092ft.) lying to the north and on the Glyders a trek is necessary to that Y Garn (940m., 3104ft.), adding considerably to the distance. Luckily Tryfan is just too low. Then, instead of the long slow plods up and down in the Lake District, the numerous Welsh peaks break up the rhythm so I found Wales more tiring. The staff in the cafe on the top of Snowdon (1085m., 3560ft.) was surprised to see us late in the evening but still sold us refreshments. I continued helping PPS Camp with erecting and dismantling the camp and leading expeditions after I had moved to Manchester but stopped when I was offered a post in the embryonic science museum.

Cambridge University Mountaineering Club

At Cambridge, the Cambridge University Mountaineering Club organised lectures and one day meets. The lectures might be given by well-known climbers with accounts of heroic deeds of daring, of tragic rescues after accidents, of summits conquered or ascents ending in failure. On one or two Sundays in term time, a coach would be hired for an early morning departure to drive up the A1 to the Peak District. The outcrops of millstone grit were the objective where rock climbing and rope technique could be practised. Stannage Edge above Hathersage with its abandoned millstones lying around was a popular destination because a public road passed nearby. On the way back, there would be an official stop for refreshments. A little later, there might be an unofficial stop in a convenient lay-by to 'stretch one's legs'.

The CUMC also organised longer meets in Britain and abroad. That for the New Year in 1958 was held at Ynys Ettws, the Climbers' Club hut in the Llanberis Pass. By that time, I had been elected to full membership of that Club. It is possible that Hugh drove me there in his Morgan, always an exciting ride, because the Army Mountaineering Association was meeting at the same time at Helyg, another Climbers' Club hut in the Llwgy valley. There was little snow but conditions were icy due to the cold. Most of our climbing was in the Llanberis Pass although we did walk over the Glyders to the Idwal slabs in the Ogden Valley. One evening, we walked up to the Pen y Gwryd Hotel where we had arranged to meet Hugh and his party. They did not appear. We heard that one of the army officers had fallen off a climb on Craig yr Ysfa above Cwm Eigiau and been severely injured. Under normal conditions, this climb would have been easy but ice made it treacherous. I had one of those premonitions, could it be Hugh? The RAF Mountain Rescue Team was on its way from Valley in Anglesey.

There was nothing I could do that night for we had no mobile phones in those days. I returned to Ynys Ettws. Next day it was confirmed that indeed it was Hugh and that he was severely injured and might not live. I was given a lift over to Llandudno Hospital where Pru was already at his bedside. Hugh was heavily sedated but still delirious. His head was swathed in bandages. His rescue by Johnny Lees of Valley Rescue team had been incredibly dangerous due not only to the icy conditions but also to Hugh fighting and punching poor Johnny. He was awarded the George Cross, thought to be the first time that such an award had been given for mountaineering excellence. The armed forces went to great lengths to rescue Hugh. It has been suggested that he was involved in some secret engineering tests. He told me that when he was stationed at Weymouth, he aimed Bofours guns across the bay and recorded how much the barrel deflected due to the heat from the sun. He made a remarkable recovery but was invalided out of the army. He was given a job lecturing about mechanical computers at the Royal Naval College until these became obsolete through electronics.

The CUMC summer meet for 1958 was scheduled in the Alps. When we arrived at Chamonix, there was too much snow to attempt anything on Mont Blanc. Instead, the High Level route to Zermatt was chosen. We started at Mauvoisin and went eastwards. On difficult or dangerous sections, we were roped together in pairs, leading alternately. On the broad glaciers, the sun beating down made us hot. A welcome treat was 'snow jam'. A spoonful of strawberry jam mixed with snow was very refreshing. We were traversing a long narrow ridge on the Grand Combin and could see that it had large cornices overhanging above the further valley. My leader kept well below the top of the cornice but to overtake him to lead I had to move above him. Suddenly my foot went through the cornice and I was looking down the long drop into that other valley. I frantically floundered down to my leader who was more concerned about my crampons piercing him than my falling over a drop of a few thousand feet.

The snow in Zermatt was still too deep to attempt the Matterhorn or other high mountains in that area. Therefore we set off for Italy by the Theodule Pass. I purchased a large block of butter for our provisions and stuck it straight in my rucksack. The day seemed rather hotter than I expected and I seemed to be sweating more than usual. I looked in the rucksack when we stopped and of course the butter had melted - what a mess. We went to Breuil and then to the little hamlet of Parayer.

Here in the summer season, Grandmother opened up the little hotel, more for her grand-children to come and stay than for climbers. I have been told recently that this beautiful quiet valley has been dammed and flooded.

Richard trying to find the way ahead

We needed more provisions and set off on the long walk down to the local shop. We bought some bread, very rough granary type, and wanted cheese. My rudimentary Italian failed me so I pointed to something on the counter that looked like cheese. The shop assistant with a baby in her arms got a knife and tried to cut off a hunk. The baby was passed to someone else to hold. It was a struggle to cut that cheese even with two hands on the knife. On the walk back to our hotel, we paused for something to eat. The person I was with found that cheese too strong for his tastes. I persevered because I thought it went well with the rough bread. Some of that cheese survived to be taken home. Audrey looked at it, 'Parmesan'. She had never seen a solid block before. We completed our circuit by the little-used Col de l'Eveque to Arolla. We camped by the stream coming from the glacier. The quick dip for a wash was very quick, the water was so cold. I left Switzerland looking forward to more Alpine adventures in better snow conditions.

Outward Bound

For March 1959, the CUMC meet was based at the RLH (Robertson Lamb Hut) in Langdale. I was glad to familiarise myself with the peaks around that valley. I had the Lancia there and may have stayed on because I felt I was lucky to have been chosen to be a Temporary Instructor on an Ullswater Outward Bound course. At that time, the Outward Bound had sea schools at Aberdovy and Burghead and mountain schools at Eskdale and Ullswater. That at Ullswater was situated in extensive grounds stretching down to the lake. In summer, the boys had their cold dip in the lake before breakfast, otherwise it was a cold shower. The grounds were laid out for various courses, perhaps for exercises or orienteering. There was a small boathouse with a launch to act as rescue boat when the canoes were out. There were a couple of sailing dinghies which could be used by staff. One evening, an instructor asked if I would like to go with him and sail in the dinghy which he had just painted. Off we went in a strong wind, neither having put on life jackets nor replaced the buoyancy bags. The centre-board sprung a leak. I pumped hard but the water gained on me. With water sloshing around the bottom of the boat, the problem was how to turn round to sail back without capsizing. Luckily we made it – one lesson learnt.

I do not know who gained most, me or the boys, from the skilled instructors. Some topics covered were mountain navigation and map reading, planning an expedition, basic first aid and rescue with a stretcher, rock climbing and abseiling as well as canoeing in smaller rivers. In addition a great emphasis was laid on physical fitness. The boys were divided into groups of ten or twelve with an instructor appointed to look after each group. Origins and ability were deliberately mixed up so that public and grammar school boys had to live with those from poorer backgrounds. One lad sent out on a map reading exercise became lost. He found a telephone kiosk and phoned his mother for help – initiative perhaps. These one day expeditions led up to a three day one when the lads were out on their own. At the end of the course, we had to write a report on each boy and they one on us. I was interested to see that the boy I had found difficult to get to know and help also found he could not get on with me.

I was given a couple of days off to join Henry Hart on his annual pilgrimage walking round the three three thousand foot Lake District peaks. He always stayed in the Borrowdale

Valley with a few specially invited Queens' men. We set out early in the morning and headed down St. John's in the Vale for Skiddaw (931m., 3053ft.). Scafell Pike (978m., 3207ft.) came next. Henry then led us by his special route past High White Stones and the Wythburn Valley to Dunmail Raise at the head of Thirlmere. By this time it was getting hot and we youngsters had long since stripped off anoraks, pullovers and even shirts. Yet Henry with his bad back and padded straight jacket walked on regardless. Helvellyn (950m., 3116ft.) was another long haul up and down. We celebrated conquering the three peaks at the pub beside Thirlmere but we had not finished for we had to return to Borrowdale. Henry was still full of energy but it was a weary me making the final stretch up the valley. The whole circuit was about forty miles. However it inspired me to attempt the Welsh equivalents in September described earlier.

In March 1960, I was with the CUMC on their meet at Helyg, climbing on Tryfan and Cwm Idwal. It was necessary to concentrate on the looming finals which I just passed with a third class honours. This was sufficient for me to be accepted on the Diploma of Education course that September.

My rooms at Queens' had to be cleared and books and personal equipment taken to Madingley Hall, a Tudor mansion a little west of Cambridge. Both myself and Humphrey Nye had been offered accommodation there. There were also the various celebrations and degree ceremonies to attend. I had been offered another month as Temporary Instructor at Ullswater. All seemed set fair for a career as an history teacher.

On my return from Spain, it was evident that the Lancia needed some mechanical attention so she was taken over to Long Melford and the Kennys. On spare weekends one or two others with vintage cars would catch the early morning train from Cambridge on the line long since closed to Long Melford where Andre would meet us to take us to Alpheton Mill. On the Sunday, if no one was driving back to Cambridge, Andre would drive us to Bury St. Edmunds because the Melford line had no Sunday trains. The last train from Bury reached Cambridge after college gates were shut which meant climbing in. I was lucky not to be caught.

I had no car for the summer. Andre very kindly lent me an Alvis 12/50 which had been converted into a van. After a bit of fettling up, I set off in it for Ullswater towards the end of July. I had heard that the 15 ins. gauge Ravenglas and Eskdale Railway was up for sale and might be closed. To see it before that happened, I drove over the Wrynose and Hardnott Passes which was fun in the Alvis with its poor lock and weak brakes. I spent an uncomfortable night in the van owing to a step in the floor. I parked at Eskdale Green station and nearly missed the train because the driver did not expect a passenger so early. I need not have made this detour because the line was saved by a preservation society.

The Outward Bound course followed much the same programme as the previous year. One of the expeditions was to practice map reading as well as rock climbing and its associated rope work. The region to the West of the Lakes was chosen. I took some camping gear over in the Alvis and we camped in the Seatoller area while the lads made their way over on foot. I was put in charge of a couple of lads for a days walking and climbing around Great Gable (899m., 2948ft.). It was a lovely summer day when we stopped at the top of the Sty

UNIVERSITY OF CAMBRIDGE

I hereby certify that

RICHARD LESLIE HILLS

of Queens' College in the University of Cambridge

was at a full Congregation holden in the Senate

House on 25 June 1960 admitted to the Degree of

BACHELOR of ARTS

Witness my hand this sixth day of August one

thousand nine hundred and sixty

P. C. Melville

First Assistant Registrary of the University

Registrary's Clerk

Cambridge University B.A. Certificate

Head Pass to examine the First Aid equipment and stretcher stored in the box there – little thinking that we would be soon using that stretcher. I had been assigned Needle Ridge on Great Gable itself, a moderate 'V' diff. quite easy climb. At the bottom, we looked out westwards down the steep sided rather gloomy Wasdale valley and up at the Needle itself. I wondered if I would ever dare to climb up the Needle and stand on the top of its highest rock. I never have...

Napes Needle

The Fifth Age
Teaching and Research

Part 1 – The Outward Bound and Cambridge Dip. Ed.

The Accident

The little prince seemed to be on top of the world as he looked out over Wasdale at the foot of the Napes Needle. He had good reason to be satisfied. The choice at the dividing of the ways for his future seemed to be settled for the present at least. He had sought advice from the Cambridge Careers Office. He had investigated the possibility of a career in industry, perhaps in a personnel department. This might combine his interests in mechanical engineering with some form of caring for others. He went for an interview with English Electric but when father heard about it, he was not pleased to say the least. 'After I had spent all that money on your education and you throw it all away for this'. He was still hopeful that I might be ordained and could not see that there might be other forms of Christian service.

The little prince had been offered and accepted a place on the Diploma of Education course at Cambridge. This way seemed the right choice as it developed. Accommodation had been arranged at Madingley Hall. He had already completed one requirement, that of spending a couple of weeks assisting a teacher in an Educationally Sub-Normal class at Impington Village College. He had had a little experience of teaching gunners at Folkestone through helping with the Army Education Service. But these children might have a mixture of physical, emotional and low intelligence quota problems and were quite different. The first task for them every morning was to practise their handwriting. The teacher had already written a short sentence on a blackboard in neat copperplate script. The board was placed across the top of a cupboard in one corner of the room so it could be seen easily. I went round checking on the pupils to see how they were progressing. One lad had written the word 'lavourite' which from my standing position I could see should have been 'favourite'. I asked, 'Why had he written 'lavourite?' 'That is correct, Sir'. Then the penny dropped. The tail of the 'f' was hidden by the corner of the cupboard. He had copied down what he saw as a sort of picture without understanding one word. To all intents and purposes he was illiterate but he had an extraordinary empathy with horses. He was a bright lad in many ways but severely lacking in others. The question passed through my mind, could he be helped by going on an Outward Bound course?

But was the future for our little prince quite so bright? There would be great competition in the teaching profession for those offering history. A third class degree was not promising. This is where my participation as an Outward Bound instructor could be a useful additional qualification. Possibly through the termination of National Service, there were various adventure training schemes being set up to give young people a taste of the outdoors. Local Education Authorities were taking more interest although few could follow the example of Derbyshire and have a centre of its own. There was Braythay Hall in the Lake District and courses run by the Y.M.C.A. In addition, the Duke of Edinburgh had launched his Award

Scheme founded on the principles he had learnt from Kurt Hahn and Gordonstoun. Many of these organisations closely resembled the Outward Bound which remained the toughest of them all. Prospects of a future as some sort of adventure or mountaineering instructor seemed attractive.

However the immediate prospect was leading the easy route up Needle Ridge on Great Gable. We roped up and set off with myself leading. We had done three or four pitches when I wanted a rope sling to belay one of the lads more safely. He confessed he had left it at the bottom of the last pitch. Three courses of action passed through my mind – forget it and hope its loss would not be noticed back at Ullswater – climb down and collect it from where we were standing – finish the rest of the climb and quickly go and get it on my own. I decided on the middle course to descend roped up so the lads would have experience of lowering someone and bringing them up again.

I came to a small drop, sat with my bottom on the edge of one rock facing out, put my right hand onto a large projecting boulder and lowered myself down. The protruding boulder or slab came away and I went down with it. There was a mighty crash. I was held by the rope and the lad but realised that the slab had broken my left leg. I do not understand how the boulder crushed about four inches in the middle of my left tibia but missed the slender fibula. In a miraculous way, the main muscles, arteries and veins were also left intact. All I knew at the time was great agony and that I could not use that leg. At that precise moment another group from Ullswater was crossing the top of the gulley and, hearing the crash, shouted if anyone was hurt – 'Yes, Me'. I found the flattest place to lie was on top of the fallen slab itself. It was 20 August, 1960.

Well, the lads were rescued. An instructor descended to try and assess my injuries. One party went to fetch the stretcher from Sty Head. Others went to the Inn at the top of Wasdale to summon help – this was well before the days of mobile phones. Others sorted out ropes and belay points in preparation to lowering me down on the stretcher. Tied onto a stretcher is not the most comfortable way of descending a rock face with every bump jarring the broken leg. The morphine injection did little to ease the pain. Then there was the further long descent along narrow mountain tracks to the Inn and the waiting ambulance. The lads were magnificent and rose to this unique occasion. Sometime later, the instructors checked out the route on Great Gable to make sure it was safe. They pitched the unlucky slab over the side, only to watch it hit the top of the Napes Needle. The top block wobbled ominously but luckily did not fall off, otherwise I would have gone down in mountaineering history. My accident did merit a brief mention in the Daily Herald but that was all.

Whitehaven Hospital

The ambulance journey, entry into Whitehaven hospital and the operating theatre are a blur. The first I remember is the dim light of the four bedded ward barely illuminating a great mound of sheet over a cage to keep the weight off my left leg now plastered up to the thigh. The ward looked over a patch of green grass to the sign of Newcastle Ales on the gable end of a pub – so near and yet so far. I lay there wondering whether I would walk again and what the future would hold. This was well before modern prosthetic limbs.

News quickly spread. The Ullswater folk kept in touch. Ralph, Chief Instructor, had to drive the old Alvis van from Seatoller back to base, learning quickly how to manage a crash gearbox and vintage brakes (it did have brakes on all four wheels but even so to a novice...). Humphrey Nye and his cousin visited me. He took word back first to the PPS Camp on the Lleyn Peninsular where I was due to be a leader and then to the Dip. Ed. course in Cambridge that most likely I would not be either at the camp or a pupil. My place at Madingley Hall was soon filled. My carefully planned life was in tatters. Lesson 1, I was not indispensible.

At first all seemed to be going according to plan but then my leg began to swell and smell. The plaster was changed and the wound dressed. I became feverish and it was obvious that all was not well. Gangrene had set in. One day, I struggled to eat some lunch. After lunch, the doctors and surgeon came to look at me and went into a huddle by the door. They sent the Indian doctor who had been attending to me to say that they were going to operate and take the leg off. My reaction was, 'Thank God'. At least the terrible pain would cease and I would have to learn how to manage on one leg. I did not know two things. First, the operating theatre was ready but the operation was postponed through the lunch I had eaten. Second, they had phoned my father for permission to operate although I was twenty-four. He said he could not agree because he could not get to Whitehaven to see me. It so happened that the parish prayer group was meeting at that time and they prayed for me. The Indian doctor packed my leg with swabs soaked in Edinburgh University Solution of Lime (EUSOL). At 3 o'clock, I was no worse so the operation was postponed. More EUSOL and I began to improve. That particular operation was never needed. I felt that it was the hand of God that my leg had been saved and that I would walk again. This belief sustained me through the many operations needed in the following months as well as in the years to come.

Whitehaven was only the beginning of a long story in which faith and patience were sorely tried. (Lessons 2 and 3). The gangrene had destroyed skin tissue and part of the major calf muscle which had to be cut away. The tibia was showing through the lacerated flesh. Because I had no family in the Lake District, it was decided to send me to East Grinstead Hospital where Sir Archibald McIndoe had pioneered various skin grafting techniques on wounded members of the armed forces. As soon as the bone was strong enough and I had recovered a little hobbling about on crutches, a special railway carriage with provision in a compartment for a stretcher was arranged for one Sunday to take me to Euston. Audrey came up to Whitehaven to accompany me. The guard was very helpful, for instance on the occasions when I needed help to go to the toilet because I had to shuffle along on one leg, having had to leave the crutches at Whitehaven hospital. By the time we reached Euston in the dark, I was shattered so do not remember how I was transferred from train to ambulance and then to East Grinstead where I was quickly put into a bed. I expect father was there to drive Audrey back home to recover from her ordeal.

East Grinstead Hospital

The following morning, I was able to take stock of my fellow inmates and begin to learn a little about the refined forms of torture the doctors had devised for these major casualties.

Some were 'bed and breakfasters' who arrived one night for a dental operation. Next day after being allowed nothing to eat that morning, they had the operation but didn't feel like eating anything that evening and went home again the following morning after breakfast. But the majority of us were long term patients, needing some major reconstruction after terrible injuries.

With my plaster removed, the doctors and surgeon inspected my leg. In some areas not too badly damaged, the skin would grow again in from the sides but this would take too long for others. In these where the flesh remained underneath, fresh thin skin grafts would be laid on top to cover them. Donor areas for this skin were selected on the thighs. Hair had to be shaved off in preparation for the operations. At this operation, a sort of spokeshave was used to peel off skin for the graft leaving patches of raw leg as if it had been badly grazed. They were very painful and sore. The thin skin grafts were applied to fleshy areas and bandaged up until they had taken. Once healed, it was necessary to be very careful for many years to avoid too much sun for they became sunburnt easily. The leg was encased in plaster again.

Such skin grafting was impossible on the place where the flesh had been completely destroyed on the front of the leg which required a different method. This would be done after I had recovered a bit. So I was sent home. I learnt quickly how to get in and out of a car by sitting on the front passenger seat facing out, sliding across to the driver's seat and swinging both legs in through the door and sliding back again – difficult with central gear and brake levers. I waited to hear when the next operation would take place. Sometimes I would be driven to hospital expecting just a check-up so took nothing ready for a long stay, to be told the op. would be the following day or conversely I would go with a full suitcase of things to keep me occupied, send the driver back only to be told there would be no op. and I could go home for another couple of weeks. The driver had to be recalled. This waiting around taught me patience waiting for the body to heal itself.

Because the depth of natural skin and flesh on the front of the shin is very thin, it was decided to take a section off the right calf and graft it onto the front of the left leg. Incisions were cut on three sides of a rectangle and a full depth slab of flesh lifted up, leaving the fourth attached. The opposite side of the 'flap' was sewn onto the front of the left leg, covering the exposed bone. The exposed areas of raw flesh on the right leg were covered with thin skin. Both legs were tied together. At first, the flap was nourished from the right leg until it had grown firmly onto the left leg when it could be cut off and finally sewn up. Variations on this theme, taking a patch of thick skin from one part of the body and 'leap frogging' it to replace a damaged part, was a technique used at East Grinstead in remarkable ways to repair many damaged bodily parts. For me, it meant being trussed up like a chicken, confined to bed for over three weeks with the leg in plaster.

There were a few plusses, because with the help of an occupational therapist, I learnt basket weaving, split cane chair seat weaving, ready-cut rug making, tapestry work and much more. Many of these crafts were useful later in life such as repairing chairs and giving demonstrations at shows and lectures. They formed useful points of contact with people. The hospital staff put on a Christmas pantomime when the chief surgeon carved the turkey.

To help build up our strength, we were entitled to a bottle of Kemp Town Brewery brown ale. Some patients did not like it so... At least I was lying down in bed. Visitors at this time included Aunt Evelyn and Uncle Sandy with their dog Gelert who, looking through the window, was pleased to see me. Someone brought a large box of apples which was left on the window sill when I was discharged and sadly rotted to the annoyance of the nurses who had to clear up the mess. At last, the legs were separated but the plaster was retained for a bit longer to protect the new 'cross leg flap'.

Activities Between Hospitalisation

If the time in hospital gave the opportunity to learn various craft skills, the time between my sojourns there gave time for other activities. I was able to go to Long Melford to work on the Lancia. I found I could balance on my good leg and operate a lathe. Present health and safety might not approve. Some visitors were surprised to see a leg in plaster sticking out from under the car. The Kennys were also helping to restore the 1831 steam beam engine at Stretham which had driven a scoopwheel to pump the water out of the Waterbeach Level. One day, they were working on the top floor painting the main rocking beam. The stone steps up looked difficult to climb for someone with a leg in plaster. The hand rails seemed inadequate. So I sat on a cabin trunk at the bottom. Boredom and cold got the better of me and I peeped inside. I found I was sitting on a box of books containing the pumping records of the engine. They changed my life and my career of which more later.

A period of recuperation was necessary for everything to properly stabilise. After Christmas, Uncle Rob was poorly so Aunt Kathleen decided to take him to Menton in the South of France for a month in February. Auntie Bee was to go and I formed the fourth in the party. Airports were probably not as used to dealing with incapacitated passengers in the early sixties. Boarding the aircraft was a challenge because I had difficulty fitting through the door standing upright on one leg with shoulder crutches. Accommodating a stiff leg in full length plaster on an airline seat was another challenge but I suspect the seats were placed a little further apart.

Dinner jacket was still the norm at the Hotel Westminster in the evenings. This dress gained admittance to the Casino at Monte Carlo but I did not break the Bank. It was the time of the citrus festival so we looked at some of the displays of oranges, lemons, grapefruits of all shapes and sizes. The good food was beautifully presented and helped me to recover but Uncle Rob did not. He passed away soon after we returned to England. This ironically was a help to me later because Auntie Kath moved to Cambridge to be near her sister so could look after me.

The London Hospital

A visit to East Grinstead saw the plaster removed and the start of building up strength in the left leg. All was going well, but one day there was an ominous noise of a sharp crack from that leg. Disaster had struck. After the accident, Whitehaven hospital had stuffed bits of bone back into the wound in the best alignment they could. The fibula acted as a sort of splint. While the bits had fused together, thin sections remained, one of which gave way, leaving the leg flapping. East Grinstead decided bone grafting was necessary and the best place for that was the London Hospital in Whitechapel. This setback was shattering to morale but faith sustained me through the next round of pain and waiting.

My leg was smothered once more in plaster but this time it was made into a long case with a lid. The leg could be taken out for exercises and then the box reinstated for safety. The leg was not painful but was bendy in the lower part. A surgeon will flex a bone with his hands to feel either the source of the break or how far it had strengthened up. I was amused at some of the trainee doctors sent to examine my leg who failed to locate the break. Yet another operation! One incision was made alongside the cross leg flap along the line of the shin. Bone slivers were cut off the top of the left thigh bone and inserted along the tibia. Uncle Stanley, who lived in London, drove over to visit me one Sunday. He was stopped at the main gates and asked where he could park because he also had a damaged leg. 'Are you a doctor, Sir', 'No' replied my uncle. 'Are you sure you are not a doctor, Sir'. 'Well perhaps'. 'Then park over there in the bays reserved for doctors'. All went well at the London Hospital and the bone grafting with more visits to check on progress.

The Subsequent Years

While outwardly to other persons, I was back on my feet again, the accident had caused permanent damage which I have had to learn how to surmount. The problem of sunburn on the skin grafting areas has been mentioned previously and still has to be watched. The left ankle joint became stiff and 'dropped' and has never bent fully again giving me a slight limp. The left knee joint has also been affected and may have been slightly misaligned during the bone grafting. This is causing more problems today, limiting how far I can walk. The damaged left calf muscle has resulted in that leg being weaker than the right so I tend to use the right leg to the detriment of the left, putting a strain on my back. I had been gardening one day at Stamford Cottage. While preparing breakfast the following morning, I opened the fridge door and reached for the milk bottle. Ouch! I twisted my back. I had little sympathy from Dr. Richard Clarke when he called. I was lying in agony on the lounge floor. He threw a few pills at me and was much more interested in my antique furniture than me. I was always very careful hand-cranking the Lancia after that.

I had to learn how to cope with other problems. Getting onto a bicycle, I first sat on the saddle with the left foot on the ground and the right on its pedal in the highest position. A hefty push on the right pedal should get me away. The Alvis van came into its own. I followed the example of 'Peg Leg' Gordon and learnt how to use the right foot on both brake and accelerator together. Starting from stationary remained a problem with the weak left leg but the Alvis was fitted with a 'clutch stop' that helped. Once moving I hoped that I could judge the respective speeds of car and engine so that I could change gear without too much crunching. One fault with the Alvis was that the magneto ignition system had no 'suppressors' so caused interference with televisions, an offence by law. One of Auntie Kath's neighbours at Cambridge complained but luckily we moved to another part of the city before I was prosecuted. The summer months were spent trying to get fit again so I could start the Cambridge Dip. Ed. course a year late. It was a close run thing. It was not the fully fit healthy young man who was able to start that autumn but thanks to the help of so many people he did.

The Diploma of Education Course

While theoretically a university degree was considered as a teaching qualification at least in private schools, the qualification of a Diploma of Education not only seemed to be becoming more and more necessary in state schools and also it was a further asset when seeking a teaching appointment. I was pleased I had been accepted on the Cambridge Dip. Ed. course, starting in the autumn for three terms. In the first term up to Christmas, the theory and practice of teaching was covered. In the Lent term, we were allocated to a school to practise what we had learnt. In the third term, our performance was criticised. We were supposed to attend the lectures, seminars and tutorials held mostly during the mornings. We looked at the varied school organisations such as grammar, comprehensive and special needs. The size of some comprehensives was enormous. One member of my class said she had been leading a lesson in stream M. There were lectures on child psychology, basic first aid, how to cope in emergencies, the legal background and much more.

We had plenty of spare time to explore the activities of the University although in my case this meant more recuperation. Most of my undergraduate friends had spread their wings and found jobs elsewhere. At first, I was rather on my own which enabled me to pursue two special interests. We were expected to submit a dissertation on some educational project. I chose as a title 'A Criticism of the Outward Bound'. I approached various schools and institutions explaining what I was doing and whether I could have a copy of the speech or lecture Kurt Hahn had given them. I assembled these in a box file in the Education Department for other students to study. Writing up this dissertation occupied part of the final term and was I was given an 'Award of Merit'.

The other interest was Fen Drainage and the Stretham engine. As I have pointed out earlier,

```
        A CRITICISM of the OUTWARD BOUND.


    Principles of the Outward Bound Schools.       Page  1

    Foundation of the Outward Bound Schools.        "    2

    The Growth of the Outward Bound Movement.       "    3

    The Discoveries of Kurt Hahn.                   "    8

    Character Training Through Adventure.           "   18

    To Serve, To Strive and Not To Yield.           "   28

    Conclusion.                                     "   37


    APPENDICES

    Daily Time-table.                              Page  1

    Course Syllabus.                                "   11

    Junior and Senior Course Programmes.            "   V1

    Athletic Standards, Outward Bound, Ullswater.   "  X1V
                        Outward Bound, Aberdovey.   "  XV
                        County Badge.               "  XV1
                        Duke of Edinburgh's Scheme  "  XV111

    End of School Report Forms.                     "   XX

    Bibliography.                                   "  XX11
```

Award of Merit

when I still had my leg in plaster, I visited the Stretham engine with the Kennys. I opened the cabin trunk on which I was sitting to discover the records of the performance of the engine. I analysed them and noted the rainfall, the hours it worked, coal consumed and employees' wages. I realised that I could produce a much better history of the engine than was currently available. Although there were the synopses of the annual accounts, other official records such as the minutes of the Waterbeach Level Commissioners had been retained by the Clerks to the Commissioners, namely solicitors. I must have explained what I was doing to one of our lecturers, Dr. J.P.C. Roach, who introduced me to Col. J.A.G. Beckett of Archer and Archer, Ely, Clerks to the Waterbeach Level Commissioners. I was able to peruse the Commissioners Minutes which gave me a great deal of new material. But the Account Book of 1815 was missing. This covered the crucial period when the windmill drainage was being extended as well as the installation of their steam engine in 1831.

Might the Cambridge solicitors have retained this crucial book? Probably Dr. Roach effected another introduction, this time to very smart solicitors on Kings Parade. The young apprehensive researcher was ushered into the office of the senior partner who was sitting on the far side of a large mahogany table with a few papers scattered on it. I got the impression that he felt I was wasting his time. I explained what I was doing. 'Could some of the Waterbeach Level documents have remained at his office?' One wall was lined with lockable wooden document boxes. I saw the magic words, 'Waterbeach Level' on one. 'No, there are certainly no Waterbeach Level records here now', the great man replied. My eyes fell and I saw on the table the vellum cover of a large book, 'Waterbeach Level, 1815'. There was the missing link. Great excitement. My fen drainage researches assumed greater significance because here was some historical work which no one else had done. But there we must leave this project of great potential and return to Cambridge for the second term of the Diploma of Education.

Teaching Practice

Owing to my accident, I was sent to the Perse School in Cambridge for my teaching practice. This is a small independent well respected grammar school with then only two streams. I was placed under the history teacher from whom I learnt a lot. One of his techniques was to have a deliberate pause in an unexpected place in something he was saying or reading. It was a technique Henry Hart used when taking services in chapel and it is surprising how it stimulates people's attention. In one lesson, my mentor allowed his students to continue a discussion which was not relevant to the scheduled topic and carried on for the remainder of that class. The students no doubt went away delighted at having successfully distracted their teacher but he commented to me afterwards that they had probably learnt more in that lesson than in most. (No lesson plans and schedules in those days.)

For me, taking history was not easy especially when one of the junior boys was son of a professor of medieval history and knew more of that subject than I did. The lad was very patient with me. The Department of Education sent assessors to see how we were doing. One of mine was a lady. We found her a chair and placed her at the back of the classroom. Unfortunately the chair collapsed, tipping her onto the floor. Her comment afterwards was that she thought that I coped with the situation very well. Another problem was my realisation that I could not see clearly what was happening at the back of the room. My distance vision had deteriorated but pride had prevented me wearing spectacles when I ought to have accepted them much sooner. At least I survived teaching practice.

Final Days in Cambridge

The third term was one of consolidation. Auntie Kath had found a house on the other side of Cambridge, just off the Trumpington Road. To help her, she employed an Italian au pair girl, Nadia. Nadia was sent off shopping and upset the best grocers in Trinity Street by asking to taste the cheese. She was asked to prepare some runner beans and showed Auntie Kath a small cupful of little beans, apologising that there would not be enough for lunch. She did not know about our strange English habit of eating the pods. For myself, I took a course for teaching mathematics up to 'O' level to improve my employment prospects.

Professor of Education:
W. ARNOLD LLOYD, Ph.D.

UNIVERSITY OF CAMBRIDGE
DEPARTMENT OF EDUCATION

17 BROOKSIDE
CAMBRIDGE
Telephone:
CAMBRIDGE 55271

Secretary of the Department:
Sir FULQUE AGNEW, Bᵗ

25 June 1962

<u>To Whom It May Concern</u>

Mr. R. L. Hills has completed a Revision Course in Mathematics (up to G.C.E. 'O' level) which should enable him to teach mathematics in the lower forms. He has passed the examination set at the end of the Course.

W. Arnold Lloyd

Professor of Education
in the University of Cambridge

Catching up with Mathematics

Cambridge Institute of Education

UNIVERSITY OF CAMBRIDGE DEPARTMENT OF EDUCATION

This is to certify that

RICHARD LESLIE HILLS

has satisfactorily completed the post-graduate course of training in the Cambridge University Department of Education, and has passed the Examination in the Theory, History and Practice of Education held in June 1962.

It is further certified that he submitted a dissertation entitled "A critical examination of Outward Bound", which was adjudged by the Examiners to be of merit.

Vice-Chancellor of the University

Director of the Institute

The Diploma in Education

The dissertation on the Outward Bound was finished and submitted, receiving its award of merit as previously mentioned. Advantage was taken of access to the University Library to find the stack with books on the history of Fen Drainage. Before the war, Andre had been employed by the Great Ouse River Board and joined me studying them. Another reader complained about the noise we were making but our research showed further possibilities for this subject. I was granted my Diploma of Education. The time had come for the little prince to fledge his wings, leave the hallowed realms of Cambridge and face the world.

Teaching and Research

Part 2 – Teaching in Schools

Earnley School near Chichester

Having obtained the Diploma of Education, it was obvious that really I needed more time for convalescence from the accident and would have difficulty coping with big classes in a large school. I would have earlier consulted the Careers Bureau at Cambridge and I expect they recommended that I try Earnley School which was situated on the Sussex coast about eight miles south west of Chichester. Earnley seemed to be the answer. It was to take pupils after Common Entrance in a brand new boarding school. The sponsor, a Mr. Betts, was said to have made a fortune out of ladies' sanitary wear. He lived in a Georgian house with peacocks strutting across the lawn. A neighbour complained that one of his blue peacocks was raping her white hen. We complained about the noise. There was a large impressive lounge inside the house where prospective parents (and possible teachers) were welcomed. Two or three boys were accommodated in this house. Autumn 1962 would be the first year of opening with two streams of a dozen pupils in each. In the spacious grounds was a brand new range of buildings for the school. There were small dormitories, a large dining room, swimming pool and gym, communal room and a range of class rooms. The teaching staff only taught while other staff supervised sports and social activities.

I was impressed with all the new buildings and was able to meet the older man who would be head teacher. So I decided to accept. Teaching staff lived out. I was placed with the Lanchesters, the husband being the son of one of the Lanchester car manufacturers. My accommodation was the original bungalow once used by a draughtsman of Henry Royce when that great man was convalescing at the Witterings. I shared the kitchen with the Lanchesters who lived in a two storey extension on the far side. Mrs. Lanchester prepared some meals for me and of course I had lunch at the school where there was a staff room. Bicycle was the normal means of transport to and from school.

Opposite the main school entrance was the little Earnley church in which I arranged a regular Sunday morning service for the boys with the Reader, John Rusbridge. He ran the adjacent farm and with his wife Yvonne wondered what had hit their previously quiet hamlet. They were both worried about the rumours that were soon circulating about the school. Yvonne was a talented artist with her own studio and pottery kiln. David, their only son, was growing up very much a farmer's lad. When a chicken was killed, he cut off the bottom of a leg, exposed the tendons and operated the claws. She had a most peculiar deformity in the base of her skull. Instead of two holes for the blood vessels to go in and out, she had only one. If she became too excited, blood would flood into her cranium and since it could not escape fast enough, was liable to drown her. She was always saying, 'I must keep quiet'. Sometime after I had left, John was driving home from Chichester and saw an emergency ambulance dashing the other way. Alas it contained Yvonne who died from her condition. I felt his loss for they had been very kind to me and helped me to get fitter with their friendship and meals. They also looked after the Lancia in one of their barns while it was being repaired.

School routine was quickly established with myself teaching history and scripture. There was a school minibus in which I took classes out to see local historic monuments. One was the Roman villa at Bignor with its tessellated pavements. Another was Pevensey Castle with its Norman fort where one boy availed himself of the gardez-loo in the wall. On a Saturday, I used to go into Chichester for lunch. I overheard some parents commenting about the prospects of their son at the Cathedral school gaining his Common Entrance to pass into a public school. The head assured them that they had a 90% success rate. I smiled because I knew that if the head thought that a boy might fail, he would not be allowed to sit the exam.

One afternoon in the New Year, I went to see the film *Samson and Delilah*. I soaked up the warmth of the cinema and the delightful gloriously sunny scenes only to receive a nasty shock when I came out as snow had settled everywhere and there was a vicious East wind. I felt I never wanted to see such a film again. But worse was to come. That was just the start of a bitterly cold couple of months. On the shore, the salt sea froze into a sort of porridge. Tidal Chichester Harbour froze over, trapping yachts which had not been taken out of the water. In holiday bungalows, water pipes, boilers and other appliances froze because their owners had not drained the systems. Even mains pipes froze because they had not been buried deep enough. What a mess when the thaw came. 'Water, water everywhere'. In the Harbour, it was low tide and the ice rushed out through the narrow harbour entrance taking all the yachts with it. I abandoned the bicycle to avoid the icy roads for the relative comfort of the Alvis van. Andre did not want anti-freeze in it so I had to drain it at nights. The nearly boiling water flowed out over the newly-laid tarmac, washing some away. Mr. Lanchester was not pleased!

I had been told that if you let your house during Goodwood Week, you could meet your mortgage charges and rates. This was much better than a longer lower priced summer let when the holiday makers would bring in sand from the shore. I looked around for somewhere to purchase but found nothing suitable. It soon became apparent that the school was not being run properly. The swimming pool turned a murky green. Even Mr. Betts' pockets were not inexhaustible. I forget when I decided to leave and put in my notice in time to quit at Easter. The school folded soon after, leaving some boys stranded. It became a sort of conference centre. My thoughts turned to my fen drainage researches and how I could develop them. Then an offer came from Worcester College for the Blind where a teacher of general subjects for the lowest class was being sought.

Worcester College for the Blind

I was surprised to open a letter which stated, 'We have met before'. It came from Richard Fletcher who had been housemaster of Hogsonites at Charterhouse. I must have told the Careers Bureau in Cambridge about my decision to leave Earnley. 'Dicky F', as we used to call him, had moved to Worcester College for the Blind as headmaster. It is possible that he also had approached them because he was looking for a teacher to fill a temporary post that summer term to replace the lady who would retire from teaching the junior class.

Worcester College for the Blind was the only grammar school for boys, taking pupils from preparatory schools through to maturity at eighteen. It was a special needs school so classes were small yet a wide range of options was offered to the senior boys. Here the term 'blind' is used to cover those with no vision at all to those with defective vision in some way or another which disabled them to such an extent that they could not cope with normal life. Visually impaired is a more usual term today. I accepted Dicky F's offer and moved to live in the school at Worcester for the summer term.

I had met blind people before because the large Wilderness House near Godden Green had been turned into a College for the Blind catering for courses for school leavers of both sexes. I remember waiting near the entrance hall at the end of a long passage. A girl, whom I knew had no vision, entered the far end and started walking down the middle towards me. She paused, then moved to one side and began walking again. She had sensed something or someone strange was there. I was intrigued. The organist at Seal church was blind and taught there. Audrey had learnt the basic Braille alphabet and wrote letters to a blind friend with a simple frame and single point punch.

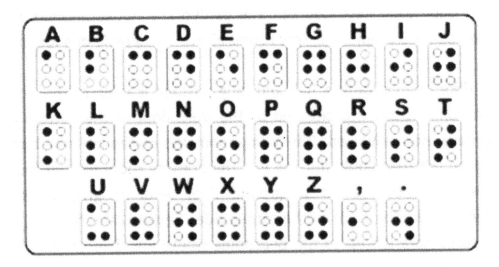

Basic English Braille

I quickly realised that it was essential though not a condition of employment that I should learn Braille. This was before the age of mobile phones, I-pads and other electronic devices although I think a few 'Talking Books' were available. Basic Braille is very simple, the alphabet consisting of a combination of six raised dots, impressed into stout paper. The dots are arranged in three vertical rows of two in each. Combinations of these cover the whole of our alphabet and punctuation marks. Audrey had a special board on which the paper was clamped and her guiding frame aligned. She wrote from right to left, impressing the appropriate dots into the paper but not piercing it, the impressions facing down. When finished, the paper would be taken out so that the blind person could 'read' it from left to right by feeling the raised dots. Therefore Braille symbols had to be memorised written one way and read the other.

Now the first ten letters of the alphabet were also used for the numbers 1 to 0 but how could a blind person tell if a single dot was 'a' or '1'. Figures had to have a special symbol before them warning when a number followed. So a single number had two symbols. Braille music was even more complicated because both length of note and its pitch had to be conveyed needing four symbols. Sight reading Braille music and playing by blind people is very difficult. There are a host of standard contractions to simplify both reading and writing. Common words such as 'the' or word endings such as '...ing' are a single symbol.

Most blind people used the 'Stainsby' Braille writer which had six plungers with a cross-over linkage for three fingers in each hand so that Braille was written as it would be read but still only one symbol at a time. The 'head' also moved onto the next space so writing with one was fairly quick but very noisy from the clatter they made. The boys generally appreciated my attempts to learn Braille except when I had to punish them by dishing out 'lines'. Three or four sheets might be written at once although the dots in the top sheet would not be as sharp as those in the bottom. A nasty sighted teacher could tell the difference. But worse was to come if a mistake were made because it would appear in all four sheets. The blind boy might try to smooth the dot down again but left a mark clearly seen by the teacher. I gained a certificate for competence in Braille.

R.N.I.B. Certificate for Standard English Braille

Soon after the start of term, the classics master died suddenly. A replacement could not be found at short notice so his lessons were shared out with me taking the junior classes. A new teacher took over my previous teaching load. I will admit that sometimes I took advantage of the boys' blindness by looking up the vocabulary at the back of the Latin text book. One boy, Peter White now a famous BBC Radio 4 Presenter, wanted to learn Greek.

I had to teach him. He had the great advantage because the Greek Alpha and English 'a' and so on are the same symbols.

Extra Curriculum Activities

The College was set in extensive grounds with views towards the Malvern Hills. I thought it was so sad that most of the boys could not see the magnificent sunsets in the summer evenings when the sun went down behind that range. There was a large gym where the boys played football on their bottoms with a bell in the ball. It made a noise while in play but was difficult to locate when stationary. The joinery shop was well equipped while outdoors there was an open-air swimming pool. A sighted person had to be in attendance to see that the boys did not dive onto each other. I was surprised at how far some could swim underwater, provided they kept in a straight line! This underwater ability was useful on one parent's day when a boy lost his glass eye in the pool and another had to rescue it in front of the parents.

One weekend, a trip was organised to stay in the Brecon Youth Hostel and walk in the Brecon Beacons. I found it very instructive to watch how different boys coped with being taken out of their usual surroundings. The first evening, I was sitting at a table in the lounge probably writing a letter. A couple of blind boys entered and started to feel their way round the room. I did not wish to spoil their fun so sat still. They came to a table, found some paper then, horror of horrors, a master! They retreated outside quickly. The College had a long dark broad main corridor with steps at the end before dividing into passages to the class rooms (no lights on of course). Some blind boys ran down it quite happily, jumped down the steps and so to their class room. One, who had an eye removed, possibly through cancer, lost the sight in the other perhaps in sympathy, found no difficulty. He was quite happy walking out over the hills and could even avoid the thin twigs of birch trees as we passed under them. Another who walked slowly down the corridor, shuffling his feet to find the edge of the steps, was not at all happy when we went out in the broad open spaces of the Brecons and I had to go and help him. One commented that he liked walking with Mr. Hills because he knew when he was lost!

So far, I have made the assumption that the boys had no vision at all but many had some 'visual impairment' with some sight remaining. The College had an 'initiative' day when the boys had to organise something themselves. A couple of older ones asked if I would take them rock climbing. One had very poor vision and needed glasses with extremely thick lenses. The other had partial vision, parts of his eyes where he could see something but in most nothing. He would look you up and down until he had you in the best part of his sight. We made a comfortable second seat in the back of the Alvis and spent the day rock climbing on the millstone grit at Stannage. This was the first time the College had attempted such an activity.

The Alvis was very useful that summer term not only getting to and from Worcester but also nipping down to see Margaret and family at Brimpsfield. I noticed that the steering wheel was sinking lower and lower. The petrol tank was situated in the bulkhead behind the engine but above the driver's knees. A cock controlled the flow of petrol by gravity down to the carburettor so no pump was needed. I found that the wooden bulkhead had rotted and no longer bore the weight of tank and petrol. The joiners' shop came into play. The old bulkhead was removed and a new one fitted in two halves. The time came to try it. The cock was turned on and petrol flowed down to the carburettor but some overflowed into the oily tray supporting the engine. I went to start the engine. A main electric lead from the battery to the starter motor must have frayed allowing a spark to ignite the petrol. Flames and smoke poured out. I was determined not to lose my handiwork, the car and the garages, but managed to turn off the petrol and put out the fire.

A small selection of tools, used to repair the Alvis and the Lancia

The City of Worcester held many attractions. I cycled down to the Cathedral for evensong and listen to the choir. I found the 'seconds' shop of the Royal Worcester Pottery and another shop on the Shambles where more was sold so assembled a dinner service from odd pieces. Getting back up the hill to the College was much harder. The City was also an attraction for the boys. They never liked using their white sticks because this marked them out as different. One fell into a hole which some workmen had left unprotected. Woe betide you if you left something in a different place from usual. Even parents had to remember to return things back to where a boy expected them to be. They would 'watch' television in preference to listening to the radio because that was what normal people did. I was left with the impression that those of average IQ could just about cope with their disability. Those below had great difficulty but some with higher IQ were able to rise above their problems. For example Peter White has been mentioned already and there was David Blunkett, a minister in a Labour Cabinet.

The end of term was approaching fast. When 'A' Level exams had finished, some senior boys formed themselves into a Group and performed in various public houses in the City. Their musical initiative was not appreciated by those in authority and they left the College early. I was helping to sort out and return library books remaining on shelves in classrooms.

When the other master picked up one book, it rattled. The boy had carefully cut out the centre pages to form a hollow space where he hid his cigarette rolling machine and tobacco. Unfortunately he had mutilated Volume 3 of *Dr. Zivhago* which would be impossible to replace. He was sent to the headmaster who rewarded his initiative with a rather sore bottom. One of my final tasks was to escort three lads on the train to Birmingham New Street Station where I had to take them to a special waiting room so that porters could help them catch their respective trains. Each boy had at least one piece of luggage in one hand and his Braille writing machine in its box in the other. I could grab two by their collars and march them along alright but the third would wander off. Catching that one allowed another to escape. This was before the days of 'doggie' leads but I managed to assemble them in the waiting room and hand them over.

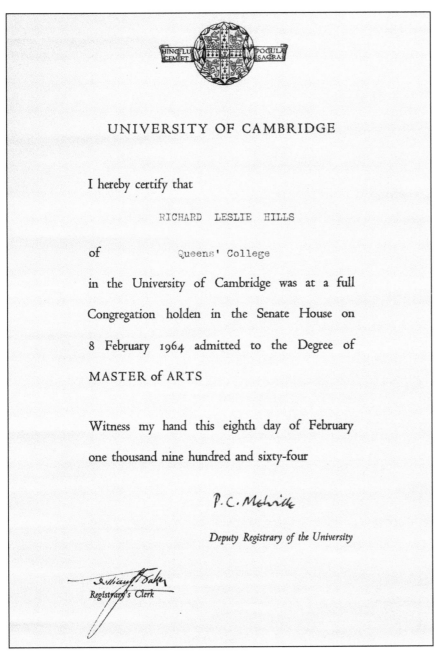

Master of Arts

The Future

Originally I had been offered my teaching position at Worcester for the summer term only. It could have been extended through the staff changes. While I was happy there, was this the place where I wanted to remain for the rest of my career? In earlier chapters of this autobiography, I outlined how many members of my families had worked and indeed were still working overseas. There was not only my mother's family, the Millers and their connections (see page 2) but also the Allisons and the Hills with John in Basrah and Uncle Stan in Bahrain (see page 77). While at Cambridge I had realised that a career in the Indian Colonial Civil Service was no longer possible (See Chap 4.1), might there be an opening for a teacher? One possibility might be with the Church Missionary Society. I went to their training college at Chislehurst for a short time. They wanted to send me to their School for the Blind at Isfahan in Iran. Knowing how specialised was teaching the blind, I said that I ought to receive proper training before working abroad. To this, the CMS did not agree and the chance of a place on a course was missed so I decided to return to my fen drainage project. It seemed strange that Iran was where later John would spend many years until the fall of the Shah.

The Alvis badge and hare mascot

Teaching and Research

Part 3 – The Lancia

CY 8115 at Prescott in August 2011

Say not the struggle naught availeth,
   The labour and the wounds are vain,
The Lancia faints not, nor faileth,
   She is back on the road again.

(apologies to Arthur Hugh Clough)

The Lancia has been mentioned various times in this narrative starting with the lady in Lydd informing me that one was for sale (page 76). I also recorded how I was besotted with her fine elegant lines (page 91). While the Alvis is a sort of sturdy tough British bulldog, the Lancia Lambda (to use her proper name) is a rather elegant Italian lady. The clean lines of its design were recognised as classic from the earliest days of its launch at the Paris Salon of November 1922.

It was immediately recognised as uncompromising and refreshing. Even those with no engineering interests at all had only to look at it to know that it was different. It was low and angular, with a quality of unity, of being 'all of a piece'. It looked deliberate, something that was designed from scratch by a team that knew exactly what it wanted. The car was a total departure from all previous practice… The Motor of November 1923 called it the 'materialisation of a dream'.

This was written by Nigel Trow in 1980 (N. Trow, *The Shield and The Flag*, David & Charles, Newton Abbot, 1980, p. 58). The Lancia Lambda still holds a certain mystique even in 2017 when this is being written and the papers are full of the advent of electric and even driverless cars. In 1958, such a car represented value for its price because it could outperform most ordinary cars.

The mechanics of the Lambda have been described many times by those better qualified than myself. There have been immense changes in automobile design over those ninety years but I will concentrate mostly on the struggles I had over fifty years to keep the car roadworthy, modifying some parts yet keeping to the original as closely as possible. I will describe some adventures with it and the effect it had on other people. Also I suspect that it helped progress my career in the museum and engineering worlds when people saw that I was capable of maintaining and running such a car. Much of the initial restoration work when I acquired the car had to be replaced over the years. That a mechanical overhaul was needed after our trip to Spain has been pointed out (page 95).

The Chassis or Body

(a)

We will start with the chassis or body of the car. Two contemporary photographs show how the Lambda body was formed with the sides pressed out of 2mm. sheets of steel. It was lightened with holes pierced through wherever possible and flanged for greater rigidity. The outside of this skeleton was covered with thin sheet steel, pressed over the main flanges. The reason for trying to describe this frame is that, unlike other contemporary cars that had a chassis on which was mounted a body that could be removed and to which other parts such as mudguards, doors, bonnets were fitted, on the Lancia, they were all fitted directly onto this frame.

Looking down on the car, it can be seen how the sides of the car are the width of the radiator at the front, broadening out for the engine compartment and then swelling more gently past the front and rear seats before swinging in again to be rounded off at the boot.

Let us take the case of the running boards which were so useful for laying out tools or engine parts when carrying out repairs, or sitting on while drinking a refreshing mug of tea, or standing on when climbing into the car. They were made from a pressed steel sheet covered with ribbed aluminium sheet, surrounded on three sides by specially shaped nickel plated brass angle. The fourth side was sealed against the frame by another plated brass angle. Rain water ran down the sides of the car, penetrated behind these brass strips, causing the steel sheet of the running board to rust. That steel sheet passed a short distance under the main frame where of course there was further rusting. The floor of the foot-wells consisted of wooden tongue and groove slats with tongues of strips of steel, covered in piled carpet. All this inevitably became wet. The steel tongues swelled with rust and burst the wood. The damp ends of the wood resting on the frame caused rust in the frame, both in the 2mm. steel sheet and the overlay. Condensation spread the rust up the side walls. The rust I had noticed on the sides of the car when I first saw it had started on the inside and penetrated through to the outside.

To begin with, the rust patches were covered with thin sheet but over the years it was feared that rust had seriously weakened the main steel frame. Robert Steeds cut out large sections and welded in new. Parts of the thin sheet were also replaced and depressions filled with tinmans solder. Each running board was supported on four pressed steel brackets, fixed at their inner ends to the propeller shaft casing and in the middle to the main frame, the outer ends left projecting to support the running board. These had rusted badly and, since no replacements were available, a length of tube was cut in half longitudinally and welded onto a piece of steel of appropriate width and length, the semicircular holes at the ends having been blocked up. They were bolted on and were much stronger than the originals.

The wooden floorboards were replaced with steel that had one odd consequence. The four seat squabs were designed to be lifted out, exposing wells for storage of tools and equipment. I had packed the front passenger seat with spare clothes. I did not worry about the slight leak in the silencer but the heat from the exhaust singed a pair of socks! The space under the driver's seat already had trays for tools. Some were vital for servicing and maintaining the front suspension for which I was exceedingly grateful. I built another tray for this seat and more for the passenger seat. Together with these trays, the box on the running board, spaces under the rear seats and the tool box in the boot, I carried a pretty comprehensive array of tools and supplies in the car.

The Mudguards or Wings

When Vincenzo Lancia designed his Lambda, he obviously expected that it would show other cars a clean pair of heels, or at least wheels. The rear mudguards end almost horizontally above the wheels so that, especially in the wet, mud and stones will be thrown up at any car daring to approach the rear too closely. I never had any complaints but wondered if they were legal. Vincenzo did not expect any other motorist to see the Lambda if they came too close in the dark. The single rear light was barely an inch in diameter and had to suffice for the number plate as well. This was soon changed with twin matching rear lamps, one for the GB sign and the other for the number plate CY 8115. These lamps also contained bulbs for a brake warning light operated by the foot pedal which was fitted later. These rear wings were bolted to the frame and to the rear of the running boards.

While looking at the rear, a few comments about the boot are appropriate. The lid of the boot was yet another steel frame covered in thin sheet, hinged along its lower edge. Inside was the petrol tank and space for a suitcase, or more necessarily the toolbox.

The tank was treated for rust both inside and out. There was no external filler so the boot had to be opened every time it was refilled. The filler hole was closed by a large brass octagonal nut that was unscrewed with a special spanner. Two spare wheels were mounted on a tube in the middle of the lid. These were quite a weight to lift, but the knack of closing it without trapping fingers was soon acquired.

The Wheels

The great weight of the wheels was due partly to the British Rudge Whitworth hubs which Vincenzo just had to modify. What has been called a 'dinner plate' was riveted onto the hub and shrouded the brake drum. When driving Auntie Kath through Tatton Park, I stopped to identify a new scraping sound issuing from the front of the car. Removing a wheel revealed broken and loose rivets resulting in a slow drive home. Auntie was not impressed. Matching tapers round the outside of the drum and the inside of the dinner plate located the inner side of the wheel. To secure the outer, a taper was machined on the hub which fitted inside the nut, securing the wheel. This also had a matching taper.

Later hub caps had 'wings' or ears which were hit with a lump hammer to secure them. Other passions of Vincenzo were fine screw threads and circular slotted nuts. In spite of searching through many engineering books, I never did find the specifications for some threads used on the Lambda which made replication of parts difficult. Often these were tightened by collars which might have slots cut in their circumference or holes drilled in their face.

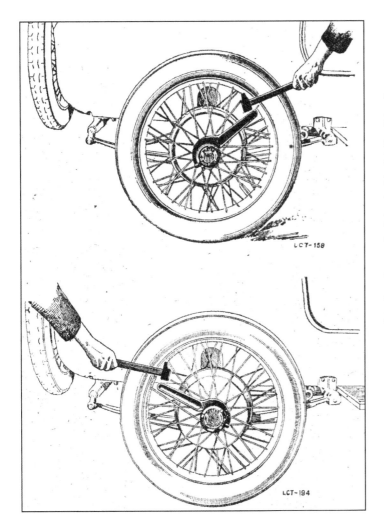

The illustration shows a 'C' spanner being used to tighten a hub nut. One came with CY 8115 but was useless because the projecting pin that fitted into the circumference for the hub nut broke off. Luckily someone had fabricated a heavy 'spanner' that fitted over the hub nut and was held in place by four bolts. It had a pair of 'wings' well able to survive being bashed by a lump hammer to secure the wheel firmly. All that had to be done then was to touch up the chipped paint.

The Tyres

CY 8115 came shod with narrow high pressure beaded-edge tyres. She was a delight to drive with light responsive steering. But in the wet, beware. Descending the steep cobbled Guildford High Street, I touched the brakes and skidded broadside across the road, luckily hitting nothing. Fitting these tyres was an art, very different from later ones. Two special spoon-shaped levers came with the car. Release pressure in the inner tube and thump one side of the bead out of the wheel rim. Pull out the inner tube, trying not to scrape fingers too badly. Lever and pull off the other side. Hopefully a replacement tyre will have been found. The proper size was 765 x 105 but was obsolescent. An alternative 820 x 120 was fatter and might foul the front suspension. Their cost became astronomical so CY 8115 had the indignity of being fitted with 19ins. well-based tyres. To fit a new beaded-edge tyre, one side was levered on and thumped into the rim. Then the other side had to be bashed into position on the rim. The new tyre had been prepared with a nick in the bead through which the air valve of the tube could pass and so to the hole in the rim. The two inner sides of the tyre should overlap each other to protect the tube from rubbing on the rim. Care had to be taken to ensure that the tube was not trapped below this overlap. Too often the tube was caught by the cover and the air valve not positioned to fit through the nick and the hole in the rim. Then the tube was damaged, necessitating repairs and trying again. The air valves were longer than later ones and the head of the air pump nozzle had to be at right angles to the delivery pipe or it would not fit on. I saw that at one garage the nozzle was in line with the delivery pipe and told the attendant that I thought he would be unable to inflate the tyre. He replied, 'I have been blowing up tyres for X years now and you are telling me...' I was right.

The Front Wings

The front wings swept up from the running boards along the side of the engine compartment. At their base on each side was a metal box, the nearside one designed for a specially shaped 12 volt battery close to the starter motor. Since this shape of battery became unobtainable, one six volt battery was placed in both sides. Later I was able to revert to a single 12 volt one as batteries improved. Then the offside box could house an hydraulic jack and hammer for the wheel nuts. Both boxes needed remedial welding to restore rust damage.

When first collecting the Lancia from East Grinstead, I had to climb along the front wing to reattach the tow rope which shows how strong they were. But their smooth paintwork was liable to be damaged by stones thrown up from underneath by the front wheels. To counter this, aluminium under-wings were fitted. But we have passed by the windscreen. As purchased, the car had a 1930s flat folding screen which looked wrong. It should have had a dog-legged one with a lower part sloping up to a pair of opening windows. Based on what I had seen on other Lambdas and from photographs, I designed a replica which was made by Austers. When asked to make a second, they declined so I was lucky.

While it was legal to drive in the rain if the windscreen could be opened, a wiper would be a great safety feature. Returning from Oxford one winter's night to London, it was snowing. The snow covered the windscreen so it was opened to see out underneath. The snow slowly slid down, leaving a clear patch. Our backs soon became crooked with bending down and up to see out of this slot. The original vacuum-operated wiper motor was reactivated until an electric one was fitted. The main hazard of the vacuum operated wiper was when ascending a long hill, the vacuum gradually decreased until the wiper stopped working, usually when at last overtaking a large lorry.

The Electrics

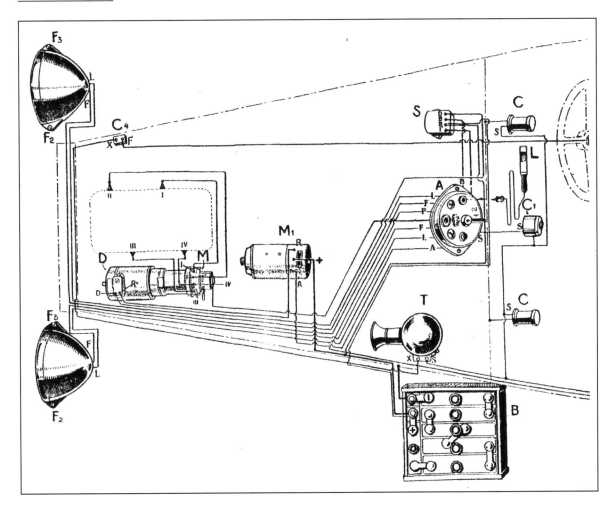

The Instructions manual devoted thirty pages to 'Electrical Equipment'. Perhaps Vincenzo felt that Lambda owners had little experience of this newfangled apparatus. He paid particular attention to the battery, explaining about the 'electrolyte which was composed of a mixture of pure sulphuric acid and distilled water'. He warned, 'Never accost a flame to look into the inferior of the accumulators as the hydrogen and oxygen remaining after the charge would ignits with an explosion'. Dangerous these modern cars! The wiring diagram shows the layout of the cells in the original Lambda battery. It also outlines the various wires connecting the switches to their apparatus. All these wires were concealed in the channels formed in the main frame and hidden by aluminium covers. These came in short lengths, bent to fit into each other and the frame. Sections had gone astray over the years so there ensued some bashing of aluminium sheet into shape to hide these wires on both sides of the engine compartment.

These early Lambdas were fitted with either Bosch or Marelli electrics. CY 8115 had the latter with magnificent Zeiss headlights which contained two bulbs. The smaller was a long festoon bulb for the sidelight. But their position was probably too far in from the side of the car to be legal. Therefore I fitted separate sidelights which stuck up prominently at the front of the wings. They were a great aid even in daylight for judging the width and length of the car when manoeuvring in tight places. The festoon bulb was adapted as a traffic indicator light when these were added latter.

The Zeiss headlights were magnificent examples of craftsman's work. The main bulb projected from the rear centre of a glass mirror reflector. This needed re-silvering. Luckily the glass was removed safely from the cement securing it into the brass mounting without breaking. The bulbs could be adjusted from a narrow pencil-like beam up to a broad beam lighting up the trees and all around. This was unsuitable for modern traffic conditions which needed a beam cut off at the top. To dip them, a spring-loaded yellowish glass cylinder was moved out to screen the bulbs from the glass mirror. It was operated by the driver through wire cables. This was too effective against the bright lights of modern cars so eventually I devised a system of switching off both Zeiss headlights and switching on a single lamp illuminating the kerb better.

The collapse of the bearing in the dynamo during our continental expedition meant that the electrics were modified to the three brush system. The automatic mechanical advance and retard was scrapped and replaced by a plate carrying a ball bearing to support a new armature. New wires led to an additional panel below the dashboard with cut-out switch, volt meter, and a charge/discharge ampere meter. This was later extended with switches to control the headlights, flashing indicator lights and electric windscreen wiper. The Marelli magneto was retained to provide the current for the spark plugs.

The Dash Board

A look at the dashboard will show how much car controls have changed over the years. Starting at the left is the round knob B for an air pump to pressurise Le Nivex fuel gauge. Round knob C is a light switch to illuminate the dials, useful also for map reading. The fuel gauge measured in litres and worked only when activated by the pump. The four-day Jaeger clock comes next (see page 91 for its return). It kept very accurate time when wound up by hand and set correctly. The centre panel A had at top an ignition warning light not functioning in between fuses for right and left lighting circuits. The main switch for side and headlights is in the middle. The small key underneath was the ignition switch and safety

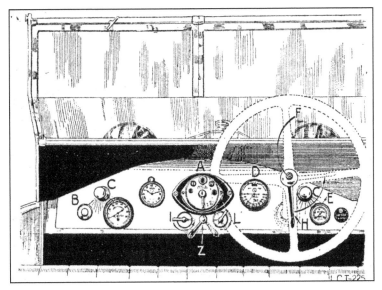

lock. A plug for a leadlight (very useful when changing wheels in the dark) went in the hole. Then at the bottom of the original panel was a carburettor control I with three settings, rich for starting, normal running and economy. The long lever Z worked the dipping cowls for headlights through cables while the right was the throttle control. The additional small box was the electric horn button. The speedometer D measured in kilometres and recorded the distance travelled. On the dial, were two red lines showing the maximum speeds for the gears. In the centre of the steering wheel was the original horn button F. The lever H in the centre controlled the advance and retard of the spark on the magneto. The steering column passed through the dashboard in a ball bearing with spherical housing to accommodate the flexing of the body. The final fittings on the dashboard were another light switch C and an oil pressure gauge E which measured in 'metri d'aqua'. And of course above this was the bulb horn, the back-up warning system which was a source of great fascination for children (of all ages). A new panel below the centre of the dashboard would have the volt meter, charge and discharge ampere meter with dynamo on/off switch and a new ignition switch.

The reason for going into all this detail is to show how much simpler driving our cars today has become. We just jump into them, turn the ignition key which starts the engine, and drive off. To start the Lancia from cold, I would make certain that the ignition was switched off and check that the advance and retard on the steering wheel was set at retard. Then with the starting handle, I would turn the engine over slowly a couple of times. The carburettor control would be set to rich for starting and the throttle control opened a fraction. The petrol would be switched on and the carburettor flooded a little. Check the advance and retard was set to retard and the magneto switched on. Return to the starting handle and turn the engine slowly over perhaps four turns. Then a quick jerk up with the handle and the engine would start (if lucky). The advance and retard lever would be advanced for general running. When warmed a bit, the carburettor control would be turned to normal and finally the throttle turned to normal running speed. And of course when stopped for the day, the petrol would be turned off and the other switches turned off and set back to normal. The joys of vintage motoring.

The Rear Suspension

The Lambda was famous for its ability to hold the road with its smooth suspension. The back axle was mounted on two semi-eleptical springs. It is possible that the offside one was strained when its bracket nearly tore away and was welded back on in Andorra for the main leaf of this spring broke. The leaf was welded together and we set off camping in, I think, Northumbria. The weld broke, the axle moved back on that side. What were we to do, as we were well out in the country? The break had happened in the front half of the spring. I realised if the spring were turned front to back, what then became the front two thirds of the broken leaf would still locate the axle while the broken part now at the rear might be supported by adjoining leaves. It was worth trying so we set to in the middle of a field. The drive back south was taken slowly but it worked.

These main leaves caused problems at the repairers. To form the eye for the shackle pin, normally the end of the leaf is bent upwards and backwards to form a circle above the leaf through which the pin would pass. But on the Lambda, the end of the leaf is first bent into the circle which is then bent back down again until the centre is in line with the curvature of the spring. If done incorrectly, the length of the leaf will be incorrect so sometimes the leaf had 'to be returned to maker'. The wheel bearings would leak a little which spread onto the brake linings. It did not seem to be a good idea and follow the instructions in the handbook that, when one wheel was braking more than the others, to oil the surface of the brake shoes with engine oil (p. 28) so the hardened felt seals were removed and sealed ball bearings fitted instead. Likewise the oil seal where the propeller shaft enters the back axle was machined to take a modern oil seal. The back axle leaked very little oil after this.

The Sliding Pillar

The front suspension consisted of the famous Lambda sliding pillar. The reason for Vincenzo's choice is said to have been due to a spring breaking, throwing the occupants out of the car. He was not the first to use the sliding pillar type since Morgan's amongst others had it before the War but he introduced hydraulic damping which transformed it.

The radiator, which Vincenzo may have designed to copy Rolls Royce or more likely from the facade of a classical temple, has to be removed for access to the main frame, a finger crunching business. It has to be disconnected from the water pipes, the mounting blocks removed and the top screw round the filler removed. Then by lowering and wriggling it about, it can be pulled out. There should be space between the track rod and the framing. The main frame over the top of the radiator had cracked and was welded up. It was difficult to alter Vincenzo's designs and there was only just room to strengthen this part by brazing a horizontal bar between the back of the radiator and the blade of the 'Ventilator' or fan.

If the line of the radiator is continued out and down, it ends in a casting securing the end of vertical tube for the upper part of the sliding pillar framing. This tube ends in another casting with one tube sloping back to the main frame and a horizontal one running right across the bottom front of the car to the sliding pillar on the other side. On these outer castings are fixed casings to protect the springs and the important sliding pillar itself. Luckily the dismantling tools came with CY 8115.

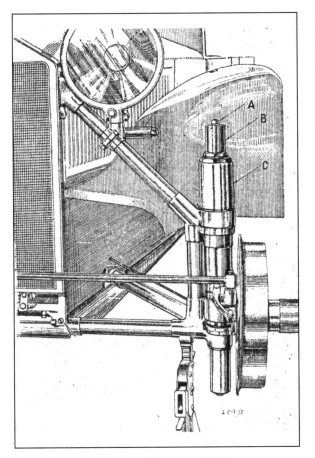

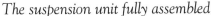

The suspension unit fully assembled

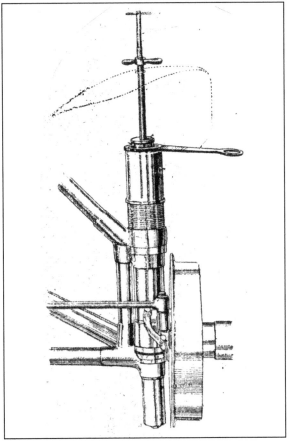

The cover being removed

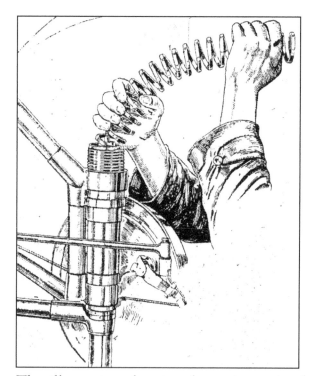
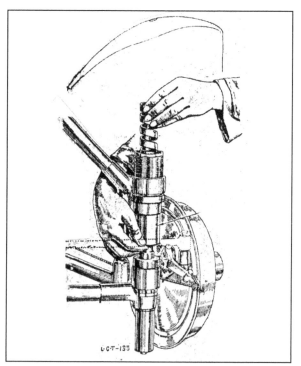

The illustration showing the major spring being removed is rather optimistic. Perhaps Italian men were strong enough to bend it, but then there was not enough space on CY 8115 below the wing to do this. I had to remove the wing. On later Lambdas, a large hole was cut in the wing fitted with a cover plate. The smaller stronger emergency spring followed.

The sliding pillar is a long tube with a complex casting near the middle. Inside is the hydraulic damping piston with its valve at the bottom of a thin rod. The oil level needed checking from time to time which involved taking off the top cap, catching the end of the piston rod before it sank into the pillar tube. On CY 8115, the special tool was inserted through a small hole in the wing and screwed onto the top of the rod. This tool was not as long as is shown in the picture so fingers were trapped against the wing. The plug had to be removed and oil poured in hopefully since there was no level gauge.

The complex casting fixed to the sliding pillar had in one direction the stub axle protruding for the front wheel. At right angles were the arms for the brake shoe pivots and brake operating lever. The steering arms fitted in another part and there was a bracket for the track rod linking the wheels.

I was always surprised at the way this arrangement performed with little maintenance but it gave the Lambda an enormous lock on the steering so this long car could be turned round in a very tight circle. While I was recovering from the climbing accident, the opportunity was taken to lift out the engine. Engine and gearbox rest on a pair of tubes running from front to back of the engine compartment. The offside tube was found to be cracked under the engine and so was replaced. The casting for the pulley guiding the brake cable to the front brake was also cracked. This was made from 'muckite', a mixture of aluminium and zinc that could not be welded. A new aluminium casting was made and all seemed well.

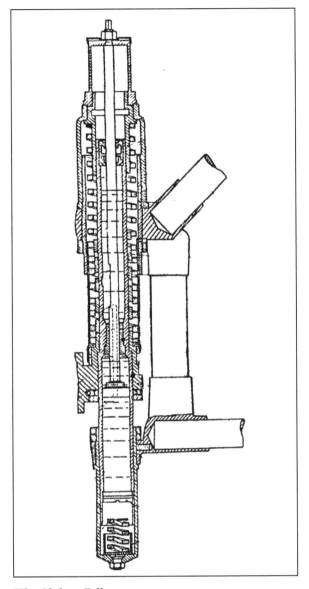

The Sliding Pillar

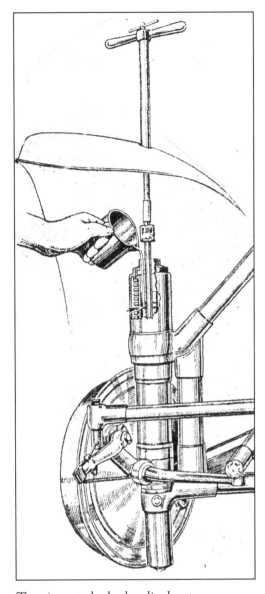

Topping up the hydraulic damper

However, during a later restoration, the suspension framing was examined more closely. The long horizontal tube stretching right across the front of the car was found to have broken inside the casting under the radiator. I suspect that before I purchased CY 8115, she was involved in some accident. The whole front frame came off. A new cross tube was fitted. A jig was borrowed from the Lambda Consortium and the castings were brazed on again by the owner of 'Dot' motor cycles just before he died. The steering was much firmer after this repair.

Front Wheel Bearings

The front wheel bearings had to withstand the sideways thrust when cornering as well as the weight of the car. Timken roller bearings had not been invented so Vincenzo devised a complex arrangement of large and small ordinary ball bearings for the weight with a double-thrust ball bearing for the sideways thrust. These bearings, which became unobtainable, were separated by spacers kept in place by screwed rings. Small bolts locked a castellated screwed ring. The whole arrangement was bolted onto the stub axle with a large castellated nut. To prevent this unscrewing, a split pin was inserted through holes tapped in the splines, closed with little aluminium plugs. The hole at the end was filled with a large aluminium plug to prevent leakage of oil. Vincenzo recommended 'filling up the cavity with extra thick oil'.

I always used grease but even so, oil and grease escaped into the dinner plate wheel centre and into the brake drum. To stop this, I decided to fit Timken taper roller bearings and modern oil seals. My Myford ML7 lathe was brought into action. The most challenging part was to turn a screwed disc that

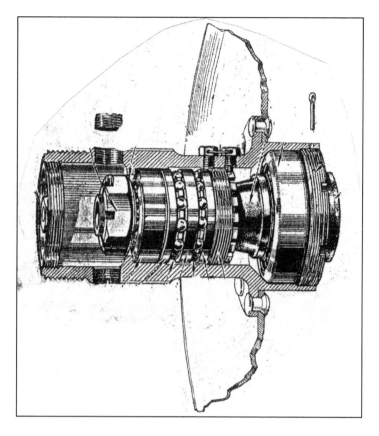

would fit into the large end of the hub. The inside was hollowed out to accommodate a modern oil seal. A small oil seal was fitted into the outer end of the assembly with a spacer separating opposed taper roller bearings. All this was a great improvement, not only stopping grease escaping but reducing wheel wobble to virtually nothing. I felt this justified such a modification which could be concealed.

The Brakes

When the Lambda appeared in 1922, few cars, even those with a high performance, had four wheel brakes. I recounted previously how I discovered the excellence of the Lambda's when first collecting CY 8115 in 1958 and managed to break the tow rope when I applied them (page 91). Both front and rear brakes were fully compensated, operated by rods and cables. The hand brake applied only the rear brakes. From one rear brake, a cable passed round three pulleys back to the other. Pull the centre pulley with the hand brake lever and the brake was applied equally to both drums. However when not applied, a strong spring on one side could cause that brake to drag so I fashioned brake stops to prevent this.

The Horizontal Bar

For the front brakes, there was a very sophisticated pivoted horizontal bar connected to the foot brake in the middle. Push on the foot brake and the bar applied the brake in each drum. It tilted as the lock was applied in the steering to compensate as the cables wound and unwound round the pillar suspension. Vincenzo had already anticipated my little addition with adjustable stops on these brakes to prevent dragging. But while the front and back brakes were each fully compensated, the two systems were not. So Vincenzo recommended that 'To adjust the brakes, the car must be lifted in such a way to leave all four wheels free to turn; then tighten the various brake adjustment nuts, until, when depressing the pedal, all four wheels are braked with equal force.' A counsel of perfection! It was necessary to check the foot brake regularly because the front brakes wore more quickly than the rear.

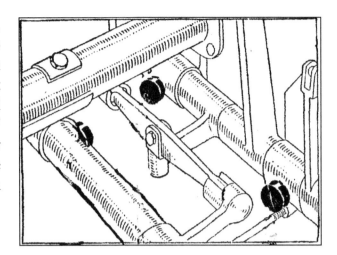

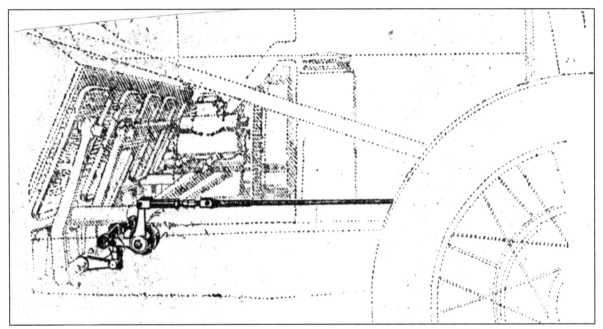

The front brake cable adjustment method

The Petrol Supply

Before describing the engine, we will look at the way the petrol reached the engine from the rear tank. A copper pipe ran along the off-side bottom channel of the main frame and up to the scuttle to a form of pump worked off the vacuum in the carburettor manifold. It was supplied by the French Le Nivex Company as was the petrol gauge which measured in 'Litres d'Essence'.

The header tank was cleaned out and given an internal coating of polyurethane varnish. The next job was to restore the seal round Le Nivex using brass screws instead of steel. Le Nivex was self-contained

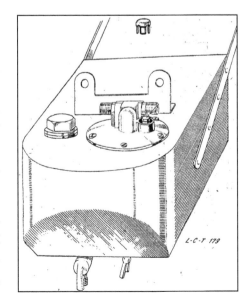

in a brass casing. Heat was applied gently. The casing fell off in a burst of flame. Inside was a cork float that had become soaked in petrol. A modern brass float replaced the cork; some worn pins were replaced and the whole sealed up again. Its innards remained a mystery but it worked, drawing up petrol into the header tank in a series of clicks.

Le Nivex worked reliably for many years until the car began to run roughly. I traced this eventually to petrol being drawn straight through Le Nivex into the inlet manifold. Once when driving the late Sonia Rolt through the Pennines, we came to a stop. Working on the Lancia with the sound of curlew calling overhead was a new experience for both of us. This was sorted out but, for the sake of mind when driving in modern conditions, I decided to fit an auxiliary electric petrol pump that supplied the carburettor directly. Underneath the header tank were two cocks. One drained the tank which gave a useful supply of petrol for cleaning purposes. The other was the main supply to the carburettor. The Instructions book shows a nice curly 'pig's tail' in the pipe. I tried this but the engine vibrations caused the copper pipe to loosen the joints, causing a leak. A modern plastic pipe gave no trouble.

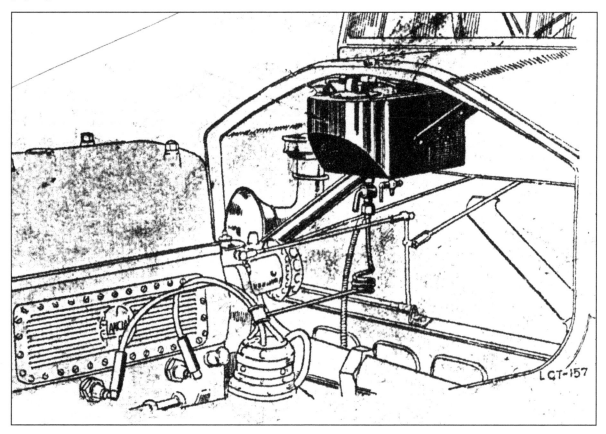

Under the bonnet

The Gearbox and Clutch

Early Lambdas had three forward and one reverse gears. They were selected by what has been claimed to be the first remote control lever in a car. The left hand dropped naturally onto the short gear stick mounted on the central tunnel. A horizontal jointed rod to allow for flexing of the frame entered the top of the gearbox. The gearbox was overhauled and the British ENV gears found to be in remarkably good shape. But here I made one mistake when I replaced a ball bearing at the rear with a sealed one. While this reduced oil escaping, it also stopped oil reaching the gears that drove the speedometer drive. Henceforth I had to oil that little gear regularly.

The clutch was the multi-plate type that took up the drive very smoothly, an advantage with my poor left leg. However it was a nightmare assembling it because there was only one strong central spring that fitted snugly into a pocket. It had to be compressed before its retaining collar could be screwed on. I was unaware of the special tool devised by the Lambda Consortium which would have removed the cause of much frustration. The clutch pedal pushed two little fingers with the inevitable ball bearings taking the final thrust. Care had to be taken when priming the carburettor to see that petrol did not drip onto them and wash out the grease.

With only three forward gears, there was a great difference in speed between top and middle gears. Perhaps this did not matter in Italy when you were driving either along the flat or climbing a mountain. In more gentle Britain, the hill you were climbing became less steep. The car wanted to go faster but you had reached the maximum revolutions for that gear. Ease off the accelerator and slip out of gear but the car slowed down faster than the heavy flywheel allowed the engine revolutions to drop. With a crash box, it was impossible to get into top gear so one ended back in middle gear again.

The Engine

The drawing of the engine through the top of the cylinders shows how Vincenzo arranged them in a narrow 'V' inclined at 13 degrees. This resulted in a remarkably short cylinder block of 16 ½ ins. (41 cm.) and 22 ins. (58 cm.) over fan and flywheel. The block was cast in aluminium, as was so much else in the Lambda, and was light enough for me to carry, as indeed was every other single part of the engine. The magneto and dynamo are across the top with the vertical drive and water pump. To the right is the fan. The oil filler cap is bottom left.

The off side view of the engine now complete with cylinder head and cover, has the carburettor, flywheel and clutch to the left. The timing mark on the flywheel should be noted. The spark plugs and priming cocks protrude from the side of

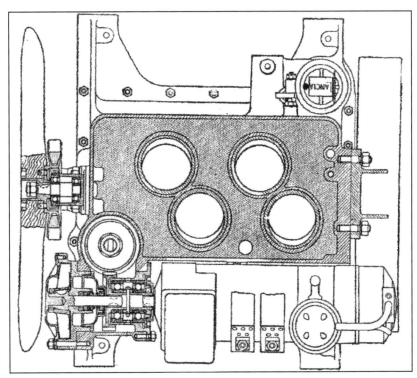

the cylinder block. Between them would be a notice saying that the oil should be cleaned every 750 miles, an expensive business.

The round filler cap can be seen between the flywheel and top of the steering box. Below this cap were gauze filters. When the engine was running, oil was taken through these filters and across the sump to the pump at the front to be recirculated once more.

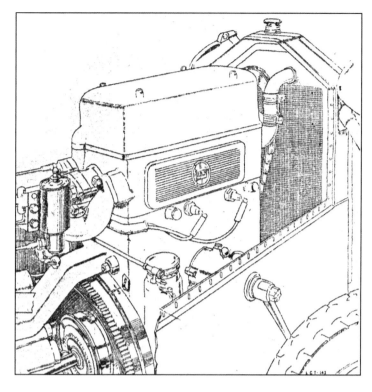

The sump was a massive aluminium casting strengthened by cross webs. I realised that the part of the casting through which the drain hole protruded was thicker than the rest, so that some oil was always left in the bottom of the sump. But it was this dirty oil which was drawn into the oil pump. So I decided to fit a modern paper type oil filter. A second copper pipe was fitted to the oil pump outlet and taken round the outside of the engine to an oil filter which we placed on top of the gear box. The oil from this was fed into the pipe to the oil pressure gauge and to the rear main bearing of the crankshaft. Not only did the engine oil show a marked improvement in cleanliness but the oil was distributed more evenly throughout the engine. Nearly hidden by the steering box was the oil level indicator which had a cork float inside the block and the oil pressure relief valve. In addition to checking oil levels in engine and gear box when maintaining the car, there were over two dozen grease nipples as well as other oiling points. What a difference with cars of today that need so little maintenance!

The near side view has the radiator and belt drive to the fan on the left. Along the bottom are the dynamo and magneto with the carburettor to the right. The exhaust pipes from the back of the cylinder head join and sweep down to a large nut before exiting under the car. This joint always gave trouble, partly through the flexing of the main frame. The final solution was to make a pair of thick square steel plates with bolts through the holes in the corners. One plate had a

large central hole threaded to fit the screwed end of the pipe from the cylinder head. The other plate had a plain hole through which the lower pipe fitted with its flanged head. The bolts secured the plates together with suitable packing. The lower pipe was brazed into a stainless steel ball joint pipe from a black London taxi cab which gave sufficient flexing and no more trouble.

The Cooling System

The fan at the front of the engine might have come off a First World War aeroplane because it was carved from wood. Over the years, it had become dog-eared and moth-eaten with bits missing. I found a suitable piece of wood and enjoyed fashioning another. At the nearside of the front of the engine was situated the water pump. The impeller shaft had become worn through the felt seal becoming hard and no longer being compressed by a spring. Vincenzo had thoughtfully provided drain holes to stop leaking water getting into the sump. Various modern face seals were tried with varying success. When driving along the M6 bound for the Isle of Man, the seal gave way and water poured out. We risked blocking up the drain holes and limped along to Port Erin. Water in the oil seemed preferable to being rescued on the M6. Another Lambda owner, Julian Edwards, and his father came to the rescue with a spare water pump.

From the pump, the water was piped to the centre of the engine near the bottom of the cylinders. There should have been adequate cooling capacity. I can remember only one time when she boiled driving normally. That was climbing up the 'Struggle' from Ambleside to the Kirkstone Pass when no fan belt had been fitted. But the old girl had a naughty quirk. When braking suddenly, perhaps when approaching a roundabout and changing down, water would spew out of the radiator top. This was probably caused by the water boiling at the rear of the head when the internal exhaust pipes had become exposed. As the cooling system did not have antifreeze, the shower of water did little harm until one day when I had added Radweld which sprayed red over cars in the next lane.

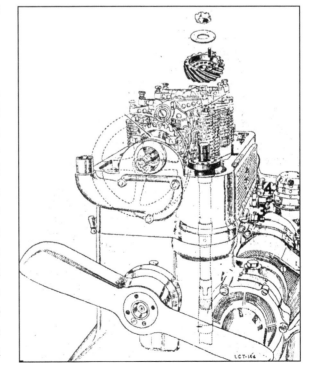

The Cast Iron Cylinder Head

'Uneasy lies the head that wears the crown'. The cast iron head was the Achilles heel of early Lambdas. Vincenzo produced a delightfully clean design on the outside by concealing a central inlet manifold and twin exhaust passages within the head. The head was bolted to the crankcase with only six massive studs. In spite of using fresh copper asbestos gaskets, spreading copious amounts of gasket sealing compound and pulling down the securing nuts with a torque bar that might have inspired Archimedes to move the world, the gasket was still liable to fail and blow. The rocker box cover with only four holding-down bolts was likewise liable to leak oil even when well sealed with compound and a fresh cork gasket.

Owing to the narrow 'V' inclination of the cylinders, there was a central camshaft operating the banks of valves on either side through overhead rockers. The ends of the long valve stems were capped which could be unscrewed with just a spanner. The tops of their locking nuts were hardened to take the blows of the tappets which should have 'the thickness of two sheets of cigarette paper' clearance. These nuts came in two lengths, probably from early and later series Lambda models. A later long one had been ground back to fit. One evening driving home up the motorway from Hyde, the engine started making a dreadful racket. I stopped under the last street light wondering what on earth to do. Luckily my neighbour happened to be passing and recognised the car. He went home and returned with a tow rope. Back at Stamford Cottage, we found that the top of one nut had been ground down so far that it had developed into a hole in the hollow screwed part for the valve steam, entirely upsetting the clearance.

To set the valve timing, the engine was rotated to the appropriate mark on the flywheel. The camshaft was rotated until one exhaust valve closed and the corresponding inlet valve was about to open for the next stroke. There was no valve overlap. The drawing shows the top gearwheel about to be dropped into place and the little peg inserted through one of the holes which matched one in the vertical shaft drive. Lock up the cover plate with the nut and, hey presto, the engine was timed! But Vincenzo did not say how the pin was taken out when the camshaft had to be removed.

I forget when I first noticed a few drops of water on the cylinder head in front of the off-side aluminium side plate cover. The drips became more frequent and hence the use of Radweld. The front bearing of the camshaft was poorly supported and it is possible that vibrations from the camshaft may have caused embrittlement in the cast iron. It quickly became apparent from other owners of early Lambdas that there was a weakness in the head design, particularly in the same area as my crack. Welding effected only a temporary cure and could lead to other complications such as distortion. Purchase of other second hand heads would, most likely, reveal the same faults. Jonathan Wood came to the rescue with a later sixth series engine. That head had design modifications with a change in the position of the gauze oil filter in the oil passage at the rear of the head as well as shorter, fatter valve springs located in shallow pockets. This engine would not make a permanent solution to the cracking so, after I was offered ill-health retirement from the Museum of Science and Industry in Manchester, I decided to look into the possibility of making new heads. An estimate from a commercial organisation was prohibitive. Luckily I still had my contacts in the engineering world from my days at the Museum who might be prepared to help. 'Where fools rush in...' It was worth a try.

The project would have been virtually impossible without the copies of the engineering drawings which Gerald Butt had saved from Turin. There were magnificent sections of the entire engine but only one detail drawing of a cylinder head. These were insufficient for either a pattern maker or machinist to work from. Being single at the time, the dining room table could be commandeered as a drawing board and a trolley used as a platform for my original head which a local firm had sawn into four pieces revealing the complications that awaited us. The result was around eighteen drawings. Fran Whitehead, a pattern maker we had used at the Museum, made the patterns, a formidable task when you look inside a head. Soon there was a stack of brightly coloured wood pieces. I decided we would go for the lowest common denominator, the early type, as later modifications could be fitted around that. I also decided to strengthen the flanges around the side plate covers which would give a slightly greater water space around the internal exhaust pipes. Fran worked in conjunction with a local iron founder who was willing to have a go. Alas the first attempt failed through the iron not running everywhere. It also showed that the patterns needed a few adjustments. The second casting failed in different places, as did another couple. It was a depressing time. It was only at the

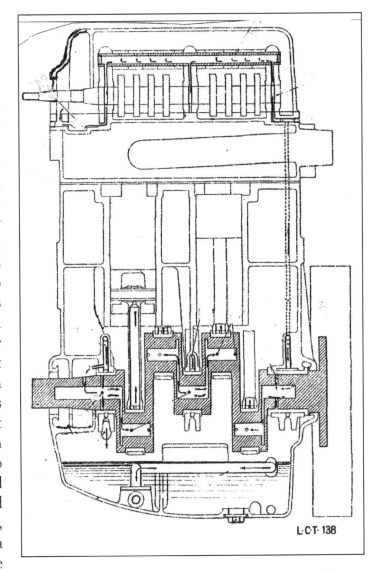

fifth attempt that we appeared to have a perfect casting which was taken to North Wales where someone who knew me through the Museum and my help on the Welsh Highland Railway undertook to machine it. All went well so it was assembled and fitted onto the car. Once again, everything worked.

But then disaster! I left the car running in the garage to warm it up when I heard the sound of the engine change. I looked in to see a flood of oily water spreading over the floor. Unknown to us, there was porosity in the casting where the oil feed to the cam shaft comes up through the head. Part had given way with the high oil pressure when the engine was still cold. Off came the head. The oil passages were filled with Wonder Weld and a by-pass pipe fitted. The head was reassembled and performed very well. It had shown that the drawings and patterns were correct from which further castings could be made. But it had also shown that casting in iron was a very tricky business. Thoughts turned to aluminium. Would the different shrinkage rate of aluminium make any resulting casting too small?

Enter James Woollard and, through him, Gary Miller. A car full of patterns went off to Suffolk, a casting appeared, slight modifications to the machining and back to Mottram for fitting on an engine. That head performed very well, seemingly making the engine run more smoothly. On early heads, the internal exhaust pipe was supported on three columns, omitted on later engines which I left out in cast iron. Although the new aluminium head was strengthened with internal plates, weakness appeared with the cylinder head gasket blowing. Back to Gary Miller who made a strengthened

The aluminium head

head for James. At this point I had to drop out through being diagnosed with Parkinson's but more heads have been produced and are running successfully.

The Flywheel

With increasing age, I found that starting the engine with the crank handle became more difficult. The handle was made stronger with a new shaft and stronger bearing blocks were fitted to the frame. I had to remember to close up the number plate which folded down for starting. The starter motor had always been unreliable and to improve matters, attention turned to the teeth of the gearing round the flywheel which had become badly worn. One possibility was to build up the teeth with weld and reprofile them. Then came some good fortune. I was offered a new gear ring. I did not know that the number of teeth on the pinions of Marelli and Bosch starter motors and likewise the gear ring differed. It was a Marelli ring so was duly fitted. However this showed that the starter motor did not mesh properly. Patterns were made and a new aluminium mounting block cast and machined. Everything fitted. It was electrifying to have an electric starter that worked without effort on my part and it saved embarrassment at traffic lights if the engine stalled so I did not have to get out and crank up the car! Before leaving the engine compartment, we must not forget that engine and gearbox were shielded from road dirt and spray by the undertray which stretched from radiator to behind the foot pedals. It enabled fords to be crossed without fear of stalling as well as collecting small pieces of engine dropped unintentionally.

Passenger Comfort

The all black interior of CY 8115 also received considerable refurbishment. Soon after arriving in Cambridge, the leather covers on the seat squabs were renewed in leather but the sides in leather cloth. The leather seat backs remained original and were treated with preservative and wax polish. The metal frames of all the seats were derusted, painted and covered in hessian. The seat springs were restrung with string to hold them in place and then sewn onto the hessian. The original padding was reused. Next came the sides. The front footboard had rotted where it touched the floor and was replaced. The disadvantage was that the warm air from the engine no longer came through the holes to heat the front passengers. Missing side panels in the footwells were fashioned from thin waterproof ply, painted and covered in leather. The panels beside the seats only needed their leather being treated with preservative. Panels in the doors were reconstructed and two missing pockets fabricated. Black pile carpeting covered the footwells and rear of the front seat. Sun and rain had rotted the tonneau so a new one was made at Cambridge. This time the front section was divided with a long zip fastening so that the driver's side could be opened separately from the rest – a great comfort to the driver when alone. Then I obtained some proper black double-duck cloth and made myself a new tonneau. Sewing this very thick material quickly produced sore fingers.

Vincenzo retained the clean lines of the Lambda by concealing the hood in a trough under the tonneau behind the rear seats. With two people, erecting the hood was easy through its remarkable skeleton of iron frames pivoted just behind the rear doors. Originally the hood was attached to a frame in the bottom of the trough but rain ran into the trough and rotted it. I was lucky that, when a new hood was needed around the year 2000, I found an experienced trimmer nearby at Marple. The new hood had fasteners and studs round the outside of the trough. Along the tops of the doors and main frame were holes into which side screens could be fixed. As purchased, CY 8115 had none. Iron frames were welded, covered with the black double duck and the centres filled with celluloid. Provision had to be made for the driver to open his door and then open the rest since all the door handles were inside. The frame round each door had special nickel plated strips.

One thing CY 8115 still lacked – a rear windscreen. With the hood down, rear seat passengers took the full blast of the air which became unpleasant at over 50 m.p.h. I had seen other vintage cars with screens that folded neatly behind the rear of the front seat. When the farmer's wife left Roe Cross farm, I penetrated the top attic and found to my surprise a rear screen off a vintage car. She said I could have it. It came in two halves. After measuring it, I found it would fit CY 8115 nicely with two front panels reaching across the car. At the front of the hood trough, wooden blocks were fitted with holes for the uprights from which side panels were also hung. It was replated and fitted with safety glass. The frames were stored vertically in a thin wooden box constructed behind the front seats. A short tonneau filled in the space behind the back of those seats and the screen to keep wind and rain off the rear passengers.

On 8 August 2008, CY8115 had her day of glory when she took my bride Bernice to our wedding at Mottram Church. The day was sunny. I drove my dear Bernice away after the reception. We used CY 8115 regularly after that but in 2011 I was diagnosed with Parkinson's and realised we would have to leave Stamford Cottage for a bungalow. Also CY 8115 was becoming too heavy for me to maintain and drive. She was auctioned at Buxton in June that year to start a new life in the south.

The Lancia in the garage at Stamford Cottage

The Sixth Age
Unlimited, Untiring Power

Part 1 – The Drainage of the Fens

In fitness for the urgent hour,
Unlimited, untiring power,
   Precision, promptitude, command,
   The infants will the giant's hand,
Steam, mighty steam ascends the throne,
and reigns lord paramount alone.

(From a plaque on the Burnt Fen Engine)

The sixth age starts with a steam pumping engine in the Fens and ends with the collection of steam engines in the Museum of Science and Industry in Manchester. It is the period when the little prince finally branched out from the shelter of other institutions to launch his own kingdom. We have seen how sitting on a trunk in the bottom of the Stretham engine with a leg in plaster my curiosity opened up a new realm of possibilities through finding the records of the performance of that engine. Cyril Clark, the superintendent, had allowed me to take some of these books away and analyse them

The Stretham engine viewed from the Old West river

The ground floor, I was sitting just to the right

while I was in hospital. (page 111) I realised that what might be called the mechanics of fen drainage had not been covered in any great depth even in H.C. Darby's great work, *The Draining of the Fens* (Cambridge, 1940).

Further research while studying for the Diploma of Education convinced me that this might be developed into an exceptional project (page 114). Leaving Worcester College for the Blind might give me an opportunity to work on it full time, but how? To qualify for a post-graduate degree at London University required obtaining a 2.1 history degree. There was no way I could do the reading for this before the exams in July 1963. But then, I heard that Rupert Hall and his wife Marie Boas Hall were coming from America to Imperial College in London to start a department for the History of Science and Technology. Rupert was willing to accept me as a research student for one year, leading to a Diploma of the Imperial College.

London, here I come! Andre, who was managing the West London Estates, rented me a flat in Petley Road, off Fulham Palace Road close to Hammersmith tube station. To get to London, it was cheaper to walk through the cemetery with its memorial for a gold-digger to Baron's Court and so to Gloucester Road or South Kensington for Imperial College. But some tube trains did not stop at these intermediate stations so you could end up at the wrong place. On days when Fulham Palace were playing at home, it would be impossible to park a car anywhere near Petley Road but Andre let me garage the Lancia in his estate depot just beyond Hammersmith. CY 8115 came into her own, taking me on many expeditions throughout the Fens looking at drainage features and to record offices. The car roused interest at some of the places I visited which helped gain access.

As a student at Imperial College, I was expected to attend the five o'clock lectures given by Marie and Rupert. Marie covered the History of Chemistry, about which I knew very little. I found her American accent very soporific. Once, Rupert was sitting next to me. My right hand taking notes ceased to move across the page. I nodded off to my great embarrassment. As Rupert's first and then only student, I was invited to attend his inaugural lecture and the dinner afterwards. I was placed next to Shell's publicity officer who was very interested in my Fen Drainage project. 'Would I like to go to the Netherlands and see similar works there?'

I met the Royal Dutch Shell representative over breakfast in the Central Hotel in Amsterdam. He welcomed the chance to see parts of his own country and drainage works which he had never visited. We toured all over the Netherlands, covering the very old and the very new. The new polders to the north east of Amsterdam were still in process of being reclaimed. Lelystad was still a small village with a massive pumping station which we were allowed inside. Reed beds with eels awaited draining on one side while fields of yellow cole-seed rape flourished on the other. We called at the little Maestenbroek steam pumping station, its scoopwheel replaced with a modern electric Archimedes screw.

Solitary pumping windmills, triple lift pumping windmills, industrial windmills such as saw mills and paper mills were seen.

The Schermer polder triple lift mills

The Arnhem Open Air Museum with its little papermill was the first of its type for me. We stayed at Arnhem in the smart hotel overlooking the Rhine. We had been eating well and the thought of a heavy Dutch dinner was too much for both of us. My guide suggested an Indonesian Restaurant. We sat at the end of a long table. I let him do the ordering. After a bit, I sat and watched him eat most of the mounds of rice and other small dishes that kept appearing. I have no idea where he put it all. We also went down to the South West of the Netherlands where the massive storm sluices were still under construction to protect the Delta region from inundation again.

My knowledge of drainage and engineering benefited enormously from this visit. We had gained privileged entry at many places so that later I was able to draw on comparative studies of British and Dutch practices in both windmill and steam engine technologies.

Let us take one small example, that of wind power. A traditional windmill will work with wind speeds varying from 6 to 12 m.p.s., but the ideal is from 8 to 10 m.p.s.

Wind Speed	The Fens	Norfolk	The Netherlands
6 – 8 m.p.s.	1,778 hours	n/a	1,332 hours
8 – 12 m.p.s	450 hours	964 hours	1,339 hours
Total	2,238 hours	964 hours	2,671 hours

These tentative figures show that the Fens have much less effective wind than both the Norfolk Broads and The Netherlands. Therefore we should not be surprised when, in 1710, P. Bateson described the Fen windmills as 'Gentle Spectators'. Again, in 1878, J.H.H. Moxon wrote, 'There is something touching about these old fellows, despite their occasional uselessness. In these days of rapid change, they still serve to remind one of the days of the past and, like musty old tombstones in a country churchyard, recall to mind the memories of bygone worthies'. Will our present wind turbines go the same way?

While on the subject of climate, through studying the Waterbeach Level record books, I was surprised to learn that February, far from being 'February Fill Dyke' was one of the driest months with more rain falling in the summer. Also the much greater amount of rain falling on the Somerset Levels explains why that area remained essentially pastoral and introduced steam power much later than the Fens.

Month	Total falling	Evaporated	Remaining	Waterbeach Records, averages of rainfall 1840 to 1925
January	1·847	·540	1·307	1·38
February	1·971	·424	1·547	1·07
March	1·617	·540	1·077	1·26
April	1·456	1·150	·306	1·36
May	1·856	1·748	·108	1·56
June	2·213	2·174	·039	1·90
July	2·287	2·245	·024	2·46
August	2·427	2·391	·036	2·37
September	2·639	2·270	·369	1·96
October	2·823	1·423	1·400	2·22
November	3·837	·579	3·258	1·72
December	1·641	·164	1·805	1·62
	26·614	15·320	11·294	20·88

Rainfall records in inches

The comparative dryness of the Fens was one reason why, with better drainage, they became a 'Wheat Growing Country' that supplied the expanding cities of the Industrial Revolution. (J.A. Clarke, *The Great Level of the Fens*, J.R.A.S. Vol. 8, 1847, p. 97). This was achieved partly by 'paring and burning' the peat which gave the ground great fertility, something that probably would be banned today through atmospheric pollution. Also the top surface would dry out and a strong wind in the spring could blow off this soil and with it any sprouting seeds.

I experienced such a blow when driving to the 'Five Miles from Anywhere; No Hurry' at Upware. The road disappeared beneath a shimmering black mass of particles.

I learnt a great deal about agricultural practices and crop rotation on both silt and peat lands. One farmer in the Waterbeach Level decided to try asparagus on his deep fertile peat. He never saw any because he got up too late. Others beat him to it. The Wisbeach and Upwell Tramway in the clay region survived hauling the summer crop of strawberries off to the London market.

The record books of the Waterbeach Level detailed the performance of the Stretham engine from almost its earliest days to the time when it ceased regular use in 1925. They had been preserved probably because the Commissioners might demand to see them at their Annual Meetings. The stoker had to load them into a wheelbarrow and trundle them through the fen to the pub in Waterbeach where the meetings were held. It is said that after the meeting someone else had to push the barrow back carrying the stoker.

Those books contained lists of wages paid to employees such as the superintendent, the stoker for the steam boiler, the mole catcher (most important to stop the moles digging through the river banks), and other casual labourers such as those who had to clear the reeds and rushes out of the drains. There were account books in one of which I found the special drainage account, so many port and so many sherry. It was a period of virtually no inflation, so the figures were much easier to assess than would be the case today.

Of more immediate interest to me were the books containing repairs to the engine, the rainfall amounts, the hours the engine worked and how much water it would have pumped. The stoker was paid a little extra from time to time for chipping scale out of the boilers. Should this deposit build up too much on the fire tubes, the efficiency would fall. I noticed that, after some years, while the stoker continued to be paid as stoker, he no longer received the occasional payments. So I asked Cyril Clark whether the stoker was a large man? 'Yes, he was.' I realised that the stoker had become too large to fit through the manhole into the boiler.

Top of a boiler at Stretham

Back in London, I made full use of the various libraries such as the British Museum and archive depositories such as the Public Record Office in Chancery Lane and Kew. Once in the British Museum, I received a book I had not ordered but luckily it was a book on fen drainage that I did not have on my list. In Kew Public Record Office, I had great difficulty ordering a book because the computer did not understand my typing when I put the figure 1 instead of a 'l'. Eventually I twigged.

Wicken Fen windmill, the last one to work in the Fens, moved here from Adventurer's Fen

I had come across the engineer John Rennie in the Waterbeach Level books when he was advising about installing a steam engine here in 1813. He concluded, 'A windmill drainage is the most imperfect of all modes and in many cases the adoption of such a mode may be said to be a useless waste of money'. Rennie's drafts of his reports are housed in the Library of the Institution of Civil Engineers. I was allowed three days when I could go and study them. There I frequently admired the marble fittings of the toilets because I was suffering from diarrhoea. However I persisted and made as many notes as I possibly could because I thought such an opportunity might not come again. In those days, everything had to be copied by hand and I might find some extra detail I would have missed if I only copied bits of immediate interest. It was sometimes very dull work.

I must have visited over a dozen libraries and archive depositories from Lincoln to London, sometimes with surprising results. The North Level Internal Drainage Board offices at Thorney produced an elderly Lancia in a shed! The tedium of the Bedford Level Corporation archives was relieved by the entry in 1698 that great harm and destruction had been 'committed by divers desperate and malicious persons, that have destroyed in a great measure the works of draining in Deeping Level... under cover and pretence of football playing'. Human nature hasn't altered!

My researches coincided with the growing interest in Industrial Archaeology and this approach paid dividends. I was able to locate the site of a very early pumping windmill. In 1555, the Commissioners of Sewers in Holland (Lincs.) complained that 'the see [bank] bilongyng to Algerkyrk and Fosdyk from the wyndemill unto Cromer Hyrn is in decay'.

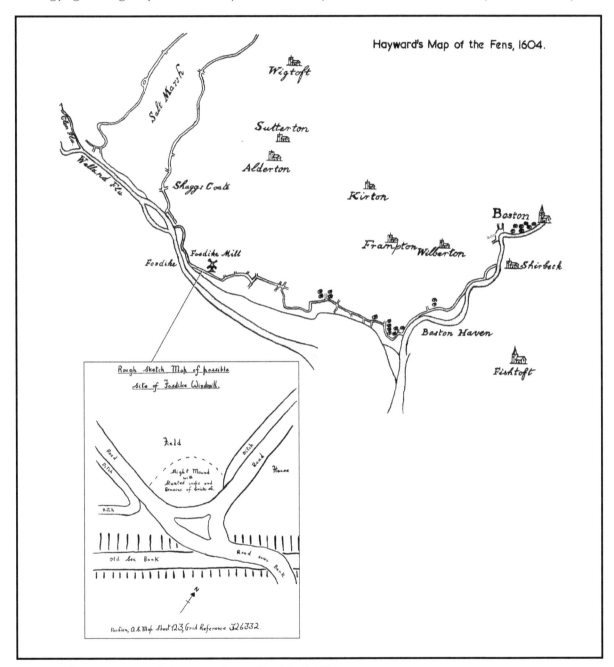

Hayward's 1604 map of the Fens shows Fosdike Mill.

An inspection of the site revealed remains of a windmill beside the old sea bank with two ditches leading up to it, so it was obviously used to pump water. Rumour that at Amber Hill there was the stump of a windmill with a scoop wheel beside it encouraged me to go and search. I was about to turn the car round when I saw the shortened redbrick round tower of a windmill with indeed the scoop wheel.

The Amber Hill Scoopwheel

It was the combination of map, records and a visit that brought me to the site of the first steam pumping engine in the Fens. When consulting Baker's 1821 map on Cambridge for the windmills in the Waterbeach Level, I noticed the words 'Steam Engine' outside the boundaries of Cambridgeshire close to Sutton St. Edmund. Part of this area was drained in 1664 by a windmill. The Littleport and Downham District Commissioners were debating whether to install a steam engine and on 21 May reported that they had been over to Wisbech and 'that from every Enquiry and Observation they could make on view of the same, they are of opinion that a Steam Engine would be most beneficial to the drainage of this [Littleport] District'. This engine was probably built around 1815. I made a site visit that showed stunted growth of crops in the vicinity and many remains of broken bricks and stones. The engine would have been made redundant perhaps after the opening of the Nene Outfall Cut in June 1830 but certainly in 1834 when the North Level Main Drain was finished. Water started flowing one Sunday morning when the congregation of the church in near-by Borough Fen dashed out of the service to see the water moving by itself, something that not even the oldest of them could remember.

While the improvement of the Nene Outfall caused the abandonment of two of the earliest steam drainage engines, it was the success of the Eau Brink Cut which showed that steam engines were essential for draining the peat lands. In 1820, Rennie wrote to the commissioners of the Swaffham and Bottisham Level,

The next Question is as to the Machine or Machines best adapted to raise the water into the Cam – on this subject my opinion has long been formed, namely that a Steam Engine or Engines is much preferable to any other machine. It has the advantage of always being ready to work when required, whereas windmills can only work when the wind blows and it is frequently calm when most wanted... No dependence can be had on Machines of this sort. (J. Rennie, Letter Books, Vol. 11, p. 31, 2 Feb. 1820)

The rivers could not be improved further. The fenmen had to turn to the steam engine for a guaranteed drainage. However, this had one unforeseen effect – the shrinkage of the peat. Whittlesey Mere was drained by a steam engine in 1851.

In 1852, the Holme Post was driven into the peat until its top was level with the surface of the peat. I visited it in about 1964 when it stood over 12 ft., (4m.) proud. Little peat was left.

These Fens have oft times been by Water drown'd
Science a remedy in Water found
    The power of Steam she said shall be employ'd
    And the Destroyed by Itself destroyed.

(Plaque on the Hundred Foot Engine, 1830)

Social Activities in London

Compared with far away Earnley and Worcester, in London it was much easier to see family members and friends from school and college. Father and Audrey came to a concert in the Royal Albert Hall one evening but had to leave before the end in order to catch their train home. Hugh was giving lectures to some army groups. He had married Shelagh, a Bartholomew's Hospital matron. They had a flat in Upper Montague Street, Marylebone, where she could practise her Cordon Bleu cookery. She bought

Photo taken on Boxing Day 1983 with Ben, Richard, Hugh and Sheelagh

an expensive cut of veal which she expected would last a couple of meals but Hugh demolished it in a single sitting. Sheelagh became matron at Rishworth School.

Humphrey Nye was teaching mathematics at Haileybury, once the East India Company College where Sir Alfred Lyall had been trained. It was always worthwhile accepting an invitation to one of the masters' Common Room dinners for the excellent meal. Once I was driving back to London and warned Humphrey that we would be calling. He forgot and we found his room empty but not his whiskey bottle. We drank one of his bottles of beer (no breathalyser in those days) and filled it from the whiskey bottle, leaving him a note thanking him for the whiskey. Luckily Humphrey spotted the swap before offering some 'beer' to a pupil.

At Petley Road, I looked round to find a local church. The nearest was a massive Victorian monstrosity almost hidden under a canopy of trees. The gutters were overflowing, blocked by leaves, and the whole place had an air of neglect. The door was unlocked. I entered.

An elderly priest apologised, admitting he could no longer cope. He was about to retire. I joined his congregation and we were able to start a small Sunday school with the help of the Church Army. One of their lady members told me how they taught the children how to pray. She would set the example by keeping her eyes shut and the children must do the same. During the prayers, she heard some shuffling and opened her eyes to find the kids had scarpered. Although we were able to increase the congregation a little, after I left the parish was merged into a neighbouring one.

I joined Christian prayer and study groups with my other friends. John Nye, Humphrey's father, was one of the Southwark Diocesan Lay Readers. He was able to arrange for me to attend one of their training courses held in a primary school close to the Oval cricket ground. For grown men, having to sit in

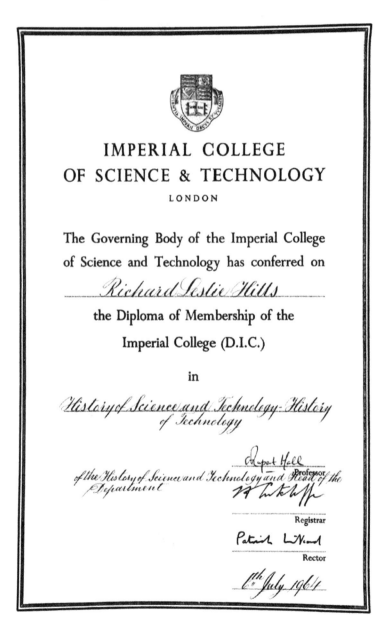

IMPERIAL COLLEGE
OF SCIENCE & TECHNOLOGY
LONDON

The Governing Body of the Imperial College
of Science and Technology has conferred on

Richard Leslie Hills

the Diploma of Membership of the

Imperial College (D.I.C.)

in

_History of Science and Technology-History
of Technology_

_of the History of Science and Technology and Head of the
Department_

Professor
Registrar

Rector

6th July 1964

such small desks was most uncomfortable but it kept us awake. We covered Old and New Testaments, church history, and the prayer book. I passed the exams and, after I moved to Mottram, Chester Diocese accepted Southwark's results so I was licensed to St. Michael and All Angels.

My First Book

My thesis on Fen Drainage was awarded the Diploma of The Imperial College which I received at a ceremony in the Royal Albert Hall in July 1964. Rupert suggested that it was worthy of publication and a bound copy was sent to the States. Perhaps it was fortunate that it was lost in view of the further research I undertook that broadened its scope considerably. As part of my research into the textile industry when I was at Manchester, I went to Birmingham to consult the Boulton and Watt Collection in the Central Library. There was the involvement of James Watt himself as drainage consultant, not only in Britain but also in the Netherlands. Rennie featured as well because, in his capacity as civil engineer improving the rivers and their outlets into the Wash, he advocated small self-contained Boulton and Watt engines to power the pumps that kept the foundations of sluices and other structures dry while they were being built.

This was followed with help from another quarter. The idea of publication was not abandoned, in fact rather the reverse with this extra material. Andre and I jointly read a paper, 'The Steam Pumping Engine at Stretham, Cambridgeshire', to the Newcomen Society (*Transactions, Vol. XXXVI, 1963 – 64*). While I wrote the paper, Andre took the photographs. They came to the attention of Ronald Clark who generously allowed me to use some of the photographs in the C.O. Clarke Collection. Once again, all these considerably expanded the scope of the thesis. It was probably Ronald who roused the interest of his own publishers, Goose & Co. of Norwich. It was they who chose

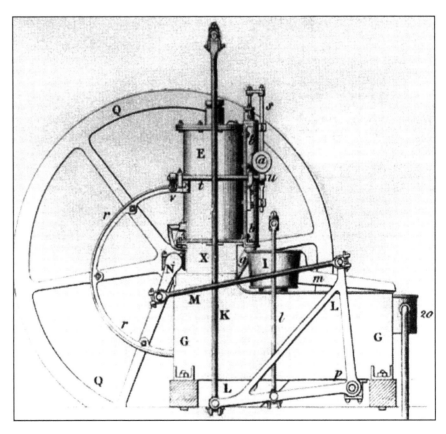

Boulton and Watt bell-crank engine which Rennie used to help his work in the East, West Wildmore Fens (Farey, Steam Engine, 1827)

the title, *Machines, Mills and Uncountable Costly Necessities*, a seventeenth century quote from Humphrey Bradley.

MACHINES
MILLS
AND UNCOUNTABLE
COSTLY NECESSITIES

A short history of the drainage of the fens

By this time, I was beginning to acquire a reputation for my academic work. The Cambridge Antiquarian Society had published an article, 'Drainage by Windmills in the Waterbeach Level' (*Proceedings*, Vol. LVI, 1964). I was elected to the august Council of the Newcomen Society, a youngster amid the venerable historians of technology.

This is not quite the end of the story of my book on Fen drainage. While in London, I had studied the paper on 'Draining of Land by Steam Power', delivered in 1838 to the Society of Arts by Joseph Glynn, engineer of the Butterley Company responsible for erecting the Stretham engine and many more. Glynn added a mouth-watering list of engineering drawings of some of his engines which he had presented. I asked what was then the Royal Society of Arts if I could see them. 'No, we certainly do not have anything like this in our archives'. There I had to leave the matter.

Much later, Peter Bower, paper historian, arranged a display of interesting paper from their archives. I was invited to his lecture. One he had selected was a sheet with along the bottom a watermark saying that no bleach had been used. I was amazed. It was one of Glynn's drawings. Peter had no interest in the subject of the drawing and had not realised the importance. The rest were soon put on show and I gave a lecture about 'Joseph Glynn and Fen Drainage' (R.S.A., Vol. 144, No. 5468, April 1996).

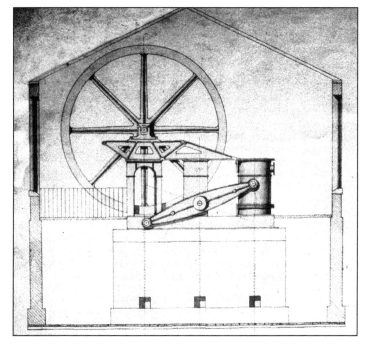

Glynn's drawing of the Prickwillow engine

Landmark had taken over the goodwill and publication rights from Goose. They wanted to reprint *Machines, Mills and Uncountable Costly Necessities*. The new 2003 edition contained some of Glynn's drawings. I had kept my original photographs which modern techniques reproduced with greater clarity in *The Drainage of The Fens*. Its sales were such that a second edition was published in 2008. It is still an important study.

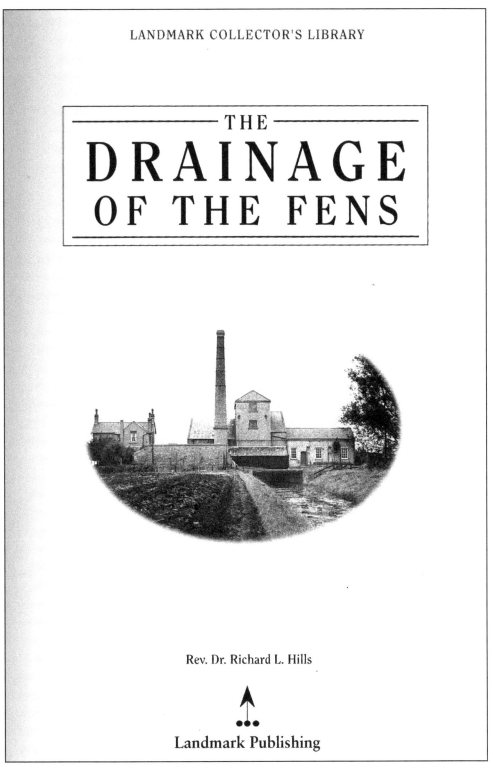

LANDMARK COLLECTOR'S LIBRARY

THE

DRAINAGE
OF THE FENS

Rev. Dr. Richard L. Hills

Landmark Publishing

The Stretham Engine from the Fen Drain

Testing a coffin for size at Crowland Abbey! During the Association for Industrial Archaeology Conference in 1975

Unlimited, Untiring Power

Part 2 – Arrival in Manchester

It was necessary to search for paid employment. While Universities were founding or expanding their departments for history of science, openings were scarce, none more so than in the history of technology. Thoughts turned to museums where there might be opportunities. Rupert Hall strongly supported my application to Norman Bertenshaw, Director at Birmingham Museum of Industry for a curatorial post there. I admired the collections which it was expected would be rehoused in a new building within about three years. It was an exciting project but I decided to turn the offer down because I saw no prospect of developing any educational potential of the collections. I am glad I did because many years were to pass before Birmingham had a new industrial museum, having spent more on architects' designs and fees than would have paid for a new building originally.

There was also Donald Cardwell who was enlarging his Department of the History of Science and Technology at the University of Manchester Institute of Science and Technology. In 1965, he offered me a Research Assistantship for three years to study the history of the textile industry. This was much more tempting because not only was there the possibility of gaining a higher degree but Donald also outlined the plans for a new science museum building on the University campus with support from Manchester University and the City as well as UMIST. It would be closely linked to a broad spectrum of educational services for all ages and abilities. The fish was hooked. When I landed in Manchester, I found the reality was no fixed plans, no finance, almost no exhibits and only a small office on J Floor in UMIST main building. Another reality was that, if there were no museum at the end of the research grant, I would have no job. O yes, there was another asset, the use of a damp railway arch in Charles Street for a store. It would require some idiot to be willing to plunge in and get his hands dirty. That idiot turned out to be me. Once again the little prince would have to start again from the bottom.

One suggestion was that the museum in Manchester would form the centre for a number of smaller satellite museums that might preserve an industrial enterprise in its original setting. These might be a corn mill or a fulling mill or a forge where they could still be driven by their waterwheels. One obvious candidate was the cotton spinning mill at Quarry Bank, Styal.

Quarry Bank Mill, Styal

The Old Order Changeth, Yielding Place to New.

(Tennyson)

When I accepted the offer to rent 28 Oak Cottages, Styal, I at first thought of it as solving for the time being the problem of where to stay. Little did I think that I would find the final days of the old cotton industry that once made Manchester the centre of the Industrial Revolution. Samuel Greg had left Belfast in 1784 to build a spinning mill powered by the

River Bollin in the bottom of a deep gorge. In order to protect their water rights, successive Gregs acquired land and woods on either side of the valley and farms on the land above. There were pleasant walks in the woods. Just before the Second World War, this idyllic pastoral and industrial landscape was threatened by the construction of a new road to by-pass Wilmslow. To preserve it, Alec Greg offered the estate to the National Trust which accepted it. Alec lived at Acton Bridge but continued to take an interest in Styal.

Old Mill

On the other side of the Altrincham road, lived Harry Greg and his co-director of the Greg Mill at Reddish, Mr. Jacks and his wife. Harry Greg could be seen watching the Styal village football and cricket teams playing on the sports ground. He built himself a bungalow with a large plate glass window giving dramatic views to the south. His housekeeper's quarters merely looked into a small courtyard and not even into the garden! Perhaps Harry did not want her watching him playing with his live-steam model railway. Mrs. Jacks was concerned with the welfare of the village.

In the bottom at Quarry Bank mill was the Georgian Quarry Bank Mill house, suitably spacious for a prosperous mill owner. The mill manager's house was minute in comparison. There had been a gas works in the mill yard was well as stables and stores for raw cotton and spun yarn. It was a good day's work for a horse and cart to take the yarn to the canal at Altrincham and return with the bales.

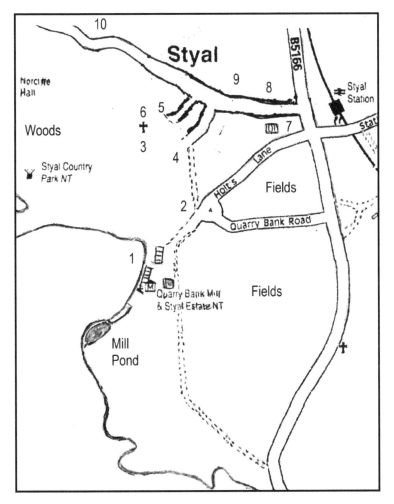

Map of Styal – Legend

1. *Quarry Bank Mill & House*
2. *Apprentice House*
3. *Unitarian Church*
4. *Farm Fold*
5. *Oak Cottages*
6. *Oak Farm*
7. *Post Office*
8. *Old Ship Inn*
9. *Playing fields*
10. *Harry Greg's Bungalow*

At the top of the hill was the Apprentice House. The apprentices had little free time for, besides working regular mill hours in the week, they had to walk to Wilmslow Church on a Sunday. The Account Books show they were fed reasonably well for that time and were given special food if unwell. However one or two tried to run away and there are entries for payment to someone bringing back an apprentice who had 'eloped'. Also there was another ominous entry, 'Lost time to be made up in winter'. Styal must have had a 'waterwheel clock', a form of clock with two dials. One was a regular time piece showing the correct time of the day. The hands on the second were set to the same time at the start of the working day. They were driven by a shaft from the great waterwheel. If the waterwheel ran slowly, the hands on this second dial would also slow down. The mill operatives had not been working full time – 'Lost time to be made up in winter' when there would have been more water to drive the mill! Later I was able to purchase one of these 'waterwheel clocks' for the museum in Manchester when Frosts of Macclesfield closed down.

The waterwheel clock

Across the fields lay the Unitarian chapel and two of the farms the Gregs had purchased. The earlier purchase is likely to have been Farm Fold which was adapted to house mill workers. For example, Ivy Singleton lived in one of the thatched old cruck cottages. She had arranged a sofa under the window in her living room so she could sit comfortably watching in a mirror on the far wall all who walked by on the main road. She was one source of village gossip. Sometimes I would notice a lace curtain twitch as I passed and said that the villagers knew what I was doing before I did. In another cottage nearby lived Reg Worthington who had taken on the responsibility of being chief spokesperson for the villagers. The brick pillars of a barn that had been converted into dwellings stood out in the pointing. The Methodist chapel must have been once another farm building, perhaps stables.

One of the last looms at Styal, weaving dishcloths

On Oak Farm land, the Gregs had built four rows of cottages that might well have been transported from the centre of Manchester. Here was the primary school and the Co-Op shop. On the wall outside was a board giving instructions about how to measure up a deceased person for a coffin. There was the Styal Burial Club into which were paid regular subscriptions. Claims on it were made when appropriate until the cheques in the cheque book ran out. It was discovered that the three authorised signatories had signed all the blank cheques, leaving one person to fill in the amount. But one person had moved away and another had died so presumably these cheques were void.

One advantage for the inhabitants of the village compared with their opposite numbers in towns were the allotments which provided a source of food when trade was slack and wages reduced. No doubt they were well fertilised with compost from the cottages. There was still night soil being collected daily from some homes but most had been 'modernised' with a flushing toilet in the back-yard. One old lady confessed she did not like going outside at night but equally she was afraid that her chamber pot might break when she sat on it. The National Trust was undertaking further modernisation by clearing away the back-yards and fitting internal bathrooms. One such was No. 28 'Bug' Row [Oak Cottages] which I was able to rent from the Trust. It had bedroom and bathroom upstairs, living room and kitchen in the middle and a cellar in the basement. A family had lived in the cellar with minimal light but I equipped it with a work bench. I was the first 'outsider' to move into Styal village, a portent of what would happen.

In fact, Styal had been even more self-contained. At one time the postman collected the mail from Handforth Station, walked to Styal and the outlying houses and returned to Handforth to pick up a second collection. When I lived in Styal, there was a proper Post Office situated in another general store. Opposite was Henry the butchers, the Old Ship Inn corrupted from Sheepen, and the village hall. Cyril, a porter at Styal station, had an allotment here from which he sold vegetables and his magnificent prize winning chrysanthemums. There was little need to go elsewhere for essential supplies.

Further away from the village centre was Styal Anglican chapel with its regular Sunday services run by Frank Smith, the 'one-armed bandit'. He had lost an arm in the First World War and been ordained after a career as a travelling salesman. He recounted how one of his main outlets rejected his wares. On investigation, it transpired that the rival had beaten him in price through selling smaller dishcloths, etc. I had not realised how much the loss of a limb could handicap someone, not only through phantom pains but even loss of balance. When holidaying with him in the Isle of Man, he had great difficulty walking the short distance from the Bungalow to the top of Snaefell. This made me realise how lucky I was to have kept my leg. He solved one problem for me, that of somewhere to garage the Lancia in return for services rendered.

The three churches in Styal, Anglican, Methodist and Unitarian, joined together in the Styal Village Fellowship for occasional Sunday services. In addition, there were regular evening meetings in the village hall during the winter for lectures, quizzes and entertainment. Through this I met people beyond the immediate village who were still at work or who had worked in local industries, particularly of course textiles.

Among those of particular importance for me was Geoffrey McComas, the Bursar at UMIST, who travelled regularly by train to Manchester. Styal station was where the Queen's train was kept overnight when she visited our area. The station staff had to place white enamel buckets under suitable places below the carriages. Styal was well blessed with three trains an hour in the rush hour and two during the rest of the day. After the Southern Region in

London with twelve-carriage trains packed to standing room only, it was wonderful to be sure of a seat on our three-carriage trains.

Sometimes I joined our Bursar and his Deputy for lunch in the Student Union. They settled down with *The Times* crossword. 'Now Monty, give us a clue'. 'Five – two – six'. McComas gave the correct answer without having heard the wording of the clue. He did this three times consecutively. We talked about museum prospects which I am certain helped to launch both myself and the museum.

Donald's hope that Styal might become the home for the science museum was dashed because the City of Manchester could not support a project beyond their boundaries. Therefore the National Trust sought the advice of professional fund raisers. I was invited to join the group and learnt a great deal. First, the whole project was examined in minute detail to see if it were viable and what snags might be encountered. Once assured that it could be a success, detailed costings were drawn up. These would cover the initial launch and development as well as what sources of revenue there might be to meet running expenses. Only at that stage was the search for influential sponsors begun who would be expected to underwrite a third of the budget. The remainder would be raised as the project grew. At last an appeal to the general public could be launched. To protect the National Trust, Quarry Bank Mill would be run by its own charitable trust and committee. A museum run by University and City authorities could not be launched in this way because the budget had to be in place before any start could begin.

HRH The Princess Royal, at the opening of Quarry Bank Mill's New Steam Power Galleries on 14th May 1998 – I am 2nd on the right.

I wrote the report outlining the scope of a possible textile museum for the cotton industry at Styal. It was a great experience collaborating with professional designers and photographers. Later I wrote reports for the National Trust on the Nether Alderley water-powered corn mill and the water-powered saw mill at Tatton. Instead of any payment, I was given life membership of the National Trust which is still being used from time to time.

The termination of my three year research grant was looming and the probability of a science museum in Manchester became more certain. I realised that I would have to find a larger more permanent home than 28 Oak Cottages. It shows how much times have changed for I could not afford a 6% mortgage on a £6,000 house on the main

Quarry Bank Mill
Official Opening of the Steam Power Galleries
14 May 1998

I thought you might like a reminder of the splendid day we had on the occasion of the visit of the Mill's Patron, Her Royal Highness The Princess Royal, when she officially opened the new Steam Power Galleries on 14 May.

I am sorry that it has taken so long to send out photographs, but I hope you will agree that it is a case of better late than never!

I look forward to seeing you again soon at the Mill.

Peter J Battrick
Chief Executive Officer

Wilmslow Road. So it was with regret that I moved to Mottram-in-Longdendale leaving many friends in Styal where I had learnt and benefitted so much. The National Trust had to develop Styal as a visitor attraction in order to support the mill. Much changed and the old Styal village was modernised. 'The Old Order Changeth, Yielding Place to New'.

Unlimited, Untiring Power

Part 3 – A New Science Museum

I have written detailed histories in my *Reminiscences of the North Western Museum of Science and Industry* and elsewhere. To repeat those here would take too long. Therefore this will not be a chronological account but instead will concentrate on the policies and rationale behind our actions. To set these in context, here are a few key dates or events.

*Lord Rhodes of Saddleworth, left and Lord Bowden (UMIST) at the opening of
the Museum*

1968 Spring. Agreement reached for the Museum and Methodists to share 97 Grosvenor Street.

1968 Autumn. First Museum staff appointed.

1969 October 20. Museum opened by Lord Rhodes of Saddleworth.

1972 July. Museum occupies whole of 97 Grosvenor Street.

1973 November. 'Working Saturdays' commenced.

1975 July. New constitution includes the Greater Manchester Council.

1978 The GMC buys Liverpool Road Station.

1980 Working Saturdays cease and Great Railway Exposition held at Liverpool Road Station.

1983 July 22, 97 Grosvenor Street closed after 500,000 people had visited it.

Manchester has been called the First Industrial City and claimed to be the centre of the Industrial Revolution. While London might be the centre for science with its scientific learned and prestigious institutions and Birmingham and the Midlands the centre for iron and steel, Manchester's claim was based on the cotton textile industry. The numerous inventions for spinning and weaving cotton driven by power captured world markets for cotton cloth. This resulted in the need to develop transport for the cotton, inventions to process the cotton, buildings to house the machines, and machines to make the machines. In this way Manchester developed so many supporting industries. I, a Kentish man who regarded anything beyond the Thames as the rugged North, had a lot to learn. I was surprised to find that it was further from Manchester to Glasgow than Manchester to London. However this ignorant southerner was awarded his PhD in July 1968.

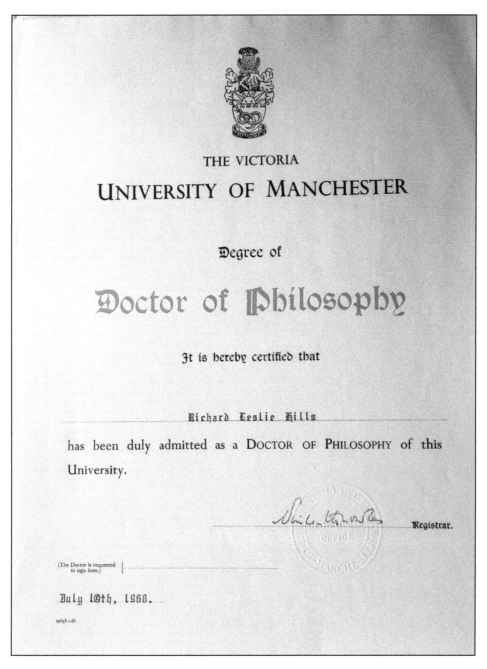

Official Support

Rumours about a new science museum for Manchester had been spreading when I arrived in September 1965 at my office in J13 at the top of the main UMIST building to take up my kingdom. Donald Cardwell had already collected a few exhibits. One was a magnificent slotting machine with a fluted column that stood about twelve feet high. After manhandling it across the floor of the Charles Street store, he was distinctly less inclined to offer help in the future with heavy exhibits. A Joint Committee consisting of representatives from University of Manchester, the City of Manchester and UMIST had been meeting regularly. One Councillor asked why such a museum was necessary when people could look at machines in UMIST – which did not go down very well in some quarters. Their report was presented on 31 October 1966 and became the foundation document for the museum (*Report on a Museum of Science and Technology by the Working Party of the Joint Committee*, 31 October 1966, Ed. D.S.L. Cardwell). The objective was to 'explain the major discoveries and inventions of history of science and technology using wherever possible exhibits made in or linked with the North West'.

Recently the Director of the London Science Museum has written, 'Our role is crucial in inspiring the next generation of scientists, technologists and engineers'. (Letter 20 June, 2013.) Michael Gove, M.P., when Minister for Education, stated that 'pupils needed a narrative of chronology that gave them a wider sense of the impact of Britain in the world and the world on Britain... Giving people a sense of chronology is the high priority'. (*Telegraph*, 31 Dec. 2013.) How was this to be done? Donald wrote,

> *Regional Museums have, I believe, four main purposes; (1) to conserve historically important machines, apparatus, records and drawings; (2) to advise on or to help with, the conservation of outside exhibits that cannot be put in the museum; (3) to teach at all levels; and (4) to carry out research and publish monographs. (1966 Report).*

Donald might have included that, wherever possible, the exhibits should be returned to full working order and demonstrated regularly. This would show not only how they were used but also would help to explain the social and working conditions of the time. When possible, mill engines would be driven by steam and cotton processed in the textile machines to make their presentation as authentic as possible. Development would be traced from simple hand-operated machines through to those in use at the present day. However inadequate 97 Grosvenor Street might have been, it was probably the last chance to start a science museum in Manchester. Salvation had come through the Methodists needing temporary accommodation for their university chaplaincy for the next three years. We had to make the best of a bad job.

Soon our part of Grosvenor Street became dangerously overcrowded with no sign of the Methodists leaving so I had to put my foot down. It was only after 1972 when we had the whole of the building that we could really show the potential of such a museum and the editor of Steam Railway wrote,

> *The Manchester Museum of Science and Industry is recognised as one of the most important educational facilities in the country, educating young and old about the industrial and scientific changes to the world. It is at the heart of a city that drove the Industrial Revolution*

in the eighteenth and nineteenth centuries developing manufacturing and commercial policies that impacted on the rest of the world.

Collecting Policies

How had this been achieved? Constraints through lack of space and finance meant that every exhibit would have to have historical significance. Once accepted, it would be entered into the Museum's register. Dr. David Owen, Director of the Manchester Museum, recommended that we kept a bound ledger with numbered pages. Each exhibit would be listed in the main index with a running number for the year received and a number showing the sequence in its reception. A hand-written description would be entered into the next space on the numbered pages. A large envelope would be prepared with the running number in which would be placed a sheet containing further details of the exhibit, photographs, and, more important, a letter from the donor stating that it was a gift. I remember once an elderly gentleman offering a genuine cast-brass model of Stephenson's 'Rocket'. I turned the engine over and saw that the name had been inserted into the mould for casting it with a strip of 'dymo' tape. We did not accept it.

In each area of our collections, we decided what would be appropriate exhibits to explain the development. For example in cotton manufacture, there might be hand spinning and weaving, the great inventions of the eighteenth century launching the Industrial Revolution, mechanisation in the early nineteenth century and the heyday of the industry circa 1900. In this case, machines might be shortened to just a few spindles showing the basic principles to save space. Again to save space with machine tool inventions, smaller examples should be collected covering the basic principles of the lathe, the planing machine, the milling machine and so on. The steam engine drove the textile machines faster necessitating the change from wood to metal construction. This in turn needed more accurate machines to manufacture them. In papermaking, small demonstration moulds would show hand-making of paper while a small machine might be acquired.

A pair of spinning mules at Osborne Mill each with over 1,000 spindles

The one exception would be the steam engines which drove the mills. Here in a few examples might be displayed the best of Manchester's engineering heritage. Because the last atmospheric engine in the region at Fairbottom Bobs had been taken to the Henry Ford Museum in America, the Mechanical Engineering Department of UMIST built a one-third replica of the original Newcomen engine of 1712 for us.

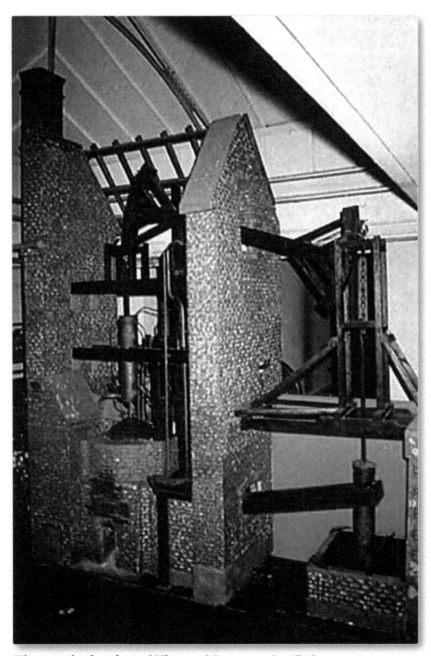

The one-third replica of Thomas Newcomen's 1712 engine

However, I was fully aware that Manchester was late in establishing its science museum. Most of the original machines that their inventors had used had been snapped up by other museums, if they existed. Because we set out to be an educational museum, we decided we would have to fill in the gaps in the historical sequence with replicas. These would show the problems faced by their creators but there was a danger. I was in the Deutsches Museum in Munich looking at their road transport section. One young boy had been playing with the demonstration gear and steering boxes laid out in a display. He then came upon the prize exhibit, the first Benz car. He climbed into the driving seat and started playing with the steering and other levers. Everything was of equal significance to him. We would have to give explanations.

Let us see how this worked out in practice. The advantage of Gove's historical approach was that so many of the early textile machines were quite simple, operated by hand. While this would demand skill and dexterity, generally there would be no health and safety issues. But what to do when a vital historical exhibit was no longer available? Should we build a replica? There were plenty of spinning wheels around. With hand spinning, the wheel could be stopped and the audience told what was happening. Visitors might even be allowed a go, too often ending in failure. But there were no original examples of the Spinning Jenny invented by James Hargreaves. Our replica was a backbreaking machine to operate and almost impossible to spin all eight threads at a time on it.

Our replica Spinning Jenny

We were lucky to borrow a very early example of Richard Arkwright's Waterframe. It needed little skill but it had to be driven by some power source so hardly qualified as hand operated.

An early example of Arkwright's Waterframe

Samuel Crompton's Mule was much easier to work but none survived from the 1780s. I had a demonstration one assembled with parts from a modern mule that we had to scrap. It was a delight to use and later I was sorry to hear that it, together with our jenny, had been passed over to a museum at Belper, leaving Manchester bereft of these vital textile inventions that helped launch the Industrial Revolution. One exception to safety on hand operated textile machines was the loom with John Kay's Flying Shuttle. The weaver could send the shuttle at great speed across the loom where it should be caught in a box at the end of the slay. But it might fly out into the audience so we installed wire mesh screens.

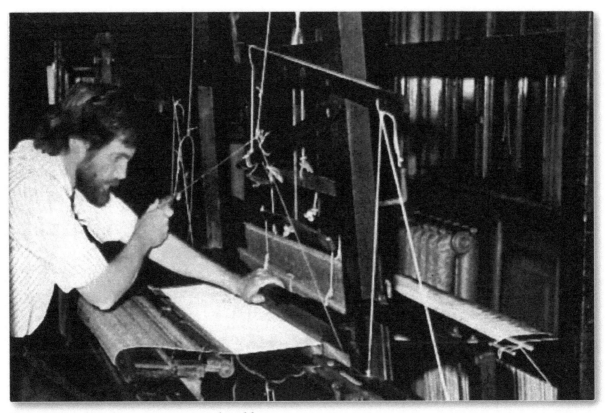

Robert Manders demonstrating our hand loom

However the next stage in textile development was power-driven machines such as the self-acting mule and the power loom. We tried to run these machines slowly or with just a few spindles. The self-acting mule was reduced from over one thousand to 120 spindles. A narrow power loom was selected for the same reason but the speed on a power loom could not be reduced too far or the shuttle might not be sent across the web. We needed skilled operatives or demonstrators specially trained. Fred Hilditch visited the museum to see what we had done to 'his' mule, the one he used to work at Elk Mill. For many years he came in two afternoons a week to run his mule for school parties as well as train Museum demonstrators.

Piecing up a broken thread on the loom

The speed of the mule could not be reduced or certain changes in the winding sequence might not happen. On the other hand, the massive mill engines could be safely reduced in speed so generally they ran at about one third of their working speed.

Textile machines were designed to process certain types of fibre. We aimed to produce a good quality cloth capable of being sold to the public. This was particularly difficult on our ribbon loom which was set up to weave a keepsake with a flywheel motif. Weaving a circle calls for a lot of adjustments to prevent it becoming egg-shaped. In this, as in so many other areas, we were greatly helped by staff from various university departments.

A keepsake woven on the ribbon loom

The Education Service

To develop the educational potential of the exhibits, the City of Manchester financed the Education Service. Robert Manders was the first Teacher in Charge. A room on the top floor of 97 Grosvenor Street became the Education Laboratory. A school party would be taken here first and given an introductory talk using demonstration exhibits. We built one to show how James Watt's separate condenser worked. It had a small boiler, the steam from which filled the cylinder, a brass tube. A piston fitted with a heavy weight hung on its piston rod fitted in the tube. Adjacent was the separate condenser in a large glass test tube filled with cold water. A couple of pumps with the air pump in the condenser drew the steam from the hot cylinder into the cold condenser where it was condensed causing a partial vacuum. This caused the piston to rise dramatically as it lifted the weight.

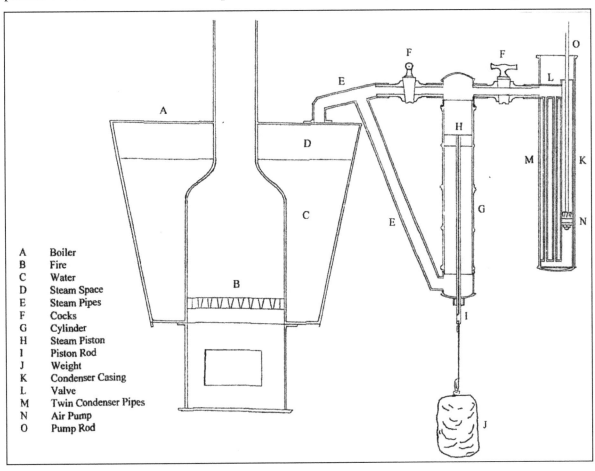

A	Boiler
B	Fire
C	Water
D	Steam Space
E	Steam Pipes
F	Cocks
G	Cylinder
H	Steam Piston
I	Piston Rod
J	Weight
K	Condenser Casing
L	Valve
M	Twin Condenser Pipes
N	Air Pump
O	Pump Rod

Watt's drawing of his first separate condenser, which was probably prepared for one of the patent trials in the 1790s

After the initial introduction, the pupils would be given work sheets and taken into the galleries. As well as demonstrating textiles, Robert learnt about steam engines, papermaking by hand and printing, turning these subjects into the three most popular courses on offer. At 97 Grosvenor Street, the Education Service grew from strength to strength until it employed three teachers, a secretary and a technician. Robert accepted the Deputy Directorship until the GMC took over the Museum. In the move to Liverpool Road, he became Adult Education Officer. One day he had an amicable meeting with our Greene Director in the morning and returned home to find a letter of dismissal.

The way our Education Service worked, together with 'push button' self-operated demonstrations in the galleries, convinced me that a special Children's Gallery was unnecessary. This was confirmed by visits to Science Centres in America and Europe. While these places had excellent models, etc., they were not connected to any narrative, or to use Gove's terminology, any chronology. In the Boston Ma. centre, the most spectacular part of the papermaking demonstration was when the kitchen soup blender mixing the pulp blew up in a shower of smoke and sparks. I wanted to link the 'Science Centre' approach to historic machines.

The Manchester Region Industrial Archaeology Society

After reaching Manchester, I soon found myself volunteered as Secretary to the Manchester Region Industrial Archaeology Society which had not long been formed. Some meetings were held in UMIST and more at the Extra Mural Department of the University where Owen Ashmore was Director. He promoted lunch time lectures on Industrial Archaeology at the Central Library as well as courses of evening lectures at the University and elsewhere. In the ensuing years, I ran courses in many places from Wigan in the west to Glossop in the east and Macclesfield in the south to Bolton in the north. Some were for the Workers Educational Association whose members were mostly not workers and the courses sometimes hardly educational. Once after a lecture at Urmston, I heard an elderly gentleman say, 'I still don't understand how the Newcomen engine works in spite of Mr. Hills' explanations'. Travelling at night could be difficult. One cold night, I was waiting for the Styal train at Piccadilly Station and decided to try a soup. I put my money in the machine, pushed the button and watched the soup pour into the drain as no cup descended. I had no more change.

MIRAS moved their meetings into the Museum where their evening lectures were held. Members helped save possible exhibits. One instance was a collection of photographs of Crossley buses found put out for waste paper. Members demonstrated some of the machines especially to school parties and on our 'Working Days'. We ran evening classes in the Museum. Our lecture room was equipped with chairs that had a writing pad on the right arm. During some of my lectures, I waited for the notes of one student to drop to the ground as he fell asleep, not through the dullness of my lecture but because he was under great strain to keep the Shirley Institute afloat.

Museum Staff

The Museum was governed by its own Joint Committee with representatives from the City of Manchester, the University of Manchester and UMIST. The Town Clerk was the Secretary. Staff appointments were handled by UMIST Registrars and finances by the UMIST Bursar. I could not run the Museum into debt although the various allocations in the annual budget might be adjusted slightly. For instance, if there were a surplus in the wages allocation, this might be transferred to exhibitions. My empire started with myself, secretary, two technicians and a cleaner. When 97 Grosvenor Street closed in 1983, this had swollen to seventeen, not counting any employed under Community Industry schemes and the like. I insisted on having two technicians so that one could help the other for health and safety reasons.

My budget for exhibitions could be augmented by gifts in kind which did not appear in the accounts. For example, Platts of Oldham estimated that their fitter taking out and re-erecting the self-acting mule from Elk Mill would cost £1,000. Their invoice was never sent. Pickfords might happen to have a vehicle that could be diverted on its journey to pick up and deliver an exhibit for us. The small Lancashire boiler from Trowbridge was one example. The National Union of Railwaymen arranged with British Rail at Horwich that somehow the railway goods wagons on which we would build the replica Liverpool & Manchester carriages fell off at Liverpool Road Station instead of the scrap yard.

There was no doubt about the appointment of my first Chief Technician. I expect Frank Wightman had tidied himself up a little when he came asking for a job. He was well known for his passion for steam mill engines and was normally dressed in oily blue overalls and his black beret. He was came with his assortment of engineering tools such as large spanners, chain blocks and the like which he was willing to use on behalf of the Museum, saving us this expenditure. He also came with his little 15 cwt lorry for which UMIST agreed a special mileage rate. In the ensuing years, we were able to put his millwrighting skills to good effect for, without him, there would not be the important collection of mill engines today. We were able to start him in a small workshop in the basement of a chapel in Rosamund Street until we could move into 97 Grosvenor Street.

While it was one thing to demonstrate replica machines, were we really justified in working historic machines? Those which were truly unique such as the early Arkwright Waterframe and the Royce motor car engine, I decided we should not.

Most other exhibits duplicated similar ones in other museums. We could prolong the life of ours by running them slowly. On steam engines, we could fit mechanical lubricators to inject oil into the cylinder with the steam. Stainless steel piston rods might replace iron to prevent electrolytic corrosion while the original would be kept for a pattern. The little vertical engine ran much better after oil passages had been cut in the crosshead slides which reduced wear. Worn bearings could be built up or replaced. Records were kept of work carried out.

I did not have to estimate restoration costs so the technicians did not usually have any pressure to complete an exhibit. I insisted that every machine be stripped down and checked over thoroughly. Re-erecting a machine on a new site would not realign the bearings in quite the same position, causing wear. Hence the need for renewal to prime condition. A roving machine on re-erection was not winding the rovings correctly. Examination showed the teeth in a gearwheel had not been cleaned properly. Cleanliness is next to godliness and showed respect for the exhibits.

Harry Applebee, who had been used to the rough maintenance of a building site, often took the attitude, 'That will do'. A short walk from Liverpool Lime Street Station brought me to a double-fronted warehouse with a loading bay in the middle giving access to each floor and the basement. I saw the printing press we had been offered which would make an excellent exhibit. The beam at the top of the loading bay slot would take its weight so removal would be easy. My second Chief Technician, Sid Barnes, a really great asset, trained in both electrical and mechanical engineering, and Harry went with a small lorry to the rescue. Ropes were attached and Sid looked at the feet of the press. 'Should we tie them on?' 'No, they look safe enough', Harry replied. Luckily Sid did tie them on for once the press was launched into the air, bang, bang, the feet dropped a few inches. The beam lowered goods into the basement into which the press would descend but railings round the drop prevented the lorry getting underneath to receive it. Volunteers from the by-standers pulled the press across with a rope as it was lowered onto the lorry. All went well in the end, but unforeseen snags frequently occurred when moving old machinery. The men working for the Museum were prepared to be adaptable. While we had an Advisory Panel for exhibits and University staff gave their advice as well, the responsibility for accepting any exhibit and its preservation ultimately lay with me. This is where those three years as Research Assistant proved invaluable.

Museum Director

> Much have I travelled in the realms of gold
> > And many goodly states and kingdoms seen;
> > Round many western islands have I been.

John Keats

I have mentioned earlier how I was able to consult the Boulton and Watt Collection in Birmingham over Watt's involvement in supplying steam engines for land drainage. His engines also formed the power source for many early textile mills. The questions over his crucial invention of the separate condenser this raised led me later to write a full biography of this great inventor. His connections with textiles formed a large section of my PhD thesis, published as *Power In The Industrial Revolution*.

At the same time, I was plunged into securing my first large scale collection for the Museum when, in the autumn of 1965, Beyer, Peacock & Co announced the closure of its Gorton Foundry where locomotives had been built since 1854. Local archive depositories took no interest in saving the firm's records. What was to be done? We had only my small office in J13, a damp store and no museum. We persuaded Lord Bowden to invite the Directors to lunch and convince them that we were genuine. 'Yes, they would tell us when we could take appropriate material when production had ceased'. Silence. One of the Registrar's staff who also worked in a pub by the main gate to Gorton Foundry heard that old letters, etc., were being destroyed. We plunged in and were able to save much of the crucial documentation covering the firm's history. The Lancia was a frequent visitor bringing back piles of ledgers, etc. The UMIST librarian was none too pleased having to find space for rolls and rolls of drawings. Harry Milligan, the Central Library photographer, was delighted to rescue a ton and a half of historic glass plate negatives. This collection still forms an important research facility for many students and even for those restoring locomotives.

Much was lost, for here I first came across a peculiar phenomenon, a sort of death wish to wipe out all record of a firm that had failed. Leonard Davenport, the last Chief Draughtsman, had set his eye on a set of nicely bound volumes of the Journal of the Institution of Locomotive Engineers. 'Are they of any value?', asked Mr. Dawes, the Chief Accountant. 'No' came the reply. 'If no one else wants them, let Mr. Hills have them'. The same applied to other objects. It has been said that Oldham Town Council wanted to sweep away all trace of its industrial past. We were publicising the Museum at an Exhibition in the Royal Exchange. A group of elderly women walked away from us because they did not wish to be reminded of the grim past. To a certain extent, this attitude still pervades Manchester where the glamorous Art Gallery is supported in preference to a dirty technological museum showing the origins of our greatest contribution to civilization, the Industrial Revolution.

Even while I was rescuing Beyer, Peacock records, I was pursuing my research topic, the textile industry. I went to Brooklands Mill at Leigh and was shown the cotton spinning machines. At the end of the afternoon, someone asked if I had seen their steam engine.

Left high-pressure side of Brooklands Mill engine

I dashed round to the engine house just in time to see the stately flywheel driven by the flashing steel of the connecting rods rotating before the mill stopped for the day. I was impressed not only by the polish and cleanliness everywhere but how quietly and

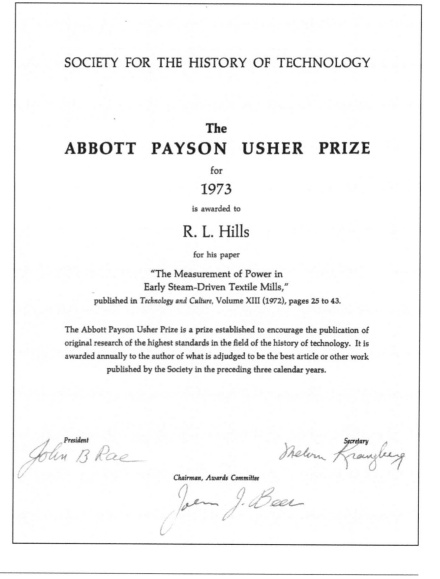

effortlessly that engine was churning out 1,000 horse power. Here was something worth preserving of which most people were completely unaware. When Brooklands Mill closed, I was able to rescue a drawing frame and an early ring frame from there. Subsequently I helped Courtaulds make films of their last engines, 'Power Behind the Spindle' and 'The George Saxon Engine at Magnet Mill'.

It was through visits like these that I was able to acquire a background of what textile machinery we would have to preserve to create a small working cotton mill and also what steam engines might be suitable. One quest in the Lancia took me with Arnold Pacey, Senior Lecturer in History of Science and Technology, to Darley Abbey Mill. While I looked at the engine, which was not suitable, Arnold examined the mill structure. We also studied their archives. By now it was well after 1 o'clock. We were offered lunch in the canteen. We gratefully accepted even though all they had left was rice pudding and rhubarb.

Arnold and I offered a joint paper, 'The Measurement of Power in Early Factory Steam

SOCIETY FOR THE HISTORY OF TECHNOLOGY

The
ABBOTT PAYSON USHER PRIZE
for
1973
is awarded to

R. L. Hills

for his paper

"The Measurement of Power in
Early Steam-Driven Textile Mills,"
published in *Technology and Culture*, Volume XIII (1972), pages 25 to 43.

The Abbott Payson Usher Prize is a prize established to encourage the publication of original research of the highest standards in the field of the history of technology. It is awarded annually to the author of what is adjudged to be the best article or other work published by the Society in the preceding three calendar years.

President
John B Rae

Secretary
Melvin Kranzberg

Chairman, Awards Committee
Joseph J. Beer

Driven Textile Mills' to the American Society for the History of Technology (Vol. 13, 1972). It was awarded the Abbot Payson Usher Memorial prize for the best article in 1972 which would be presented at the Annual Dinner in San Francisco.

The chance to see the States and Canada was not to be missed so I went with Donald who also was receiving an award. I returned home by Washington D.C. having visited many museums and science centres. By Lake Ontario, there was a Victorian steam pumping station. On the wall between the two engines was a picture of Queen Victoria in full regalia. Our Queen was due to visit there one afternoon. A teacher took her pupils along that morning and sat them down in front of the picture. 'Now children, whose picture is that?' Silence. 'Children, I am ashamed of you. Our Queen Elizabeth II is coming here this afternoon and you do not recognise her mother, Queen Elizabeth I'. I wish I had told our Queen that when I showed her round the Goods Shed at Liverpool Road. I am sure that she would have been amused.

Her Majesty visits the Goods Shed in May 1983

Participation in conferences served two purposes. One was through contributing a paper and the other was to learn more about museums. The Museums Association held its annual meeting in Manchester in June 1968 when I presented a paper, 'Manchester Museum of Science and Technology, An Experiment in Education' (*Museums Assoc. Journal.* June 1968.) Our museum did not exist at that time! At the First International Conference on the Conservation of Industrial Monuments held in conjunction with the Iron Bridge Museum, I noticed how it was supported by the local gentry, something which I rarely achieved in Manchester. A later similar conference in Sweden covered many blast furnaces, foundries and forges. Each town vied to entertain us, generally with the lavish Swedish cold table. I never thought I would tire of smoked salmon. In Ireland driving up from the south when going to speak in Belfast, I picked up a hitch-hiker with a rucksack. We came to the border and, seeing my English car registration, we were waved through. I had never thought what he might have been carrying.

At the former textile town of Lowell Ma., we were given a guided tour. We set off in a street car (tram), looked at a display in a mill, saw the dam and sluices controlling the river for water power, looked at the river lock, jumped on a boat down the canal to the next mill where we had another talk. I had not realised two hours had passed, such was the way our interest was held. Short bursts of activity were better than one long one.

I learnt a lot about museum displays. First was the need to orient people at the very beginning and guide them through the display. In the London Science Museum, I stood on the gallery above the locomotive hall and watched people entering. Most paused, looked confused and moved away to one side and not the open spaces in the middle. Displays had to be arranged so that people were drawn from one section to another in a planned sequence. Colour could help here, with labels in the same section the same colour. At 97 Grosvenor Street, we had brown for textiles and pale green for internal combustion engines. This might apply to floor coverings, a different colour in each section, perhaps with footprints to show the way. Lighting could highlight important exhibits. Labels might have an easy to read section in large print for the basic description and smaller print for the specialist. I took care to see that the Museum accession number was added so we could supply further information if required. All these little changes helped prevent our visitors becoming tired with 'museum feet'.

I was able to experiment with some of these ideas when we could plan more permanent displays after moving into the whole of 97 Grosvenor Street in 1972. A boiler in the basement supplied steam to three small engines, a grasshopper, a vertical and an horizontal. We found the cylinder of the grasshopper had worn bell-mouthed through misalignment of the supports for the beam. It may have been like this from new! We made a small alteration and it has run satisfactorily ever since. Our replica Newcomen engine remained the centre piece of that display and contrasted strangely with a steam turbine. The engine was the subject of undergraduate reports and other lectures.

It was the collection of internal combustion engines that changed the fortune of the Museum. We used one of the two solid

Crossley's original Otto Langen patent atmospheric gas engine

ground floors at 97 Grosvenor Street to display our Crossley engines, the atmospheric gas engine and the early four-stroke horizontal gas engine. They were connected to the town gas supply. The shaft of the atmospheric gas engine was twisted so I complained jokingly to the Crossley Service Manager that this was poor design on an engine one hundred years old. He sorted it out for us free of charge. Then we watched fascinated as this engine clattered and banged away. The contrast with the 'silent' four-stroke was dramatic. In the autumn of 1973, the Museum was due to change to North Sea gas with different characteristics and the engines might not work with it. To give the general public a chance to see them running, we held three 'Working Saturdays' when we demonstrated these engines and other exhibits as well. These Saturdays were so popular that they became a regular monthly feature. After the change-over, Ken Barlow, later our Keeper of Industry, was able by various means to adapt the engines to this new gas as part of his M.Sc. thesis.

Liverpool Road

In 1978, the GMC purchased Liverpool Road Station. Was this the last chance for a permanent home? We were still stuck in 97 Grosvenor Street but would it be a sort of death trap? Increasing visitor numbers showed how popular it was and faith in our vision had enabled us to carry on with their support. The station itself was unsuitable for a good museum of industry and it was with much soul searching that I pointed out how unsuitable the 1830 warehouse would be for many of our exhibits especially the mill engines. I stuck my neck out and suggested that the Goods Shed would provide excellent accommodation for the Great Railway Exposition when the GMC was planning to celebrate the 150 anniversary of the Liverpool & Manchester Railway and that afterwards it would be suitable for mill engine and railway displays. The Goods Shed was purchased and we started preparing the mill engine display in what would be called the Power Hall. This was where it was fortunate that I had helped with the preservation of our mill engines because when the time came for their re-erection, I was the only person who had seen them in their original settings. For only one, the Barnes engine, did we have the manufacturers' drawings so we had to prepare drawings for the architect to lay out the Power Hall.

The Durn mill engine being erected in the Power Hall

Moving Stationary Mill Engines

The Barnes Engine from Firgrove Mill

Looking along the line of the tandem compound engine with the low pressure cylinder nearest

The Lumb governor and regulator

The low pressure cylinder

Dismantling the high pressure cylinder

Half of the flywheel being moved into position in the Power Hall. The crane touched the roof beam.

The crankshaft being lowered

The Haydock Beam Engine

Inside the engine house with the governor in the foreground, and panelling concealing the flywheel

A crane lifts the cylinder out of the parially demolished engine house

The cylinder being taken away for storage

The cylinder erected in the Power Hall

The flywheel and connecting rod ready for trials

The Elm Street Mill Engine

The engine when still at work in its engine house at Elm Street Mill

The hydraulically operated valve gear of the high pressure cylinder

Ordered chaos when dismantling

The low pressure uniflow cylinder being lowered onto a Pickford's trailer to go to store

Home at last - the low pressure cylinder in the Power Hall

Only for the Elm Street engine could we go and measure up the original engine bed. Galloways, the engine manufacturers, had used imperial measurements. The architect wanted metric. The contractor wanted imperial. In spite of this confusion, there were few mistakes with the massive concrete foundations.

Erecting the Galloway Elm Street Mill Engine

I insisted that there should be overhead cranes because only with these could the engines be erected safely and accurately. 'Why are they necessary and could you not use temporary ones?' the GMC asked. 'We will need them for maintenance afterwards' I replied and this has been the case. We must have shifted nearly 400 tons of exhibits mostly with the help of men on unemployment schemes.

The Railway Collection

The new Power Hall presented us with a dilemma. We would have to have a significant railway display. In addition to our archive collections such as Beyer, Peacock, there was a collection of samples of railway and tram rails. The latter was the work of the eccentric Stanley Swift who lived in a Salvation Army hostel and played classical music. He looked in every road works in Manchester in his search for tram rails and would cut out a section if he saw a significant one. With the help of another enthusiast Dr. Paul Spriggs, we had amassed a comprehensive array of railway signalling apparatus from signals to lever frames to control apparatus. Many items were accessioned in the Museum registers and were displayed in 97 Grosvenor Street and at Liverpool Road. I had hoped to construct a working signal box in the station yard but left before this could be done. On Paul's death, this very significant collection was disbanded.

One of our two replica Railway Carriages

So far, we had neither rolling stock nor locomotives. I am still surprised that the design of second class 1835 railway carriages I based on Nicholas Wood's contemporary *Treatise on Railroads* was never queried by either any railway authorities or Health and Safety. Two bodies were built by Community Industry teams with wood supplied free from a local timber merchant. Surprisingly I found they fitted nicely onto British Rail standard open goods wagon chassis that came from Horwich. I am proud that these carriages have been enjoyed by many thousands of visitors and are still running today.

Ideally I thought that we should have at least four locomotives. One to represent the opening of the Liverpool & Manchester Railway, the next to show the first mature designs of 1860, then improvements around 1900 and finally one of the last steam locomotives of around 1950. There would have to be a Garratt as well. Most steam locomotives were securely lodged in museums and the like when we were planning the Liverpool Road display but perhaps there was one area where we could contribute to the general preservation scheme, that of British locomotives built for export, a feature of the North West industry.

For the 1979 re-enactment of the Rainhill trials, Mike Satow had built replicas of 'Rocket', 'Sans Pareil', and 'Novelty'. Novelty might solve two requirements because it was designed by a Swede, Ericsson, and had local connections. Satow was looking for a home for it, 'Would we like to buy it?' We were overhauling Novelty in one of our workshops when the Swedish Railways asked whether they could borrow her for their 125 anniversary celebrations. So we sent her off and I went with her. The Museum had no allocation for travel abroad so I paid for most of these trips myself.

Getting up steam in Novelty in Sweden

I demonstrated Novelty for some days at the Gavle Railway Museum and came to the conclusion that the boiler and firebox design were too dangerous for regular use and, although developing a good turn of speed, Novelty would not be powerful enough to haul our two replica carriages. I was relieved when the Mayor of Gavle stated they must buy Novelty and passed the hat round. We were able to borrow the London Science Museum's reconstruction of Novelty with some original parts. We motorised the wheels with an electric motor so they could be rotated.

Sometimes our exhibits just seemed to fall into place at the right time when we could cope. For the 1860 period, my eyes wandered across the sea to the Isle of Man where Beyer, Peacock locomotives based on a design for the Norwegian Railways formed the main-stay of the Manx Railways. To bring one back to Manchester would mean dismantling it at Castletown harbour and craning the parts onto a boat. We had neither staff nor money to do this. Then the Isle of Man Steam Packet Company introduced a roll-on roll-off ferry. My cousin Elspeth Quayle, member of the House of Keys, introduced me to the Manx Minister for Transport. In return for my submitting a report on their railways' industrial heritage, we could have a locomotive providing we did not restore it to full working order.

While at the Lucerne Transport Museum, I had been impressed with the educational potential of their sectioned engine. I realised we could do the same with our Manx exhibit. We waited anxiously in Douglas one September afternoon for the Ro-Ro to dock and Pickfords' low loader to be driven off, because we intended to show 'Pender' in Manchester at the parade to celebrate the 149th anniversary of the Liverpool & Manchester Railway.

Loading 'Pender' at the Isle of Man

The boat was delayed. In order for 'Pender' to leave on the next ferry early in the morning, we had to winch her onto the low loader in the gathering gloom. We finished too late for the booking to be confirmed. 'Pender' left a day late but still took part (together with the Lancia) in the parade through Manchester celebrating the 149th anniversary of the Liverpool & Manchester Railway. Another Community Industry team sectioned her in Beyer, Peacock's old boiler shop. Sid Barnes arranged for the driving wheels driven by an electric motor to be mounted on rollers. She became a popular working exhibit in the Power Hall.

The British Overseas Railways Historical Society helped us bring back from Pakistan a typical 1900 British express passenger locomotive. This design had been built in the North West by Beyer, Peacock, Nasmyth Wilson and the Vulcan Foundry. After protracted negotiations, President Zia ordered that we could have one built by the Vulcan Foundry. It was loaded on board ship for Liverpool before I knew about it. The mammoth steam crane hoisted it out of the hold and Pickfords brought it to Liverpool Road. We had laid a third rail to accommodate the broad gauge of the Pakistan Railways. As it was being run off the trailer, I suddenly realised that I had not checked the height of the door into the Power Hall. It fitted. The Duke of Edinburgh specially asked to see it on his visit with the Queen on 5 May 1982.

The Pakistan Locomotive being offloaded in Liverpool

After this, a Black Five was a tame exhibit for our final period. That left a Garratt, arguably Beyer, Peacock's most important contribution to locomotive design. When Gorton Foundry closed in 1965, I had seen there K1, the first Garratt design. It was the usual story, nowhere to house it, no money to buy it. Luckily the Ffestiniog Railway stepped in and saved it. The Overseas Railway enthusiasts had been endeavouring to repatriate various locomotives including the mighty East African Railways 59 Class. Negotiations were in hand but transport from Mombasa would cost over £150,000.

Then I heard that the South African Railways had decided to scrap their strategic reserve of locomotives. I drooled over the list and spotted that a GL Class was included. This was the most powerful steam locomotive built in Britain. I have written a full account of bringing one back to Manchester in *The Railway Magazine*, May 1984, No. 997, Vol. 130, 'What a Whopper, Moving the South African Class GL Beyer-Garratt'. A letter I sent to the South African Railway authorities asking for a Class GL went astray so a further approach was made in August 1983. By then, Michael Bailey, who was working for the Manchester Ship Canal, knew that GEC was shipping some heavy transformers and electrical equipment to Richards Bay on Wynns heavy lift trailers. Overseas Containers Ltd. quoted a price of £30,000 to bring back the Garratt. GMC provided extra funds. All agreed to cooperate. The trailers had left for South Africa by the time a telex was received on November 18 from the South African Minister of Transport agreeing to donate 2352. Airline seats were being booked for Christmas. Trains were busy and shipping would soon be full of oranges. 2352 was at Germiston, Johannesburg, and would be shipped from Richards Bay, five hundred miles away. Wynns trailers were not allowed on the South African roads. 2352 was vacuum braked so could not use the new direct coal line to Richards Bay but had to travel at 20 m.p.h. via Durban. This alone took a lot of organisation.

I flew out to Johannesburg to meet the railway authorities and express our thanks. Apartheid was still in place so it was quite a new experience for me. The Ro-Ro ship, Elgaren, arrived at Richards Bay late and was due to leave in less than twenty four hours. But already we had separated 2352 into three parts and worked out how we could load them. Wynns men worked into the night to take the electrical equipment off the trailers and prepare them for loading the Garratt through the stern of Elgaren the following morning. All went well. I hurried back to Durban and Johannesburg to fly back to England. Soon after Christmas, this whole area was devastated by a severe hurricane which would have prevented us loading 2352. We were just in time.

The boiler unit of 2352 on the trailer on arrival at Tilbury

2352 was delivered after Christmas to Tilbury, quickly unloaded still on her three trailers and moved to Stafford. The 160 tons of the three sections of locomotive made a splendid sight as they were taken up the motorway. H.M. Customs demanded £2,000 as value added tax, value added to what I never discovered. Delivery to Manchester was delayed by a savage snow storm because Wynns men were engaged in delivering supplies to repair the damage. So it was not until into the New Year that 2352 was delivered to Liverpool Road.

Wynns performed miracles fitting 2352 into Liverpool Road Station and the Power Hall. Not only did the units have to arrive in the right sequence and the right way round but space had to be allowed to draw out the trailers and free the tractors. The rear unit was placed well down the station yard and its tractor and trailer taken away so it sat on a set of rails. The front unit was run off onto rails by the entrance to the Power Hall. Backing the boiler unit from Byrom Street past the gantry and over the railway tracks to position it between the other two units was a masterpiece of manoeuvring. The massive multi-wheeled trailer was drawn out from under the boiler, leaving it mounted on special stillages. After cleaning up all the units and some initial restoration, rails were placed under the boiler unit and connected to those beneath the other units. These were pushed under the boiler and the boiler lowered onto them and connected up. 2352 assembled once again could be moved into her permanent position in the Power Hall.

2352 under restoration at Liverpool Road

The return of 2352 was perhaps my greatest triumph but also my finale. The GMC had set up its own Trust to run Liverpool Road as a new museum to which I was appointed Curator Designate. I had not pleased some of the GMC officers by insisting on the purchase of the Goods Shed, or the installation of overhead cranes and that steam and other supplies for the mill engines should be fitted from the start. It would have been they who decided that the post of Director should be advertised. I know they approached people in other museums to apply. So I was not unduly surprised when a person with no knowledge of the history of science and technology, Patrick Greene, was appointed. I received a number of letters expressing regret. People were also astounded when he was awarded the OBE after barely a year in post. I suppose I should not have called him 'Our Greene Director', nor referred to the display of which he was so proud, 'Underground Manchester' with its stuffed rat, as the 'Sewage Museum'. I think the successful return of the Garratt was the final tipping point. He was jealous of my achievements and of my award of the Fellowship of the Museums Association. I had been overworking far too long. My application for a sabbatical to write up some of my research was turned down. I realised the knives were out.

I decided that it would be best if I accepted the enhanced terms of an ill-health retirement, surrendered my crown and left the Museum. This may well have saved my life.

I could look back with satisfaction at our achievements. Public awareness and appreciation of industrial history had increased enormously since 1969 partly through our work in Manchester. We had saved important artefacts of the Industrial Revolution for Manchester and the North West. We had laid firm foundations for future growth. With minimal funds and an inadequate building we had assembled the greatest range of working historical exhibits probably anywhere (See Appendix IV). In addition, we had established 'one of the most important educational facilities in the country'. That such a museum had been needed was proved by the rapidly increasing numbers of visitors who were thrilled with the displays. In 1976, there were 45,095 visitors at 97 Grosvenor Street. In 2005 at Liverpool Road there were 481,039, such was the potential we had created.

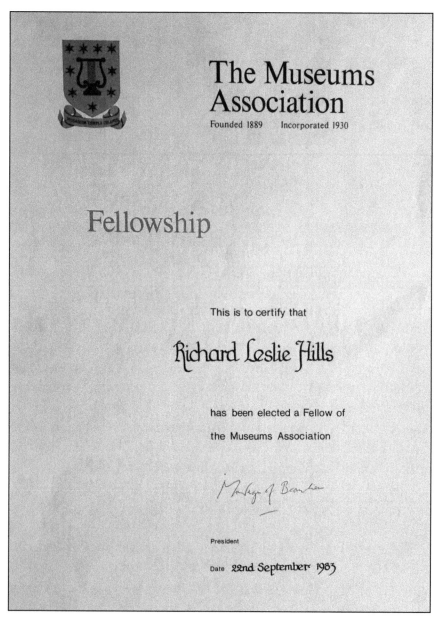

Awarded 22 September 1983

The Seventh Age
The Reverend Doctor

Part 1 – Author

Leaving the Museum in 1984 was, at first, a form of bereavement at the loss of what I had established. In fact, I left behind the drudgery of running a large establishment. Instead I was able to create another kingdom based on my abiding interests of mechanical engineering, railways and mountain walking. These I was able to share with others through lectures, demonstrations and by writing. They would lead me to many countries across the globe in a way that would not have been possible as curator at MOSI.

> Much have I seen and known, cities of men
> And manners, climates, councils, governments,
> Myself not least, but honour'd of them all.

> Tennyson

First of all, I had to get fit again as well as consider what to do with my life. I realised that I had the wrong experience to work in a general museum. I had no direct experience of teaching in schools so that was out. A university lectureship could be a possibility but where in the history of technology? There still remained the possibility of working for the church in some capacity. After all, I had been a Reader at Mottram for some years.

I realised that Manchester had many advantages. I had friends in many societies so was well known. The City had many excellent libraries, including Chetham's, the University and the Central Library. The latter had its local studies section as well as the patent abridgements on open access. Then there were good travel facilities such as the International Airport and the steadily expanding motorway network. Local transport with trains and buses was good also. Probably Manchester had the best facilities of any city outside London.

I needed a house to the south of central Manchester for ease of access to 97 Grosvenor Street so I drew an imaginary semi-circle from Lymm in the West, past Alderley Edge and round to Stalybridge in the East. I was sent details about a wing of Bugsworth Old Hall, a seventeenth century house. It sounded interesting so I went to see it. 'Needs some restoration' was the warning on the estate agent's brochure. I borrowed the key, opened the door and looked up through three gutted floors to the underneath of the roofing slates. Well I suppose this was correct but not precisely what I was looking for.

When I was in Mottram in Longdendale one day, I thought I might as well pause to see at least the exterior of 'A delightful small country house'. It was a three storey weaver's cottage. I was unimpressed with the little I could see of Stamford Cottage through the trees and shrubs as well as ivy smothering the walls. I drove on and searched elsewhere. Sutton's must have contacted me again about inspecting it so this time I went inside. I

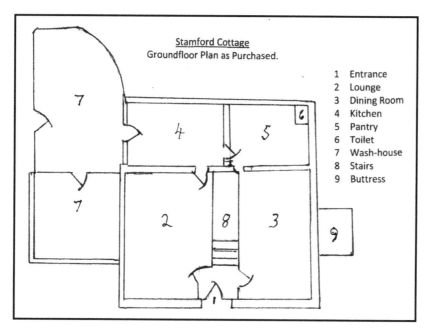

Stamford Cottage
Groundfloor Plan as Purchased.

1 Entrance
2 Lounge
3 Dining Room
4 Kitchen
5 Pantry
6 Toilet
7 Wash-house
8 Stairs
9 Buttress

wanted two garages, workshop, study and then the usual accommodation. There seemed to be possibilities. 'Fools rush in where angels fear to tread'. (A. Pope)

Stamford Cottage

The offer I made was accepted and so began forty years of restoration work. In fact, Stamford Cottage proved to be a much better base for my new kingdom as the home of an author, lecturer and preacher than I could ever have anticipated.

> I will arise and go now and go to Innisfree,
>   And a small cabin build there of clay and wattles made.
>   Nine bean rows will I have there,
> And a hive for the honey-bee.
>
> W.B. Yates

Stamford Cottage was situated on the Old Road where it passed over the top of the deep Mottram cutting so it was not overlooked at the front.

The road had plenty of space for visitors to park cars without interfering with neighbours. This was useful for visitors coming to meetings. Through the cutting passed the No. 6 bus to Ashton and the centre of Manchester. The Limited Stop 125 came up from Manchester to Hyde and Mottram, ten minutes walk away. Forty minutes walk would bring me to Newton for Hyde station with its regular Glossop commuter service to Manchester Piccadilly station and beyond while a similar length walk took me down to Stalybridge for trains to Leeds, York and beyond.

The rear of the property opened onto fields, first with horses and then sheep grazing in them. The lambs delighted in sticking their heads through the wire mesh and, finding they were stuck, had to be rescued. These sheep were a source of wool for spinning. A few minutes further up the hill were paths to Hobson Moor quarry frequented by rock climbers and into the open country. Here I could get some fresh air, get fit and work off my frustrations. Perhaps it was soon after I had left the Museum and was depressed about prospects, that one evening I was approaching the summit of Hobson Moor from the east. The sun was setting over Manchester and I saw against the red glow in the sky that someone had planted a make-shift cross. It was made from a pole. The horizontal cross beam had chains dangling from the ends. I felt it was a sign that all would be well and took heart to face my problems. A couple of days later and it had gone.

FOR SALE
by Private Treaty

MOTTRAM-IN-LONGDENDALE.

W. H. SUTTON & SONS

Chartered Auctioneers and Estate Agents

60 SPRING GARDENS
MANCHESTER 2

Telephone : 832-3103 (STD 061)

and at WILMSLOW, DISLEY, CHEADLE

There was a modern concrete garage at the bottom of the garden. Gradually I hacked my way through the overgrown garden and found the distance to the garage much further than I had thought. The two boundary hedges needed trimming twice a year, quite a task, but I appreciated the soft fruit bushes which I planted. Their crops included gooseberries, raspberries, strawberries, red, white and black currants and rhubarb. They helped to fill the freezer and some were given to people to make jam to sell at church fetes. I became well known for Seville orange and lemon marmalade, sometimes raising over £100 for the church in a season. There was a small vegetable garden, later turned into a car park. In the greenhouse, which I had built, those tomatoes which failed to ripen became green tomato chutney. This produce almost paid for the rates! Many garden parties were held in the restored garden. I understood what marginal farming must have been like before the Industrial Revolution as Stamford Cottage was almost 800 ft. above sea level and why people supplemented their income from textiles.

When I went inside, I felt there was great potential to create what I wanted. I saw I might be able to move the kitchen into the pantry to improve that. The kitchen would become the workshop. The wash-house might be re-configured into a garage for the Lancia while the weavers' attic would become the study. Luckily for me, Stamford Cottage had not been listed as an historic monument which happened in 1983. It was surprising what had been done before that! The old Longdendale Council was sympathetic to alterations. For instance, double glazing was obviously fitted before that date. The wash-house was turned into a garage with a concrete floor raised to ground level outside. The original window was enlarged for the garage door. Most of an internal wall was removed and the concrete extended into the adjacent covered area where there was storage for garden tools and stores for man and beast including a chest freezer as well as being a work area. This became Lancia's lair with enlarged wrought iron gates onto the road.

The Lancia was a tight fit into her lair at Stamford Cottage. Getting her in or out was hazardous owing to the postion of the gate posts and garage door. Coming from Stalybridge direction, she ended up parked at an angle. The best way was to come up from Mottram, get out, switch off burglar alarms at front door, open gates and garage door, then drive in. When backing out with hood up and side -screens in place, it was difficult to see other traffic coming!

The old kitchen became the main workshop with bench, lathe, pillar drill and milling machine. A toilet was squeezed into the corner. The pantry became the kitchen with a large plate-glass window and door overlooking the garden. Originally Stamford Cottage had only two entrances, the front door and the one through the wash-house. Inside I made a doorway from the new kitchen into the dining room which otherwise had to be accessed past the front door.

Maintenance of the structure of Stamford Cottage was a steep learning curve. Plasterers were at work on the new kitchen. They slapped the plaster on with gay nonchalance. The attic needed attention so I bought a bag of plaster, mixed some up in a bucket and staggered up to the attic. By the time I had climbed the stairs, the plaster was already going hard and could not be used. Too much water and the plaster would crack as it dried. I cheated by adding some lime and managed to achieve passable results. 'Water is supplied from a private reservoir' the brochure said. The bathroom was modernised and some central heating fitted. This water was mildly acidic from the peat moors. The soap in the bath turned the water a pale blue. The acid also ate into the copper pipes so they sprang leaks. The pressure was insufficient to extend the central heating into the attic where night storage heaters and a gas fire were installed.

The new kitchen had a flat roof, useful for standing ladders on to access the slates on the main roof. The ridge here could be reached with a second ladder. I had been writing in the attic one Sunday evening when water fell on my typing. Perhaps it was a gentle warning that the roof needed urgent repairs. It was a very long way looking down from the ridge to the bottom of the deep cutting. The local stone slates were heavy to carry up but the top rows of slates were lifted off, insulation put between the joists, woodwork treated with preservatives, the whole covered with roofing felt and the ridge and chimney breasts cemented in.

Stamford Cottage had been built with dressed stone for outside walls pointed with lime mortar. The alkaline mortar reacted with the acidic millstone grit so the outside layers shrank and pulled away from the inner ones built from random stone. The garden end was supported by a large buttress covered with ivy. Even with the ivy removed, the buttress kept that wall damp so buttress was taken down and the whole wall was rebuilt.

The front wall began to bulge ominously. Remedial action was taken and collapse averted. Liquid waterproof cement was injected into the walls which were further tied together with stainless steel rods. It was a costly job, but Stamford Cottage was saved for posterity.

The Attic

Over the years, I amassed a large book collection on the history of engineering and theology. Book cases were built in the attic to house a complete run of the Journal of the Institution of Civil Engineers. Books were stored in more book cases and on vacant spaces on the floor along the walls. Books began to creep out into the first floor passage as well as in the lounge down stairs. Instead of struggling into the centre of Manchester, ordering a book in a library, waiting only to find it had been already lent, to have instant access in one's own home was so convenient.

The attic also had sufficient space for construction and storage of lecturing equipment. Boxes of slides were mostly kept in the warmer conditions of the bathroom airing cupboard. A proper architects' drawing board was extremely useful for producing diagrams. A photographic enlarger was adapted as a copying stand for making slides. It was up here that an experimental draw loom finally took shape. All this was in addition to the two desks, one for an electric typewriter and the other eventually for a computer. The whole was watched over by the grandfather clock ticking in the corner.

Some Publications

After I had replaced the glass in the blocked-up attic windows (through window tax when weaving ceased?), the attic became an inspirational place for an author. I could look across to Mottram church and the hills and moors beyond. I was able to spread papers and pictures over the floor and, of course, grab books for reference. *Machines, Mills and Uncountable Costly Necessities* was prepared at Styal but my early books on the textile industry (Power in the Industrial Revolution and Richard Arkwright) were launched from Stamford Cottage.

Grudgingly the Museum governors granted me a couple of months' time away to recover from the Great Railway Exposition and write *Beyer, Peacock, Locomotive Builders to the World*. David Patrick, a retired Beyer, Peacock Director, gave advice. I doubt if such a work would be viable today because I had free run of the Beyer, Peacock archives and photographs. Had the Museum charged a fee for each photo, the cost would have been prohibitive. I produced a well illustrated book which I felt was essential for a history of technology reference volume. It has been reprinted and been more profitable for second-hand dealers than the author.

Another pioneering book was the *Life and Inventions of Richard Robert, 1789 – 1864*, the first full biography of this amazing and prolific inventor whose patents covered machine tools, textile machines especially his self-acting spinning mule and a multitude of smaller inventions. While his road vehicles and his first two designs of railway locomotives were unsuccessful, perhaps with the help of Beyer, he founded the famous firm of locomotive builders, Sharp Roberts.

Centaur was the first of the redesigned Sharp, Roberts locomotives delivered to the Grand Junction Railway in 1837

The background research for these two books was carried through into many other publications and lectures. There were illustrated guides for the Museum, lists of engines built for Beyer, Peacock and, more particularly, series of articles for the K1 Garratt restoration group and the Welsh Highland Railway. K1 had been displayed at York Railway Museum but when the Ffestiniog Railway was able to proceed with the reopening of the Welsh Highland Railway, K1 was an obvious candidate for running on that line. Volunteers undertook her restoration first at Tyseley, Birmingham, and then at Dinas, Caernarfon. There were articles for *Pioneer* about K1 and then more general ones for the *Welsh Highland Snowdon Ranger*. Sponsorship was sought for missing parts of K1. I chose the whistle. Castings were poured in Hyde. The equipment in my little workshop was stretched to its limits but the challenge was met although the whistle sounded a little too shrilly for use in service.

One involvement led to another. I made some small parts for the later Garratts but I saw that my volunteering might be better applied in tidying up the neglected garden at Dinas station. Stamford Cottage again proved useful because, with a nil budget, I was able to take cuttings and grow on seedlings from my garden. I found a delightful bed and breakfast at the corner of the road leading down to the station. John and Sheila Simpson were admirable hosts, Sheila being a good cook. I would drive over on a Friday evening and return on the Monday when the traffic was lighter. One of these visits was the only time (so far) when I have been breathalysed. I was having dinner at the home of Raj Williamson and Tom Jones. Because I had to drive back to the Simpsons, I declined another glass of wine. Tom said, 'No, you are quite safe'. He disappeared into his study and returned with a breathaliser. He was its inventor. He tested me and I was well under the limit. It was through Tom that I took the controls of an aircraft for the only time in my life. He kept a small plane at Caernarfon airport where we went one afternoon. I sat in the co-pilot's seat. We were over Anglesey when the pilot said to me, 'She's all yours'. Panic. I quickly learnt the basic controls and we had fine views of Parys Mountain and the remains of copper mining there. I was not allowed to land the plane. In those days it was great fun working on the Welsh Highland Railway, perhaps because it was a pioneering effort when the tentacles of Health and Safety did reach so far.

K1 whistle

Creating the collection of mill engines and installing them in the Power Hall showed how correct was the title of H.W. Dickinson's *A Short History of the Steam Engine*. Much was omitted so I set to work writing *Power from Steam* while training for ordination. Cambridge University Press took a risk with it that has been justified since it still continues to sell a few copies annually. I aimed to write books with good notes and indexes so they could be used by students as reference works. Like the Beyer, Peacock book, it has become another classic.

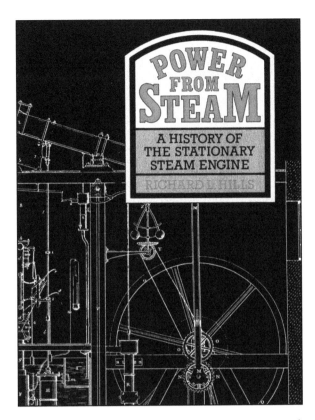
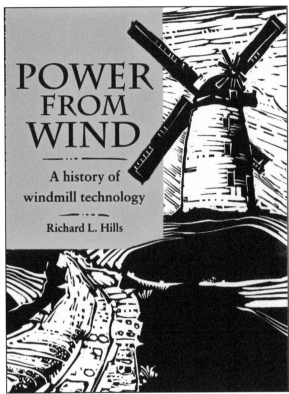

Power from Wind arose from my fen research when, to my great surprise, I discovered there was no general history of wind power. While driving to and fro to Great Yarmouth, I would divert to look at windmills across East Anglia. On an earlier trip, Frank Wightman was with me so I stopped to show him the Heckington eight-sailed mill. He called himself a millwright and to my surprise he admitted this was the first windmill he had ever entered. The miller told us how, as a lad, he returned after a dance at midnight to find his father about to go into the mill. 'Wind is rising, get into t' mill and set her on'. *Power from Wind* is still selling even though wind turbines have advanced so much recently.

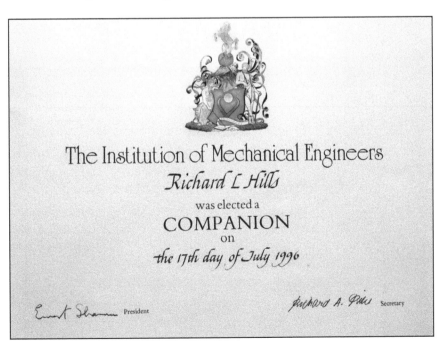

Perhaps it was through these books and my founding the Museum that in July 1996 I was elected a Companion of the Institution of Mechanical Engineers, a rare treasured honour because there were only twenty other Companions.

In my textile research, I could not avoid James Watt and his crucial inventions to the steam engine. I was puzzled by his claim, 'It was in the Green of Glasgow. I had gone for a walk on a fine Sabbath afternoon... I was thinking upon the engine. I had not walked further than the Golf house when the whole thing was arranged in my mind' (*J. Watt, Vol. 1, His Time in Scotland*, 2002, p. 339). This was probably in April 1765. That September Watt wrote to his friend James Lind, 'I have tried my small model of my perfect engine, which hitherto answers expectations, and gives great, I may say greatest, hopes of success' (Ibid, p. 364). If indeed Watt had invented his perfect engine, why was it a further ten years before he achieved success?

The more books I read on Watt, the more I found large sections of his life had never been tackled thoroughly. There was Watt the family man with the loss of his first wife and so many children. There was Watt the physician promoting the Pneumatic Institution. There was Watt the chemist helping the Delftfield pottery, inventing his copying machine and bleaching. Then we have Watt the civil engineer with his canal surveys. Watt the mechanical engineer made his fortune with his steam engines and we have Watt the natural scientist in the Lunar Society and Royal Society. This started me off on research which took me up to Inverness in Scotland where Watt was surveying the Caledonian Canal amongst other canal surveys as well as planning early tramways, an era of his life little studied before. This led to my lecturing about Watt to today's engineers in the Channel Islands. I went from the Cornish copper mines to the privileged haunts of the Royal Society in London; from Watt's Letter Books in the National Library of Wales in Aberystwyth to the enormous Boulton and Watt Collection in Birmingham.

It was a fascinating experience to be allowed into Watt's Garret Workshop in the London Science Museum. There were so many relics from the different periods in the great man's career, such as his early attempts at navigation and surveying instruments to a calculating device. Why did he have a pair of textile hand cards hanging on the wall? I hope no visitor peering in through the window mistook me for Watt's ghost.

In Cornwall standing on the hilltop by the site of the Chacewater engine, I pondered on how the enormous cylinder and wooden beams arrived on the site so far inland. I found no mention of the means of transport in the archives. I saw Cosgarne House in its delightful rural setting.

No wonder Watt preferred to be there than in Birmingham. The Gibson Watt family had given permission for me to study the volumes of Watt's copy letter books deposited in the National Library of Wales. Although tedious making notes, it was preferable to looking at microfilms all day. But getting to Aberystwyth could be a problem with an early morning drive of over two hours. Once in winter, I took the train. The River Severn was in flood and might have scoured the foundations of a bridge near Welshpool. The river was too high for investigation by divers so temporary platforms were built either side. We detrained, walked over the bridge and jumped on a second one on the far side.

Birmingham was much easier to reach by train and the buffet car attendants came to recognise a fairly regular traveller. The archive security system was to weigh the documents you had ordered, issue them and weigh them again on return. Soon after I finished my research there, the Collection was reorganised and the cataloguing numbers changed. It was too difficult to alter my notes. However they did accept my card index files with lists of names, etc.

Research in Edinburgh took me to the top of Arthur's Seat with its fine views but more prosaically the Register House with its magnificent entrance or the less pretentious National Library of Scotland were my usual haunts. In the latter were some Rennie papers which I listed for the archivist. The Royal Scottish Museum had among its artefacts a magnificent Watt barometer. A pilgrimage had to be made to the remains of Watt's workshop at near-by Kinneil house with its cylinder from a Newcomen engine. Space restricts mention of exploring many places in Scotland where Watt had surveyed the lines of potential canals. Kintyre was especially interesting because here was built the sole canal to Watt's design. It would take coal from the mines at Machrihanish to the port of Campbeltown. Traces can still be seen. I went in the comfort of a modern car but Watt had to use a horse or boat.

As well as being becalmed, he was once caught in a whirlpool near the notorious Corryvreckan tidal rip. I used many of my trips as source material for local history societies and my own work on Watt.

While Watt was in Scotland in the summer of 1775, Boulton had been installing the new accurately bored cylinder from Wilkinson for their engine at Soho. On his return to Birmingham that October, Watt replaced the surface condensers in which he had been trying to make a perfect vacuum with a jet of water into a large condenser. He found this 'operates beyond my ideas in point of quickness and perfection' as Thomas Newcomen had before him. Gilbert Hamilton commented just before that Christmas, 'I am glad to hear your Engine Scheme is going so well. I hope it will continue' (James Watt Papers, 4/20.20, G. Hamilton to Watt 23 Dec. 1775). Watt had been seeking perfection with complex surface condensers. The answer lay in a simple jet. My puzzle had been solved as well as Watt's.

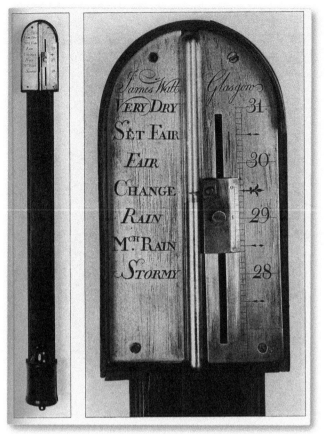

The Watt barometer

Australia

After so much travelling around Britain, it is surprising that I should consider joining the visit of the Newcomen Society to Australia to celebrate the centenary of their Engineering Society. I heard about the attack on the Twin Towers in New York the evening before I was due to leave but thought nothing of it. Manchester airport was busy but we took off on time, only to circle round Heathrow before landing so we were delayed. Everywhere was in chaos. I checked in at the desk for our flight to Perth half an hour before it was due to close only to be turned away. All planes to North America had been cancelled. I was lucky to be able to book a flight to Bangkok and then another to Perth but had to sample the delights of Heathrow Promenade for eight hours. Eventually I arrived at the hotel in Perth at midnight.

Then I discovered that the party would be taken to Kalgoorlie in a minibus and not by plane as I had booked. Quantas Airline crashed at the same time so Australia was also in chaos. I tried to cancel my ticket only to find I was number 775 in the queue. I decided to join the party in the minibus and did not go to the airport. It was only when I arrived in Kalgoorlie and tried to confirm our next onward flight to Adelaide that I discovered that all my internal flights had been cancelled! Luckily most could be reinstated but that to Adelaide was fully booked. The trains were full as well but at least I was able to get the last seat on the overnight bus. Travelling for a day and a half across the Nullabor Plain is not something I would recommend but at least I could join the rest of the party for Adelaide, Melbourne, Sydney, and Canberra. It was a great experience. What I realised from this Australian visit was the importance to British industry of our colonies because most of the equipment we saw in museums and on historic sites had come from Britain.

Manchester Association of Engineers

In my position as Director of the Museum, I was elected to the Council of the Manchester Association of Engineers and was able to contribute some papers for their sessions. The Council felt it would be appropriate if I, an historian, should be their President in 2006 which was their 150 Anniversary. It fell to me to deliver the speech thanking the Deputy Lord Mayor of the City of Manchester for the reception hosted in the magnificent setting of the Town Hall.

The Deputy Lord Mayor of the City of Manchester, Councillor Glynn Evans, requests the pleasure of your company at a Buffet Reception in the Town Hall, Manchester on Tuesday, 10th October 2006 from 7.00 p.m. to 8.30 p.m., to celebrate the 150th Anniversary of the Manchester Association of Engineers.

Rev. Dr. R.L. Hills

The Last Book

We come to the last major work, *Development of Power in the Textile Industry from 1700 – 1930*. In it, I sought to compare the different industries of flax, wool, silk and cotton and examine when industrialisation occurred. It drew from visits to many mills and places were textiles were manufactured. It was based on my experience of establishing the cotton demonstrations in the Museum and setting the spinning and weaving machines to work there. Then at Stamford Cottage in the attic I had my own spinning wheels, warping frame and small hand looms as well as other demonstration equipment. I would often take a bag of raw wool to Dinas at weekends where I could prepare it for spinning. I was offered many different types and colours of wool from which Leslie Kenny and others kindly knitted pullovers for me. At the Museum, I had learnt with much trial and error how to set up a Jacquard loom. But I knew that larger patterns had been woven long before 1800 so I determined to build my own draw loom with pattern harness. While weaving on mine was slow work, at least it showed the principles.

All this was incorporated into the book as well as an appendix at the end with photographs of many of the last mill engines. The pictures in the main text were often smaller than perhaps I wished but it was copiously illustrated with explanations. Sadly it came on the market just as the financial collapse of 2008 struck. In the general turmoil, Landmark the publishers, folded. I have no idea how many copies were sold. Perhaps one day it will be reprinted.

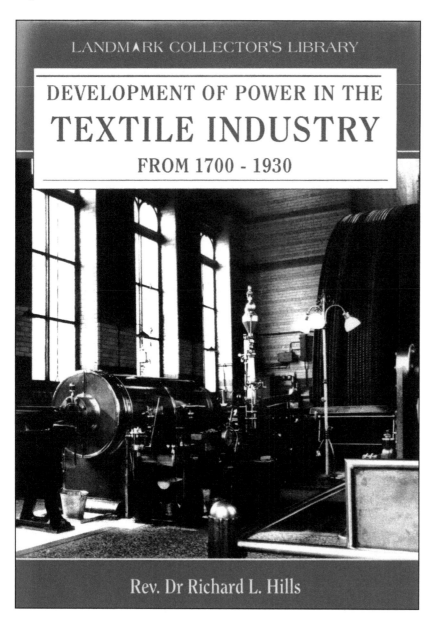

The Author spinning
and working on the
horizontal loom

Working on the draw loom with a finished piece from that loom

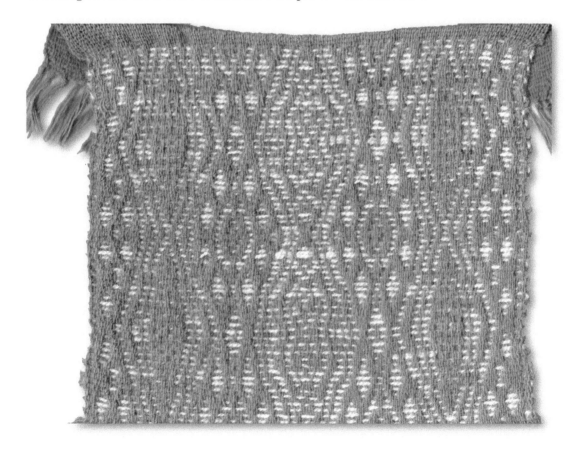

The Reverend Doctor

Part 2 – Paper Historian

The National Paper Museum was established by Jack Barcham Green in a paper mill at St. Mary's Cray with the support of the Technical Section of the British Paper and Board Industry Federation. The mill closed and the artefacts were stored in another mill nearby. In 1968, looking for a permanent new home and hearing about a science museum that was being planned in Manchester, the Secretary approached the Paper Science Department in UMIST to inquire whether that Department might accept the collection. That letter landed on my desk.

Accordingly I went to St. Mary Cray and viewed the exhibits. It was far from encouraging. The river Darenth had flooded where they had been stored and covered everything in a layer of mud. But I realised that there were some important exhibits covering the early history of technology that we would be lucky to find elsewhere such as the papermaking stampers showing the use of hammers to prepare not only pulp but fashion iron and much more.

Papermaking stampers at 97 Grosvenor Street

We accepted the collection and selected some such as the papermaking vat to go immediately on display at 97 Grosvenor Street while most of the rest were stored. A few too large had to be scrapped.

When the exhibits arrived in Grosvenor Street, two packing cases I had not expected came with them. We opened up the cases. Inside was an amazing selection of books, samples of watermarked paper and different types of paper. I realised that here was a significant collection of rare books not only on the history of paper but also on the history of technology. Among them for example was a copy of Vittorio Zonca, *Novo Teatro die Machine*, Padua, 1607. There were other early illustrated books such as the Dutch windmill books and the pictures on papermaking from Diderot, *Encyclopedie*, 1779. Then there were books printed on special paper such as Baskerville, *Virgilii Maronis Bucolica...*, 1757, the first book printed on wove paper. Not only was there the first 1800 edition of M. Koops, *Historical Account of... Paper*, but the second edition as well. We would be unlikely to ever be able to afford to purchase some of these with our funds. The books especially stood me in good stead since I could refer to them quickly as a major source in my later research. At the time, I had little interest in the history of papermaking but this collection would change all that and lead to a new chapter in my life. Little did I think that I would go half way round the world chasing paper history.

The International Association of Paper Historians

With some of the National Paper Museum exhibits on display for the opening of the Museum in 1969, it was suggested that I should attend the Arnhem conference of the International Association of Paper Historians. Here I met many who would become friends later among them the Dutchman Edo Loeber, a retired paper salesman with the ability to speak a wide range of languages. He wanted his profound knowledge of papermaking by hand to be recorded and shared with others. He accepted me as a sort of apprentice so I spent many weekends at his home in Hilversum studying his archives. British Airways offered a cheap weekend in Amsterdam with accommodation in the package. My friends

were amused when they saw the name of the hotel in an area well known for something other than papermaking. He could not drive so I acted as his chauffeur as we toured sites and functioning mills in Italy, Spain, France, the Netherlands as well as England. Once staying at a highly recommended hotel in Ivy Bridge near Plymouth, he was not pleased with the selection of cheese because it contained only continental ones and no English. The information I gained served as the basis for many later articles. It also helped me to edit his Dutch English in his book, *The Paper Mould and Mould Maker*.

The next IPH Congress was at Fabriano, the place where so many developments in papermaking happened, for example the art of water papermaking around 1282. A Britannia Watermark is shown here.

The printer of fine quality books on papermaking with the Bird and Bull Press, Henry Morris and his wife, were staying at the same place and we were both invited to the home of the head of the papermaking school for some entertainment at 9 pm. We decided we had better eat first, thinking we would have only a snack there. Instead we found the local pop group and a full evening meal! We dare not refuse. At the final grand dinner, song birds were on the menu to our disgust.

George Mandl

It may have been there that I first met George Mandl, a Czechoslovak refugee, who had had to leave his family mills to the Communists and built up an empire with mills in Switzerland, Denmark and England. Since no one was willing to host the IPH Congress in 1972, he suggested that, if I would organise it, he would seek the support of the papermaking fraternity in England. I always found paper historians much more willing to help each other than say economic historians, perhaps because it was not a recognised academic subject. The Congress started in Manchester with the display in the Museum and UMIST Paper Science Department before transferring to Wells for Wookey Hole where paper was still made by hand and St. Anne's Board Mill in Bristol. George asked his colleagues who had supported him to the formal dinner. Maj. Pitts, a mill owner from Exeter, appeared in proper evening dress being unaware that this was unusual on the continent. We had great difficulty in persuading him to stay, he felt so embarrassed. We had booked one of the halls of residence in South Manchester which the participants appreciated but I had forgotten about the beginning of the Feast of Ramadan and the mosque at the end of the road.

There was chaos everywhere with cars trying to park so their occupants could worship. Our coach could get nowhere near to us and which delayed our leaving. At St. Anne's Board Mill, George whispered to me that it would soon close. He had quickly deduced from knowing the costs of wages, raw materials etc. and sales that it was running at a loss. It did. He was a shrewd operator.

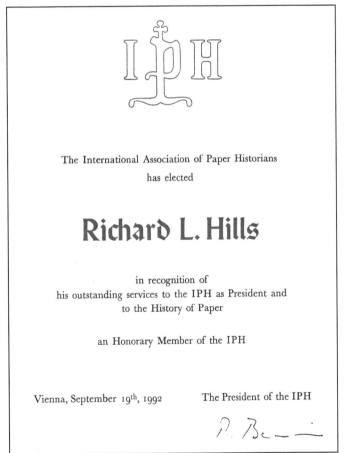

The International Association of Paper Historians

has elected

Richard L. Hills

in recognition of
his outstanding services to the IPH as President and
to the History of Paper

an Honorary Member of the IPH

Vienna, September 19th, 1992   The President of the IPH

IPH President

The first result of my collaboration with Edo was my article in 1980 on papermaking in *History of Technology*, 'Water, Stampers and Paper in the Auvergne, A Medieval Tradition'. It also appeared in the IPH Year Book that same year. The 1980 Congress was held in Basel. One attraction was the International

Garden Festival. We went to look at the plants used for papermaking. The poor hemp or cannabis plant had only a single leaf, all the rest had been picked. Because nobody was willing to become President, I volunteered. It was a very difficult assignment due to my inadequacies in foreign languages and not helped by the clashing personalities of the various nationalities in the organisation. Trying to cope with that and the development of the Museum in Manchester was really too much. I struggled with the production of their *Information* which should have been issued four times a year. We did manage it but, luckily for me, Henk Voorn came to my rescue. After ten years, I resigned at the meeting in Malmede when I was elected an Honorary Member.

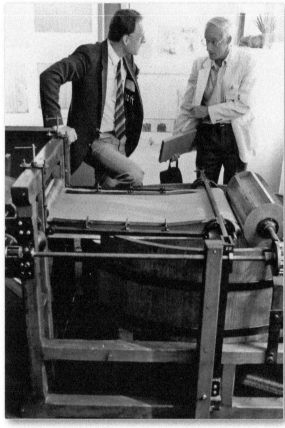

The picture shows one of a number of Robert machines I had made, both full and half size, for various museums based on the original drawings of 1801 which John Gamble brought over from France. He was introduced to the Fourdrinier brothers who agreed to finance the construction of a machine. Five out of the original six drawings passed down the Fourdrinier family until they were offered at auction in the 1980s. Leonard Schlosser, an American paper history enthusiast, bought them. The London Science Museum declared them to be of no national historic importance so permitted their export. Schlosser had copies of the drawings made reduced in size and presented me with a set in return for one of the replicas we had built by Severn Lamb. A full size one went to the Museum in Manchester at no cost to the Museum.

A half size model of N.L. Robert's papermaking machine at Malmede

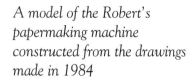

A model of the Robert's papermaking machine constructed from the drawings made in 1984

Paper 500

In the meantime, George Mandl was anxious to celebrate becoming Master of the Stationers' Company with a tribute to paper history. One result was my *Papermaking in Britain, 1488 – 1988, A Short History* which was published in 1988.

The first year of the actual production of paper in Britain still remains in dispute but that year seems as good as any from the available evidence. Once again the IPH met in Britain. We started in Durham where I was allocated the magnificent suite of the bishop in the castle. We went to Fourstones paper mill near Hexham which George owned and where he had preserved the old papermaking machine then no longer in use. I had the honour of cutting the white tape and declaring the display open.

Sadly one night there was a break-in and some of the precious metal dandy rolls and brasses were stolen. We then adjourned to Hertford and the site of the first definite paper mill in Britain, Sele Mill. Henry VIII visited this in 1498 but it had been established a little earlier. A blue plaque was unveiled on the side of the mill.

DR RICHARD L. HILLS

PAPERMAKING
IN BRITAIN
1488–1988

A Short History

The Master Copy,
Richard L. Hills

THE ATHLONE PRESS
London and Atlantic Highlands, NJ

Back in London, George had been organising a stained glass window to commemorate 'Paper 500' in Stationers' Hall. It was unveiled on 22 June 1988 at a small ceremony.

At the special banquet in the Guildhall later in October, George asked me to say the grace, a somewhat terrifying experience in front of so many people.

> Almighty God, for the great achievements of our past inheritance, we thank you.
> For the future of our papermaking industry, we pray for your guidance.
> And on this meal, we ask for your blessing, through Jesus Christ our Lord.

Founding the British Association of Paper Historians

The 1988 IPH Congress had been well attended by people from Britain so a meeting was called at Butlers Court in the following February to see whether there might be enough support to start a British Association of Paper Historians. We launched the BAPH with a meeting in Manchester November 1989. One of its most important functions was the publication of its journal, *The Quarterly*, which still continues to go from strength to strength under the editorship of Peter Bower who is well-known internationally for his expertise as a forensic paper scientist. This has provided the outlet for over forty of my articles, covering the history of various mills, watermarking techniques, the early paper machine, James Watt's uses of paper and much more.

My Activities in Paper History

Over the following years, as well as helping in the church at Mottram, I was actively helping and running various conferences, societies and lecturing. I will give brief synopses of two years, 1990 and 1993. In 1990, I was invited to the celebrations of 600 Years of Papermaking in Germany at Nuremberg. At the IPH Congress in Belgium I retired as President after ten years and gave a paper on 'Steam Power in Papermaking'. At the BAPH Conference at Wookey Hole, I gave a paper on 'The Cylinder Mould Machine' which was later published in the BAPH *Quarterly*. For *The Quarterly*, I also wrote an article, 'Some Notes on the Matthias Koops' Papers'. That autumn I replaced Joe Marsh at UMIST during his sabbatical and took over his lecturing duties. In addition, for many years I gave lectures to the third year UMIST Paper Scientists on the history of papermaking. In 1993, for the Mottram WEA, I gave a 10 week course on 'Architectural Achievements at Work and Worship'. I was invited in February to lecture to the Stationers' Company on 'John Tate, England's First Papermaker', which was subsequently published.

For the BAPH, I organised the Oxford Conference in September and presented papers on 'The Use of Straw in Papermaking' and 'James Watt and His Copying Machine'. For *The Quarterly*, I wrote, 'The Schoolmaster Mill, the Netherlands' and 'James Watt and Papermaking'. I was elected onto the Council of the Newcomen Society and chaired a meeting at Liverpool on

John Tate talk follows on from Cakes and Ale

THE TRADITIONAL 'Cakes and Ale' Ash Wednesday luncheon on February 24 was attended this year by nearly 200 Company members and their guests, reflecting the increasing interest in Company functions following the improvements and refurbishments of the Hall during recent years and the excellent standard attained by our in-house catering staff.

After lunch the Company procession headed by the Beadle, Renter Wardens, Master, Upper & Under Wardens and Court in ceremonial mediaeval caps and gowns followed by the large number of members and guests attracted unusual attention from the visitors on the front steps of St Paul's as we entered though the side entrance for our service in St Faith's Chapel underneath the Cathedral.

George Mandl with Dr Richard Hills.

Service

The service was conducted by our Chaplain, Canon John Oates, but the Sermon was given unusually by The Right Reverend Edward Holland, Suffran Bishop of Gibraltar in Europe, who has a roving commission throughout Europe and happened to be in London at that time. In deference to our publishing connections he expressed the importance of the correct use of language which he felt had been devalued in recent times and stressed that words are precious things citing 'God's word, trust and love'.

Our Company choir directed by Liveryman Arthur Fosh was particularly effective and added greatly to the enjoyment of the service.

On return to the Hall approximately 90 of those present attended a lecture in the Court Room where the Master introduced the speaker, Dr Richard Hills, a distinguished authority in the field of papermaking and President of the International Paper Historians Association.

His subject was 'John Tate, Britain's first papermaker' and he traced the history of the Tate family and John's foray into papermaking 500 years ago and his family's association with the City. Dr Hills showed all known John Tate watermarks but the Master played a trump card by producing an actual sheet of paper made by John Tate taken from a recently acquired leaf book in the Company Library.

'Engineering Biographies'. To help celebrate the 900 anniversary of its oldest watermarked sheet of paper in its collections, the paper museum in Fabriano invited me to speak on 'Light and Dark Watermarks; Some English Contributions to their development'. This was printed in *The Quarterly* for 1994 along with 'Christmas at Matthias Koops' Mill'. I edited and prepared the triple index for A.H. Shorter, *Studies on the History of Papermaking in Britain* published by Variorum. For the Buxton WEA, I repeated the course of lectures on 'Architectural Achievements at Work and Worship'. I received a travel grant from the Royal Society for my Watt researches. In 1996, I was elected an Honorary Member of the British Association of Paper Historians.

The British Association
of Paper Historians

Please reply to

Richard Hills
Stamford Cottage
47 Old Road
Mottram, Hyde
Cheshire, SK14 6LW

ALAN & GLENYS CROCKER
6 BURWOOD CLOSE
GUILDFORD, SURREY
GU1 2SB   (01483) 565821
NGR TQ 025 506
A.CROCKER@PH.SURREY.AC.UK

13 August 1996

Dear Richard

I am delighted to be able to inform you that, at the Annual General Meeting of the British Association of Paper Historians held at Edinburgh on 7 July, it was proposed and agreed with acclaim that you should become an Honorary Member of the Association in recognition of your contributions to our knowledge and understanding of the history of paper making in Britain and elsewhere and, in particular ,your work in establishing and supporting the Association.

We hope very much that you will agree to accept this position.

Yours sincerely

Professor Alan Crocker, DSc CEng FSA
Chairman, BAPH

Italy

Much has been omitted but this takes me to Italy where I was able to present some significant papers and received perhaps my greatest recognition as a paper historian. In 1991, I was invited to present a paper at the prestigious Economic Historians' Annual Meeting at Prato organised by the Istituto Internazionale di Storia Economica 'F. Datini' on 'Early Italian Papermaking' to be followed the next year by 'From Cocoon to Cloth'. I took advantage of being close by to see the Leaning Tower of Pisa and that cathedral. Another attraction was Florence with the statue of David, that cathedral and baptistery, other churches as well as the little science museum at the end of the Ponte Vecchio with its magnificent collection of British late seventeenth and early eighteenth scientific instruments. Almost as important, I discovered where in the University there was a free toilet!

It was in Italy that I would receive the final recognition of my work as a paper historian. The great paper mill of Cartiere Miliani at Fabriano was supporting the museum there and was preserving its own history as well as that of papermaking generally. In its basement were the original stampers of around 1300. With their heritage of introducing watermarks, they still produced a few of their fabulous three-dimensional or shadow watermarks.

At Christmas, I looked forward to receiving one. People there would have known about my papers at Prato as well as my leadership of both IPH and BAHP. In addition to the IPH Congress at Fabriano, I went to other meetings organised by the mill. In 2006, they printed my 'Importance of Early Italian Paper and Papermaking in Britain' in their *Congress Book of European Paper Days*. I was surprised in 2014 to receive a letter from the

Gianfranco Fedrigoni Foundation of the European Institute for the History of Paper and the Science of Papermaking that their Administrative Council had conferred on me Honorary Membership. This was in recognition of the excellence of the research and promotion of the study of the history of paper through my many publications. However by that date, my Parkison's was affecting my ability to travel so I could not go to receive it.

China

As an historian of technology, the high point of my papermaking interests came in 2002 and 2004 when I joined the visits to China organised by the Americans, Dr. Sydney and Elaine Koretsky.

Their passion for studying the origins of paper in China led them to travel extensively throughout that country and elsewhere in Eastern Asia where they sought out handmade papermakers and techniques in places quite unknown in the West. I will merge the two trips into one for brevity. We went on a sort of pilgrimage to Lei-yang in Hunan province where it is claimed that Tsi-Lun the eunuch first made paper in AD 105. His descendants still make

paper by hand there today! From Singapore and Hangchow in the East we would go to Chen-du in the West on the borders of Tibet. We were the first Europeans seen by some villagers where the toilet facilities are best not described. Our accommodation could be equally variable from modern hotels in tower blocks where the thirteenth floor was left unoccupied (as being unlucky) to rooms in remote villages with just the basic needs.

I was struck by the variety of papermaking that we saw. For example we in the West made our paper sometimes from straw, more usually from cotton or linen rags but the bulk from wood. Perhaps due to the remoteness of their mills, the Chinese made greater use of local materials. For example in Tibet, the root of the Stellera Chamaejasme was dug up. Bamboo, Gramineae, was a common material for cheaper papers. Dragon's beard grass was another. Better quality paper was sourced from the bast fibres on the branches of the String Bush, Wikstroemia Delavaye; the best came from the paper mulberry, Broussonetia Papyrefera. The old folk in the villages could be usefully employed stripping off the brown outer bark and any other impurities. Softening the fibres might be achieved either by soaking them in water-filled pits or steaming them in boilers with soda ash.

While in the West the roll or Hollander beater became almost universal, nearly every mill we visited in China had a different method of pulping their fibres. Beating by hand with a stout stick or mallet was a woman's task. A man operated a single head stamper while a woman, presumably his wife, pushed the fibres under the heavy stone head, hopefully keeping her fingers well out of the way. More usually it was the kollergang or edge runner with a single vertical stone. At one place, the river was dammed and diverted to turn a horizontal impulse wheel. The rocks in the water were extremely slippery so unfortunately the person carrying Sydney's cine-camera fell in and the camera was ruined. Other power sources were oxen, water buffalo and even electric motor.

At nearly every mill we visited, a formation aid was added to the pulp. This was a sort of treacle-like viscous liquid derived from a variety of plants such as wild kiwi, cactus, hibiscus, pine bark or roots. Some shavings were cut off a branch of pine and put in a bag. After a few minutes of immersion in the papermaking vat, the juice was squeezed out and stirred into the pulp. It delayed drainage of water while the sheet was being formed.

A primitive method of sheet formation was seen in the remote village of Dimen, south West China, about two hundred miles from the place where Tsai Lun lived. We were welcomed by the village band and a drink from a teapot which proved to be strong rice wine. The Dong villagers turned out in all their traditional dress and I was given an escort of two young ladies.

My boots were considerably larger than their shoes! Pulp was poured into a mould which took about five minutes to form the sheet. It was 32 ½ ins. (81 cm. square), considerably larger than most paper made by hand in the West where the largest hand-made sheet, Antiquarian, was 53 in. (135 cm) by 31 ins. (79 cm).

After lunch, we were proudly invited into a house to see their new electric light. One bulb glowed feebly in the ceiling. They had forgotten about voltage drop over long distances. Another time, we joined in the festivities of the Miao people. The elderly lady sitting next to me was amazed by my hairy arms and could not resist stroking one! We were invited to dance with the locals.

We flew up to the city of Cheng Du in North West China where a visit to the giant pandas was obligatory. Here we saw some of the largest sheets of paper being made by hand. At Jia Jiang, one man was regularly making sheets 60 ins. (152 cm.) by 33 ins. (84 cm.) Two men were needed to manipulate moulds 8 ft. 6 ins. (259 cm.) by 4 ft. 3 ins. (130 cm.) taking about two minutes to form a sheet. They even produced sheets about 13 ft. (396 cm.) by 6 ft. (183 cm.) which must be the largest sheets of paper made by hand. Such sheets were far too large to handle in the usual way so they had devised special methods of handling and drying them. Here we may find clues about the way the large sheets of paper seen in eighteenth century Chinese wallpaper were made which were bigger than any manufactured in the West.

Dege

What was undoubtedly the highlight of both visits to China was the printing house at Dege in Tibet. It took three days to drive 600 miles across passes of 14,000 and 16,000 feet. We made the journey after the snows had melted but even so had to battle through snowstorms. We were glad we were not pilgrims making their way to Lhasa by prostrating themselves and then crawling those couple of yards. As our coach struggled up the mud roads over the high passes, we had plenty of time to admire the skill of the engineers who laid out the routes to maintain a steady gradient around mountain spurs and zigzagging up the steep rocky sides. But this had been achieved at great loss of human life, in some parts one person for every metre. A spring on our coach broke and another time a tyre burst but both repairs were carried out in quite remote villages, something we could not have done in our civilised west.

On reaching Dege, we saw a temple being reconstructed with modern electrically driven tools such as

routers and sanders fashioning the new tall wooden pillars supporting the roof. These were magnificent pieces of timber. The interior walls were painted with brightly coloured scenes, contrasting with the darkness of the interior. Nearby, paper was being made on the floating mould from the root of the Stellera Chamaejasme. The mould 39 ins. (90 cm.) by 27 ½ ins. (69 cm.) floated in a vat of water. Pulp was poured in, spread across the surface and lifted out carefully otherwise the pulp rushed to one side. Ten sheets were made a day and left to dry over night.

The printing house was founded in 1729 by King Tempa Tsering and later enlarged so it now has over 270,000 wooden printing plates. This treasure was almost destroyed in 1966 during the Cultural Revolution but saved by two people locking themselves in the library. It was authorised to reopen in 1979, printing on Chinese machine-made paper, and in 1987 reopened for worship. Every morning, people would walk round the outside, whirling their prayer wheels around with the prayers written on slips of paper inside.

The handmade paper here is used for larger prints. One of the smaller printing blocks takes about a day to carve by hand. Red ink is used for Buddha's words translated into Tibetan and black for most other texts. These texts are read in monasteries. The printers work in pairs sitting opposite each other. One bends over to ink the plate. As he straightens up, his partner bends over and places the paper on the plate. As he straightens up, the first runs a roller across the paper, pressing the paper onto the ink, bending over and straightening up again to allow his partner to bend over once more and lift the paper off. With this alternate bobbing back and forth, they could print a thousand sheets as day. As in other buildings connected with Buddhism, the interior walls were decorated colourfully.

The opportunity was taken to visit other craft industries and see early techniques. Rice fields were irrigated by 'norias', undershot waterwheels that lifted water from the river into the fields. Streams were also diverted to power simple corn-grinding mills with small horizontal wheels similar to those found in Scandinavia and the one on Shetland. Textile manufacture was also seen. Weaving plain cotton cloth with an ordinary shuttle or making beautiful silk carpets by hand were other crafts. But perhaps it was the dyeing of fabrics that interested me most for we saw both batik and tie and dye methods. I came home laden with samples not only of textiles but also of paper. We celebrated a birthday of one of our party with both a cake and a sort of candle in the form of a bud of a flower. The candle was lit and suddenly the bud burst open eight petals, each with a candle. Then it started playing 'Happy birthday'. We told our guide how impressed we were with the device. On the morning of our departure, he pressed a package into my hand. I put it into my suitcase which was not examined at the airport. Only when I opened it at home did I realise that I had been carrying an explosive device. There was not the same terrorist threat in those days.

The reason for carrying back loads of paper samples was that I wanted to examine why paper triumphed over its main rivals, papyrus and parchment. Experience gained over the intervening years led me to write *Papyrus, Parchment and Paper* which looked at mainly writing materials across the world. I hoped that it might be published together with samples and photographs taken during my many visits abroad. It would have augmented *Papermaking in Britain* by showing how papermaking spread from China until it arrived in our country. However it was a dream not fulfilled in its entire concept as the economic situation deteriorated into a world-wide slump. The colour slides went to the Mills Archive in Reading and the paper samples to the Conservators. The text was serialised in *The Quarterly*. So all was not lost.

The Reverend Doctor
Part 3 – Ordained Scientist

O love that wilt not let me go, I rest my weary soul in thee;
I give thee back the life I owe,
That in thine ocean depths its flow may richer, fuller be.

G. Matheson, (1842 – 1906)

Looking back over my life, I can see how God has guided me throughout although I did not always recognise it at the time. How often did I wish that,

Thy hand, O God, has guided thy flock, from age to age;
The wondrous tale is written, full clear on every page.

C.H. Plumptree, (1841 – 1891)

So often the way ahead did not seem clear yet when I looked back I could see how fortunate I had been. First there were the three families, Tomsons, Millers and Hills, all of whom went regularly to church and expected their offspring to do likewise. Not only was there the background of an ordained father who hoped his son would go into the church but there were the bishops in the Allison family as well. There was the recognition that we should serve the community, for instance in the case of Audrey helping at the Time and Talents Club in Bermondsey and Uncle Stan working for the Sheikh of Bahrain.

At both Rose Hill School and Charterhouse there were firm Christian traditions with regular morning prayers and scripture lessons. It would be at school that I first met other boys who doubted the Christian faith. There were some who had not been baptised, in the case of one because his parents wanted him to make a definite commitment. Others were more hostile. But this was more than balanced by the PPS Camps where there were active definitely committed Christians professing a more liberal view such as John Habgood who became Archbishop of York. National Service was a definite eye-opener where scepticism was much more forthright and I was grateful for the support of other Christians in the barrack rooms.

At Cambridge, I was more involved in the Liberal rather than the Evangelical wing of the church where I felt more comfortable. Here again there were opportunities for helping church organisations in various ways such as the Church Missionary Society. This was where I wished that the tale was written 'full clear' because I had to make difficult decisions about a future career whether at home or overseas. The climbing accident gave me a definite assurance of the Love of God that He would not let me go, even if the way ahead was sometimes shrouded. At Earnley, I was able to establish a tradition of worship for the boys and assist at Worcester College for the Blind. If going overseas did not work out, there was plenty I could do at home for example helping with the Styal Village Fellowship.

Office of Reader

When I first moved to Mottram, I did not at once offer as a Reader because there was so much to do for the Museum and the house itself. Therefore it was not until September 1971 that Chester Diocese officially licensed me to serve at St. Michael and All Angels under Canon Roch.

While we did have the occasional curate, these became less frequently allocated to Mottram so the sort of pattern we established was that I would take the morning service at St. Mary Magdalene, Broadbottom, while he took the communion service at the main church. We swapped round the following Sunday which saved preparing one sermon. I also helped in other ways such as the Lent evening services with their series of talks. I had been out to the Holy Land in 1972 with father and Audrey and taken many colour slides. I suggested showing them one evening as part of the Lent course. I could see Canon Roch thinking, 'Not slides in church' so we adjourned to the

---

Certificate of Admission to the Office of a Reader

WE, G E R A L D   A L E X A N D E R , by Divine Permission Lord Bishop of Chester, do make it known unto all men that on the day of the date hereof we did admit our beloved in Christ

RICHARD   LESLIE   HILLS

(of whose godly life and conversation, training, and knowledge of the Holy Scriptures and of the Christian Doctrine, we were well assured) to the Office of a Reader in the Church.

IN testimony whereof we have hereunto set our hand to these presents.

DATED the   25th   day of   September ——— in the Year of Our Lord one thousand nine hundred and   Seventyone and in the   Seventeenth ———   year of our Translation.

Gerald Cestr.

This Certificate of Admission gives no authority to exercise the Office of a Reader in any Diocese except under Licence from the Bishop of the Diocese.

---

school near-by. When later I did show slides in church, the screen had to be placed high up for people to see and the projector was at a steep angle. I pressed the button to change a slide. Disaster, the slide carrier fell out of the back of the projector onto the floor, scattering the slides.

That trip to the Holy Land was one of two which gave me a great insight to the background of the Bible which has helped to bring to life much of my teaching about Christianity. They occurred at different times of the year which meant I saw the country in spring at Easter and in the autumn when it looked quite different. Easter in Jerusalem was memorable with all the Palm Sunday processions and re-enactment of the Passion of Christ. The financial backing of my ill-health retirement meant that I could give my services to the church free of charge. With so much to do as Reader, was there any point in being ordained priest?

This must be answered in two ways. First, there were the limitations of a Reader when certain services such as Holy Communion and marriages were prohibited for me to take. Second, there was the possible call from God that this was the course that I should follow. This had to be tested by the diocesan authorities. First I had to see the Director of Ordinands to confirm that I had a genuine vocation. Then I was sent over to Bishop Gerald of Chester who gave me another grilling but was willing to sponsor me to attend a Selection Conference of the Advisory Council for the Church's Ministry.

General Synod of the Church of England
ADVISORY COUNCIL FOR THE CHURCH'S MINISTRY
Church House Dean's Yard London SW1P 3NZ. Telephone 01-222 9011

WMJ/PFM   30 January 1985

Dr R L Hills
Stamford Cottage
47 Old Road
Mottram
Hyde
Cheshire SK14 6LW

Dear Dr Hills

        I am pleased to hear that the Bishop of Chester wishes to sponsor you for a Selection Conference.

        I am writing to invite you to a Conference to be held at Chester, from April 29th to May 1st, 1985. The Conference will start at 2.15 pm on the first day and you will be free to leave by 4.30 pm on the final day.

I was unable to attend one at the end of April 1985 at Chester possibly through being committed to helping at a parish mission in Mottram. Instead I went to Riding Mill, Northumberland, later that May. Further grilling by their teams followed before I learnt that I had been recommended for training for the Church's Ministry. I was hauled before Gerald again who, being an evangelical, told me to sell up Mottram, buy a house in Nottingham and go to St. John's Theological College. He had no idea of my library and contents of Stamford Cottage and I disobeyed him.

St. Deiniol's Library

Instead, I remembered Frank Smith, the one armed 'bandit' of Styal showing me where he had been trained for his ministry, St. Deiniol's Library at Hawarden. This was a residential library set up by William Gladstone, the former Prime-minister. He filled it with his theological books and equipped it with a splendid reading room, small chapel, dining room, lounge and bedrooms where visitors with a suitable recommendation could stay while studying the books.

Saint Deiniol's
RESIDENTIAL Library
Hawarden

DEESIDE
CLWYD CH5 3DF   0244 53 2350

The Revd. P.J. Jagger, M.A., M.Phil., F.R.Hist.S.
Warden and Chief Librarian.

Peter Jagger was the somewhat formidable Warden while I was there. His bark was worse than his bite. He was trying to bring the place up to contemporary standards with plumbing in the bedrooms, better lecturing and dining facilities and, after I had left, a proper lecture room and larger chapel. He established a book conservation department to better equip the Library. He advertised the Library both in this country and especially in North America. We met many interesting people from the Bishop of Portsmouth to the Bishop of Alaska. He was running two courses for ordinands, one full and the other part time. The part-timers came every other weekend during term for lectures and tutorials on a longer course than the two-year full-time one. Full-timers were there during the week and the alternate weekends. This enabled me to return to Stamford Cottage every other weekend to see all was well. I had lodging there the former caretaker from the Museum who had just retired from being a Purchasing Officer at UMIST. At least the place was occupied.

St. Deiniol's Library teaching staff seated with Peter Jagger in the centre. The full and part time ordinands stand behind with myself fourth from right.

My fellow ordinands came from a great variety of backgrounds. There was the Professor of Gynaecology from Liverpool University, a retired police officer, a school teacher, an engineer, a librarian and others. Most of these could easily leave their former occupations but I found that my advice was constantly sought about history of technology. The full-timers had tutorials and seminars during the week. There were singing lessons so we could lead services properly. Morning and Evening Prayer were held in the chapel at which we took turns to officiate. Once when I was setting up the altar, I found the candles had almost burnt away so I searched in the vestry for new ones. There was a pair of rather brownish ones which I put on the altar. Our Deputy Warden, Michael Burgess, was furious when he saw them. He thought we were playing tricks with him and had put pink candles out to celebrate his birthday. We were unaware that he was colour blind and could not see that I had inadvertently chosen special pure beeswax requiem candles.

In the afternoons, we were expected to do some community work. Help in the garden was one where I was able to improve the performance of the lawn mower with parts from Stamford Cottage. We also went further afield with our pastoral training which took us to a local Primary School. How could we help? One suggestion was swimming lessons. The teachers had to supervise from the edge of the pool and were not allowed to go in the water. Could we join the pupils in the pool and keep the learners' noses above the water? I volunteered for this and stayed on after the school lessons to improve my swimming so that eventually I was able to cover seventy five lengths.

I had my first computer while at St. Deiniol's, an Amstrad. Peter Jagger said it was no excuse if the computer swallowed an essay so it could not be handed in on time. I found the theological use of some ordinary English terms a strange new language to be mastered. Some of our Welsh colleagues found it very difficult to write their essays in English because written Welsh can be quite different from spoken. It was here that the bulk of *Papermaking in Britain* was composed to meet the deadline of publishing ready for 'Paper 500' in 1988. Also I was working on *Power from Steam*.

St. Clements, Urmston

I left St. Deiniol's having passed the General Ordination Examination (God's Own Exam) with yet another academic hood to be ordained Deacon by Stanley, Bishop of Manchester, on Sunday 27th October 1987, in Manchester Cathedral to serve in the parish of St. Clements, Urmston.

I well remember the first Communion service I took at St. Clements and the sense of awe I felt as I lifted up the bread and the wine. As curate, I was expected to assist at the Sunday 8 o'clock Communion service. One Sunday, our vicar failed to appear. I prepared everything and waited. He had forgotten the change in hour. Christmas was always a busy period. There could be problems when people left the pubs

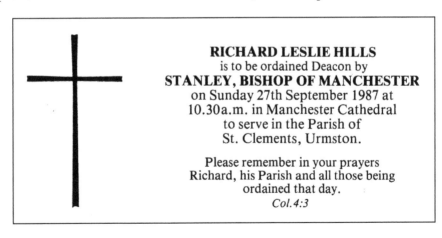

RICHARD LESLIE HILLS
is to be ordained Deacon by
STANLEY, BISHOP OF MANCHESTER
on Sunday 27th September 1987 at
10.30a.m. in Manchester Cathedral
to serve in the Parish of
St. Clements, Urmston.

Please remember in your prayers
Richard, his Parish and all those being
ordained that day.
Col.4:3

and came to church for the midnight service. The Reader and I were assisting with the chalice, taking it in pairs down the line of kneeling communicants. I came to a man I did not recognise. He seized the chalice and before I could stop him, drank most of it. I carried on and noticed he did not return to his seat. The Reader came to him and before I could stop him, he drank most of the second chalice, put his hands up in thanks and left the church.

I certainly learnt how the other three quarters of the world lived while I was in Urmston. I took communion to the sick and housebound and visited many others. There was a complaint that I had not been when I knew I had. I realised that my visit had triggered that person's memory about communion but had forgotten I had been. I made my peace with my vicar. After a year, I was ordained priest, again by the Bishop of Manchester, in the Cathedral on 2nd October 1988. This time, Audrey, Margaret, Bob and John were present.

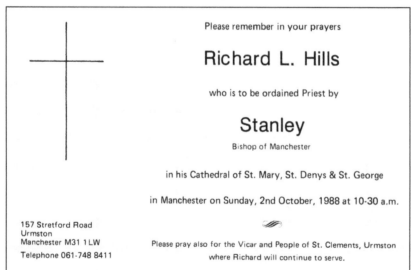

Please remember in your prayers

Richard L. Hills

who is to be ordained Priest by

Stanley

Bishop of Manchester

in his Cathedral of St. Mary, St. Denys & St. George

in Manchester on Sunday, 2nd October, 1988 at 10-30 a.m.

157 Stretford Road
Urmston
Manchester M31 1LW   Please pray also for the Vicar and People of St. Clements, Urmston
Telephone 061-748 8411   where Richard will continue to serve.

The parish was split in two by the motor way. My curate's house was on the main road on the St. Clement's side but on the further side was the Branch Church. This had been some sort of sports pavilion before being converted into a place of worship. Housing had grown up all round it so it had its own community with local shops. The roof was leaking and the space outside overgrown. My building experience at Stamford Cottage was useful here because we had the flat roof resurfaced and the front parapet over the toilets, kitchen and vestry rebuilt. On Saturday mornings, a coffee morning might be held but, for the finances, more important was the Miniature Car Club run by the organist, Alan Crossland. A track was laid out and the model cars raced against each other. Their hire of the room and other assistance such as tidying the garden helped support the Branch Church.

The Branch Church had a strong youth group which I surprised with one sermon saying that I could convert water into wine. Only I needed sugar and yeast and took a few weeks which Jesus did immediately. I took the confirmation class for the twelve year olds to find that there was no suitable confirmation course literature available. So I proceeded to produce my own. I offered it to the diocese which showed no interest although other priests did. Every week at the parish church, there was an evening surgery to which people came wanting to arrange baptisms, weddings, etc. One couple came with three children, one a baby in arms, inquiring about baptism. Having arranged for the baby, they discussed about having the other two baptised and then 'Now for the wedding'. I nearly fell through the floor.

Edwin Banks, Alan Crossland, David Barron & Richard

One person who helped at the Branch Church was David Barron. He was orphaned and brought up in a mental institution so had no formal education. He lived on his own but had taught himself to read slowly. He had an amazing memory of his early life and managed to have it written down in various books. He went around giving talks about the conditions in those institutions. He helped me by cleaning the curate's house and later after I had left Urmston, he was pleased to come to the peace of Stamford Cottage and help there. He was just one of the many friends I made at Urmston whom I missed when I left for Great Yarmouth.

The National Three Peaks climb.

Climb Every Mountain!

Try sleeping with 1960's pop music blaring as you are sitting jammed upright to prevent you sliding off your seat when the minibus screeches round another sharp bend on the highland roads, racing at mid-night from Ben Nevis back to England. It's quite easy really if you have just climbed 4,500 feet up Britain's highest mountain.

Ben Nevis was the first peak tackled. Problems such as no jack for the minibus and our walking leader, Geoff Howard, having to take a funeral, were overcome so nine out of ten climbers reached the top of the Ben at 9 o'clock in the evening. Wonderful views for quite remarkably there was no cloud on the summit.

The darkness held off long enough for us to return to our transport but all too soon in the grey light of dawn, we left Seathwaite for the long trek of Scawfell. Only the swallows watched us leave at 4.15a.m. There was no sign of our leader in the car and we learnt later that it had started to make expensive sounding noises but reached Seathwaite soon after the main party had left where it was abandoned. The score on Scawfell was seven out of ten. Those who did not manage it missed a glorious dawn with clear summits

everywhere. However, the cloud was gathering, pouring like a glacier over Skiddaw and filling the valleys. We descended into the mist with the sheep bleating like foghorns to guide us on our way.

The Miner's Track up Snowdon at two in the afternoon become hotter and hotter. Clouds hovered menacingly overhead like vultures waiting to pounce but remarkably the summit remained clear and once again we had splendid views. Is this a record, three clear peaks? Nine climbers plus one drive made Snowdon.

Congratulations to Sam for climbing after the support car had broken down. Congratulations to Jenny for being the only lady to manage all three peaks, and also Jonathan for being the only person going to India to do so as well. Above all, our many thanks to Keith Smalldon for organising the trip with his splendid driving and, of course, arranging the excellent weather.
Richard Hills
(Curate, St. Clement, Urmston)

Confirmations

Sunday September 12th: 10.00am, CLIFTON GREEN, St. Thomas (Hulme)

But before leaving Manchester, I was able to assist the diocese by being one of the leaders on two of their sponsored National Three Peaks climbs. We left Manchester in the afternoon for the drive up to Fort William. We reached the top of the Ben at 9 o'clock in the evening with wonderful clear views. An overnight drive in the 'comfort' of a minibus took us to Seathwaite which we left at 4.15 am for Scafell. That dawn was glorious with clear summits. We started up the Miners' Track up Snowdon at 2 o'clock where the summit again was clear. My walking time was 12 hours 7 seconds, a memorable finish to Manchester diocese.

St. Paul's, Great Yarmouth

After two years at Urmston, it was time to broaden my experience. The possibility of being an industrial chaplain in the oil industry attracted me to accept the curacy of St. Paul's, Great Yarmouth. This was one of four churches that were joined together under the mother church of St. Nicholas, claimed to be the largest parish church in England. I was licensed by the Archdeacon of Norwich on 14 December 1989.

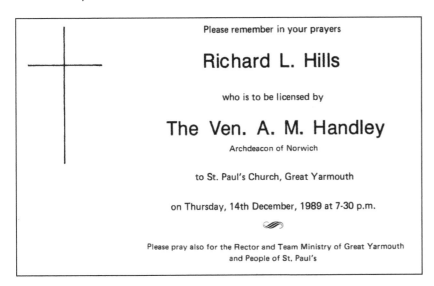

Please remember in your prayers

Richard L. Hills

who is to be licensed by

The Ven. A. M. Handley

Archdeacon of Norwich

to St. Paul's Church, Great Yarmouth

on Thursday, 14th December, 1989 at 7-30 p.m.

Please pray also for the Rector and Team Ministry of Great Yarmouth
and People of St. Paul's

St. Nicholas had been bombed during the war and restored with sand dug up from the shore. The salt it contained caused the cement to rot so that St. Nicholas was in urgent need of repair. Naturally the Rector considered this to be his first priority but the licensing service showed that St. Paul's also was neglected with the buckets put out to catch the rain pouring through the roof.

St. Paul's consisted of two buildings, the main church, a wooden framed building in Tudor style, and an adjacent brick church hall. I was able to convince the Rector that it would be best

to spend a small sum and make St. Paul's weather-tight to prevent further deterioration. He agreed and then to concentrate on St. Nicholas. As well as reroofing and treating the timber, part of the interior was redecorated and a microphone system installed, which was a great help to me as well as others. A disabled group held meetings in the hall. I was concerned about all the mess the resident pigeons made which might bring disease so I waged a constant war against these persistent birds but we were able to clean the hall up as well. In the yard outside, we held fund-raising events such as fairs and barbeques manned by our small gang of devoted supporters. At the great summer fair at St. Nicholas, Leslie Kenny demonstrated weaving while I was spinning. Both created much interest.

The members of the clergy team were expected to attend Morning and Evening Prayer at St. Nicholas. On Sunday evening, adjournment to the near-by hostelry followed. I realised that the best means of transport around the town was bicycle and even the Rector followed my example. It was useful to get to the swimming pool on the front for an early morning dip or even to go further afield to the coast at Horsey where there was bird-watching on the marshes and swimming in the sea. To assist in the preservation of Norfolk churches, a sponsored bike ride was organised. I covered fifty miles and must have called at over twenty churches, all needing restoration funds. It was tragic to see murals from the Middle Ages deteriorating on the walls.

There was the usual parochial work of visiting the sick and others. Perhaps we had rather more funerals than most parishes through the many people who came to retire in Great Yarmouth. There were also weddings and baptisms. At one baptism, I tried singing to a recording of 'All things bright and beautiful' but the speed of my domestic tape recorder was too fast for the congregation to keep up. One advantage was the fresh sea-food available in the shops as well as Yarmouth bloaters. The town would have been very run-down but for the holiday trade which saved it from further decline. The parish hired a house temporarily for me but could not find another suitable one for a permanent residence. The industrial chaplaincy in the oil industry never materialised. I realised that I was becoming overworked with parish duties and the constant requests for my historical knowledge. When I learnt that UIMST was looking for a temporary replacement for Joe Marsh in the History of Science and Technology Department, I decided to apply. The Bishop of Norwich sent me a nice letter of thanks for all I had done at St. Paul's.

BISHOP'S HOUSE
NORWICH

1st October 1990

Dear Richard,

    As your last few days at Yarmouth are approaching I wanted to send you my warmest good wishes, and to thank you for all your work during your time with us. I hope all the arrangements for your move will go smoothly, and that you will find the coming years both fulfilling and rewarding.

    With all good wishes,

        Yours sincerely,

Society of Ordained Scientists

It must have been while I was at Great Yarmouth that I heard about a group of Ordained Scientists who sought to sustain each other in prayer and fellowship. John Habgood was their visitor so I decided to apply for membership. But I had no degree or similar qualification in science so I was rejected. I do not know why the Committee reconsidered my application yet their minds were changed and I was admitted as a Life Member in 1989. I went to the Annual Gathering at Launde Abbey that year, the first of many. This story will be continued later because it was a case of 'The stone that the builders rejected has become the head corner stone'.

Return to Manchester

Leaving Great Yarmouth was another instance of saying good bye to many friends. When I took Bernice there, she was surprised at how many I had. I arrived back in Manchester just in time for the start of the new academic year which left little time to prepare the courses of lectures I would be giving. These included a general History of Science Course for first year undergraduates and another one for the mechanical engineers as well as the four lectures I gave annually to the paper science students. In addition, there was research on windmills because *Power from Steam* had been published and it seemed that a sequel, *Power from Wind*, might be worth considering based on all the windmills I had seen in East Anglia. The main point was that History of Science and Technology continued at UMIST until the return of Joe Marsh.

Having ascertained that there was nothing untoward about my leaving the diocese of Norwich, I was granted permission by Chester to be a non-stipendary minister for them. During this year at UMIST, my clerical duties were confined mainly to taking the early 8 o'clock communion service at Mottram because the tradition there was just a plain service with no sermon. However when full-time teaching finished and I was giving lecture courses for the WEA, I realised that there was a niche I could fill for the deanery. With the number of full-time priests declining and curates being scarcer and scarcer, I could help take services when the regular clergy took well-earned holidays. In addition, for many years, there was an interregnum in one parish or another and I found a welcome ministry in helping take communion services when no other priest was available. In this way, I became known to the congregations of around a dozen parishes in the Mottram deanery. For me, it was interesting to meet so many people.

I had to be careful to help Mottram itself. I reused some of the courses I had prepared while at Urmston in discussion groups as well as seeing that I took at least one service a month. In my sermons, I aimed to give some teaching about the background of the Bible because I found that even long-established members of our church had very little knowledge of our faith. The Holy Land visits featured and in addition I turned to my classical background with my knowledge of Greek. The greater wealth of meaning in the Greek was useful material in a sermon. Stamford Cottage was a comfortable place in which small groups could meet while garden parties could be held outside.

Mountainwalking Leader and HF Holidays

While I was working for the Outward Bound, my competence in the mountains was vouchsafed by that organisation. If I were to take groups of parishioners, I realised that I would need some sort of official recognition. Therefore I registered for a Mountainwalking Leader qualification and joined a Basic Training Course at Plas-y-Brenin in July 1988.

THE

MOUNTAINWALKING

LEADER TRAINING

BOARD

MOUNTAINWALKING

LEADER TRAINING

SCHEME

(Summer)

LOG BOOK

Their Mountaineering First Aid Course that I attended in November 1989 I found very helpful. The much tougher conditions prevailing in mountaineering accidents meant we had to be more self-reliant compared with ordinary first aid where help could arrive quickly. A weather course taught me a lot and I went for assessment in 1994 but failed on rope work. It was difficult to practise this without being on rocks for abseiling but, with more training, I passed in November 1997. Later, I helped my vicar in Mottram to gain his!

In the meantime, I had heard about HF Holidays. In those days, it was still following the vision of its founder through providing reasonably priced walking holidays with a Christian Fellowship background. I saw an advertisement for their holidays abroad and went for a week to Telfes, Austria, in June 1991. I soon found myself helping the weaker, less experienced members and enjoyed searching for the Alpine spring flowers. I followed this that September with one of their Ridges and Scrambles weeks around Glen Coe and Ben Nevis. Someone suggested that I should become an HF Leader. Accordingly, I attended a Leader Assessment Course at Bryn Corach, Conway, in June 1992. With my interest in industrial history, I thought I might run some special interest weeks on that subject. In addition with my experience of travel abroad, I offered to be an Abroad Leader. That required a probationary period leading in Britain before a second assessment course at Monks Coniston, Lake District, in February 1992. I had been taking evening classes in French at Glossop to refresh that as my foreign language and was accepted.

I organised a few special interest weeks in North Wales and around the Brecon Beacons combining short walks with a visit to a place of industrial archaeological interest. While successful, they were in competition with railway weeks which were firmly established. I was able to arrange services on a Sunday and prepared some lists of prayers which other leaders might use. These were appreciated by some but others were hostile.

Where was I sent for my first week's leading abroad? Mayrhoffen in Austria. My German was negligible. On the first morning, we waited at the bus stop but none came. Someone kindly pointed out the notice that the bus route had been diverted so there was a mad rush down to the station. Usually I offered to go for a couple of weeks at the beginning of the season in June and again at the end in September. While travelling was easier with fewer passengers on the flights, there might not be enough guests to justify a holiday. Once I took advantage of this and flew out to Switzerland on the original flight and explored the Swiss National Park in the far East of the country. For over fifty years, forestry, farming and hunting has been banned. Few paths traverse this natural wilderness. Even deer seem to know they are safe here when they are within the boundaries. In spring, I took a small ice axe in my rucksack in case of emergencies which I found useful struggling through this park, such was the state of the paths.

Mayrhoffen was a popular HF centre. The hotel was frequently voted the best by HF guests among those used abroad. The town had recreational facilities such as miniature golf, a bowling alley and open-air pool. It was an excellent centre for walks with good transport such as the narrow gauge railway, buses and cable-cars. Walks ranged from easy to strenuous. HF normally offered three grades of walks with criteria laid down for distance, ascent and descent and particular hazards. It was always difficult leading some of the guests particularly those going to the Alps for the first time. I had to remember that what seemed easy to me was terrifying to a newcomer. One guest, who should have known better because he worked for the World Council of Churches in Geneva, was terrified of heights and exposure so I had to walk behind him.

HF Holidays may have had a policy of moving leaders to different centres. I will admit that had I remained leading at Mayrhoffen, I would have missed seeing many other places and having different adventures. At Les Diablerets in Switzerland, I arranged a sort of cheese tour. A walk took us to a high Alpine farm where we saw cheese being made straight from the milk. This contrasted with the commercial production at Gruyere on a coach trip which returned by the caves where the cheeses were regularly washed with salt water and matured. At near-by Château d'Oex, I was able to help the local English community by taking an afternoon Sunday service in their Anglican church. At Torbole on Lake Garda in Italy, we climbed up to the gun emplacements high up in the mountains where the Italians and Austrians fought each other in the First World War. On the first morning here, I was slowly getting up when I put on my wrist watch. Horror of horrors, I had forgotten to change it for continental time! 'We wondered where you were', the guests said. I grabbed some breakfast and just caught the service bus to go to the start of the walk.

While most guests appreciated our efforts at leading and evening entertainment, there were inevitably some complaints. One lost her baggage on the flight. We went to the railway station to meet every train that evening to see if it had arrived. We arranged for her to buy toiletries and for the other guests to loan items of clothing. Her report said 'Mr. Hills did nothing to help'. On a non-walking day, we laid on a coach to Annecy where I was expected to be a mine of information about the town in spite of having never been there. On the other hand, I met many interesting people, some of whom wanted to know why we were leading when we received only travel expenses and free accommodation. This might prompt a deeper conversation. I decided to cease leading when HF Holidays became more and more an ordinary travel agent and lost its Christian foundation.

Society of Ordained Scientists

The aims of the Society were to support other ordained scientists with fellowship and prayer in our role of exploring science and technology in relation to both religion and to the world. My interest particularly lay in the effects of the Industrial Revolution. Members were expected to attend the Annual Gathering which met from lunch on a Tuesday to after lunch the following Thursday. There were also meetings of what were called 'Chapters', consisting of those members in a particular area who met on a day for discussion and prayer. The worship was based on the practice of the Anglican Church with Morning and Evening Prayer and, when appropriate, Holy Communion. The annual meeting would have led meditations, periods of silence and discussion. Depending upon the venue, there might be a walk in the surrounding countryside during the middle afternoon. Retreat houses such as Launde Abbey, Scargill or Sneaton Castle Convent at Whitby might be chosen for the Annual Gathering where about fifty members might attend. As the Society became better known, members from overseas, particularly North America, would come too. For me, it was a great experience to meet, listen to, and discuss with some of the leaders in 'Science and Religion'

SOCIETY OF ORDAINED SCIENTISTS

PRAYER CARD 2016-2017

such as Arthur Peacock and John Polkinghorne. In addition, the leader of the meditation would normally be some prominent theologian.

In 1993, I was elected Secretary. There was the Bulletin to produce four times a year, committee meetings to arrange, minutes to write, invite the speaker for the Annual Gathering, notices of the Annual Gathering to dispatch and list acceptances, attend to new applications for membership, invite a bishop to be our 'Visitor' and so on. Here again this brought me into contact with so many like-minded clergy. I continued to be secretary for six years until 1999. Then in 2008, at the Annual Gathering at Scargill, the Warden stepped down. Since no one else was willing, I took over that role until 2011. Here again it was a great privilege to meet so many people and share their concerns. I think that Bernice was not too pleased with my acceptance at first but members welcomed her lunches at Stamford Cottage for meetings of the committee. She was also welcomed into the fellowship and came to the Annual Gatherings. We went together to Northern Ireland to launch a 'Chapter' in that country and expand the work of the Society. With the closure of St. Stephen's Flowery Field, I was offered their set of Holy Communion vessels which were presented to the Society and are still used. It was a wonderful way to end my career in the Church for, in 2011, I was diagnosed with Parkinson's which changed our lives.

The Reverend Doctor

Part 4.1 – Getting Married

'Thou hast kept the good wine until now'.

(St. John, ch.2 v.10)

Our marriage on 08.08.08 was perhaps the most memorable for a long time in Mottram. It was between a decrepit bachelor well past his sell-by date and a widow not quite so elderly. At first sight, it must have appeared to many that they were an ill-assorted couple but in fact they shared much in common which might be described as running in parallel lines, complementing each other. The challenge in their marriage would be to see how they could make their individual gearwheels mesh smoothly into each other.

Let us look at some of their interests. First and foremost, both were committed Christians, whose faith had sustained them 'Through all the changing scenes of life, in trouble and in joy'. Bernice was a regular worshipper at Mottram church which was then, I suppose, liberal Anglican. Both had suffered early bereavement, she losing her father when she was only fifteen. Both knew the scourge of cancer with her much loved Geoff dying in January 2004 after a traumatic battle with the disease.

In our earlier lives, I had been expected to help with household chores and in the parish during school holidays at Seal, while she had to assist running the pubs, 'The Navigation' and latterly 'The Old Dog' in Haughton Green. Bernice had to carry the coals up to their flat as well as dealing with the customers. We were both very practical, me with gardening, model making, etc; she with more crafts such as knitting and needle work and of course cooking. We both liked being in the open air, she with her Guides and me walking over the hills. Swimming too we both enjoyed. Both had experience of youth work, me in teaching, she in the Guide movement. This was combined in both with a love of travelling especially abroad. Luckily she had a sense of humour which she needed when dealing with me for both could be equally strong willed. I managed to avoid being slashed round the legs with a wet tea towel. She had a much easier way of dealing with people with her broad smile. Possibly through the early loss of my mother, I was always more reserved. Yet we managed to get on with each other.

Prostate Cancer

It must have been in 2005 that I was having a flu jab at Mottram surgery when I complained to nurse that I was frequently waking up in the night to go to the toilet. Dr. Burke was free at that moment. She sent me straight in for a consultation. He decided his preliminary investigation needed to be examined further. Then it was off to Tameside Hospital for further tests, scans and so on. Cancer.

Next it was Christies for a course of 12 sessions of radiotherapy. How could I get there because I was warned that the effects made it inadvisable to drive? I tried one route by driving the short distance to Newton station, train to Manchester Piccadilly, walking into the centre and bus out to Christies. Return was by the same route. That would be more hazardous than driving. I learnt that there was a special car park at Christies for those who had appointments at specific times so I asked whether members of Mottram congregation might take me in return for lunch at Stamford Cottage. A certain Mrs Pickford volunteered to fill the last vacant slot.

I had known of her through her involvement with the Guides, cleaning the church and helping at various fundraising events. I had met Geoff and knew that he had died from cancer. She was one of the row of femmes formidables who always sat together in the same pew near the back of church. Under her circumstances, it was brave of her to take me. Neither of us realised the consequences. She had been happily married to Geoff for forty three years. How would another marriage turn out? Marrying me would mean a drastic upheaval leaving her home and perhaps moving to Stamford Cottage.

My appointment at Christies was delayed a little so we had time to chat. As she took me back to Stamford Cottage, she pointed out some of her childhood haunts such as the Grammar School in Hyde for she had lived in the area all her life. Lunch that day consisted of sardines on toast. She must have felt that this bachelor was a poor cook for a few days later she appeared with some frozen meals she had prepared herself. I discovered that she was Senior Technician at Hollins School of Catering in Manchester, a definite plus. I offered her some blackcurrants from the garden if she came to pick them. She had the advantage over me of being shorter so picked them more easily, looking attractive even in the rain with her hood up. I used to say she needed her legs pulling to make her a little taller.

At some stage, she realised that I was finding in her a potential partner. Apparently she consulted our mutual friends, the Jubbs. Bill was born one day after Bernice. They must have given her some assurance by inviting us both to meals. I gave Bernice a copy of Rudyard Kipling's *Just so Stories* and marked the tale of 'The Cat that Walked by Himself' with its picture of the cat 'walking by his wild lone through the Wet Wild Woods and waving his wild tail' as a sort of warning about how independent a person I was.

I discovered that Bernice liked swimming. I frequented Copley baths most Saturday mornings with a neighbour who was a Cambridge half-blue. But I changed to Dukinfield baths having inspected the outside of 6 Dale Brook Avenue which I found well kept. I told Bernice that I had heard about a cafe in that road which served excellent breakfasts. She took the hint. We both went swimming early in the morning and afterwards breakfasted and prayed together. Sometime later, Bernice asked if she could call one evening at Stamford Cottage. She appeared with a blonde bomb-shell, her younger daughter Alison. She seemed alright and I must have been acceptable to her. It took a little while before my proposal of marriage was accepted in front of the rest of her family over one Christmas. Through marriage I would acquire an instant family of two step-daughters, Gill and Alison, a step grandson, Christopher, a step granddaughter Hannah, and later a son in law, Nigel Ashworth with his two daughters, Kirstie and Sophie.

Bernice Pickford

Who was this fish I had caught? She was well known for her prominent role in the local Guiding organisation. I do not know whether she had been a Girl Guide in her youth or how she became interested in that movement. In 1974 she set up a group at Hattersley, the Manchester overspill estate in part of Mottram parish after having her arm twisted by the then Commissioner, Eileen Underwood, a close friend. Here some of her Guides became Queen's Guides and still continue to work for Guiding. While at Hattersley, she organised trips to Luxemburg, Switzerland and the Lake District. Perhaps it was through their camping with those in Mottram that she became linked with that parish. While camping at Waddow, she had to go as an emergency to hospital for a bad abcess under a tooth. She helped for many years in the shop at the Seven Springs camping ground. Her organisational skills were much in demand as was her skill with finances which she kept with great precision. She took on the responsibilities of District Commissioner for the Mottram, Broadbottom Hattersley area and was twice Division Commissioner for the larger grouping of Hyde.

She loved organising trips both at home and abroad. For many years, she took parties to the Christmas Extravaganza at North Walsham near Norwich. Once the through train on which they had been booked was cancelled. Instead she had to organise wheelchair and luggage assistance from one platform to another and two changes of train with her dozen or so elderly Guiders. She liked going to the Guide house at Adelboden in Switzerland. While the equivalent house at Sangam in India was enjoyed, she was appalled at the poverty she saw elsewhere in that country.

Sangam

In 2011, I went with her and a host of Trefoil Guides to a Regional Meeting in Cardiff which was interesting for me to see that city again. We went to the Open Air Museum at St. Fagans which I thought had become very rundown with few demonstrations. Theoretically she had to finish at 65 but she carried on helping at meetings and keeping the finances for many more years at Mottram Guides and Brownies. She started a Trefoil Guild at Mottram in 2005 which was intended for those over 63. This apparently left a gap for those who had retired so she was asked to start a 60+ group. Contact with these was through a newsletter distributed throughout the County.

She went to London with our great friend, Pat Hall, who had been invited to the Annual Service at Westminster Abbey for those who had achieved forty years of service to Guiding. Poor Bernice, because there seems to have been some mix-up in her guiding record, I had to return her invitation to commemorate her forty years after her death – a sad end to all the years of her devoted support for the Guiding movement.

Preparations for Marriage

The cat was out of the bag, or perhaps the 'wild lone' cat waving his 'wild tail' was truly caught. To prepare for our marriage, we had to settle three areas. One was to show our future partner to other members of our families and friends. Second was to make a new home where we would live. Third was to prepare for our wedding day.

Meeting Others

Meeting relations and friends took us on many happy breaks away from Mottram both before and after our wedding. It was a nice change to have a companion on these trips. There were Geoff's relations at Bournemouth, a town foreign to me. We stayed at a comfortable hotel and met Di Broddle, Geoff's sister and Lyn her daughter who showed us around. I still use the pair of mugs decorated with birds that we purchased in Christchurch.

Of course the Hills family, or rather I should say the Bishop family based at Brimpsfield, was a must. We were not so fortunate with the overnight accommodation at the Royal

George Hotel in near-by at Birdlip, because while smart downstairs, the bedrooms were dingy and scruffy. We did no better with a bed and breakfast advertised in their parish magazine where there were no washing facilities in the bedroom, no space in the wardrobe or drawers to put anything and a garrulous deaf old husband who insisted on talking all evening. For later visits, we settled on the Cheltenham Regency Hotel easily accessible from the M5 motorway and where Gill from Bristol and Michael and his girl friend Pat from Cheltenham could join us for a meal.

We were lucky again at Minehead to find a small hotel where the proprietors were establishing their reputation for good cooking. There was of course the steam railway as well as Taunton being within easy reach to see Duncan Robertson's tribe and the Quayles who came over from Stroud. We saw where Hugh and Shelagh had lived at Axminster. On these trips, we took advantage of our National Trust membership to visit places such as Dunster Castle, Stourhead, Lacock Abbey and the Swannery at Abbotsbury.

Mottram Agricultural Show in the middle of August, with the wedding planned for the beginning of the month, may have been the reason why we postponed our honeymoon till later. We both exhibited there, Bernice with her baking and me with wine and marmalade as well as demonstrating spinning.

We briefly toured West Sussex to see Lavant and the area around there. The not so Little House at Winchelsea where father and Audrey retired came later. We stayed just outside Rye so I could show Bernice the olde worlde character of that town before crossing the Romney Marsh to arrive at Canterbury for the BAPH meeting held in the cathedral close.

Luckily permits had been arranged for us to park there. As we returned home, I pointed out to her the warning sign at the entrance to the Dartford Tunnel under the Thames, 'The North'. She never really shared my enthusiasm for the history of technology but gallantly came to meetings of my various societies.

Where to Live

Two into one won't go. With all my books, archives, machine tools and Lancia, it was obvious that 6 Dale Brook Avenue would be too small as would Stamford Cottage with Bernice's added interests of Guiding, crafts and cooking. Could we enlarge Stamford Cottage? Next door in Roe Cross farm lived Gwyn Davies, an architect. Would he help prepare Stamford Cottage for its new bride? Could we extend the kitchen into the garden in an orangery? He drew up outline plans for submission to Tameside Council's Conservation Officer because the house was a Grade II Listed Historic Monument. The opportunity was taken to refurbish the bathroom with a walk-in shower which caused no problem other than the mess of the builders.

The fun started in the kitchen. Bernice did not like washing up looking at a blank wall. A window could have been reopened to look into the scruffy back passage but we moved the sink so she could view the garden. I mentioned earlier that the kitchen had a flat roof but, at one time, it must have had a sloping slated roof, the outline of which could still be seen. The Conservation Officer allowed us to retain the flatroof and install a non-original skylight in it. The layout of the kitchen was reorganised to Bernice's satisfaction.

Gwyn produced a plan for extending the kitchen into the patio. The rear wall would be solid, the south wall would be mostly glass with double doors into the garden while the west wall would be mainly glass. Tameside made encouraging noises but no formal approval.

Then the Conservation Officer changed. A new broom... Something traditional to match the main part of the house was required. I argued that the extension at the north end reflected the era in which it had been built, namely late Georgian with large sash windows

so too the south end ought to be contemporary in style. No, it had to match the small windows of the old weaver's cottage. We had to comply. Luckily I had already installed double glazing elsewhere otherwise it would not have been permitted in the extension. Talk about going green and saving energy!

Planning permission was granted, prices were agreed and work commenced. I was trying to slim down my books and archives to fit into the attic. Eventually my historic collections found homes in at least ten museums or archives. With no kitchen or bathroom, I retired to Dale Brook Avenue at night to return at 7 am the following morning to open up. Delays occurred. It was a nail-biting experience but all was finished, just.

Marriage Preparations

Meanwhile Bernice was sorting out the wedding. She went to many places before she found a dress that suited, and of course the hat. I was sent to Bradford to a bespoke tailor for a new suit. Bridesmaids had to be kitted out; bouquets and buttonhole flowers ordered. The flower ladies in church sprung into action with early visits to markets, remembering that Bernice was allergic to lilies. Participants in the service had to be briefed, bell-ringers, choir, ushers, etc. Bishop Rupert Hoare, who was my 'Visitor' when I was Warden of the Society of Ordained Scientists, agreed to preach. Then of course there was the wedding breakfast. It was difficult to find a suitable place for an hundred guests at comparatively short notice. Being on a Friday helped. Having thought that we had succeeded, Peruga Restaurant found it had made a double booking and we were the second. Whatever to do? Somehow agreement was reached. They would erect a marquee in their large car park and hire portable cooking facilities and toilets, something they had never done before. It all fell into place so that invitations could be printed.

Transport was not forgotten. Robert helped to prepare and polish the Lancia. It was lucky that he was at Stamford Cottage when our new king-size bed was delivered. The men started to carry it up the stairs but they could not twist it round at the top into the bedroom so they abandoned the bed downstairs. Inspiration – would it fit through the much larger window in the Georgian extension into the little spare room? We measured

the window – the bits might just go through. We split my long extension ladder into two, rested one part either side of the window and together climbed up with the pieces of bed. They just fitted by an inch or so. The firm was contacted before they had gone too far and we had a bed to sleep on. On the great day, Robert drove the Lancia with my best beloved and Gill up to church while John Glithero kindly followed in his 1930 Alvis with the two bridesmaids while I was waiting in church, having been taken by the best man John in his BMW coupe.

The Wedding

> In summertime on Warhill
> The bells they sound so clear...
> Oh, peal upon our wedding,
> And we will hear the chime,
> And come to church on time.

A.E. Houseman (adapted)

The Lord looks on those he loves. In a month when there were many wet days, we were blessed with sunshine for our wedding. The photograph of John and myself standing in the sun outside St. Michael and All Angels shows a worried elder brother, perhaps concerned for his sibling's fate. He was not nearly as worried as I was, wondering whether the Lancia would behave herself and get Bernice to the church on time. Inside, we listened to the wise words of Bishop Rupert, exchanged rings, with luckily nobody dropping one as happened once when father was taking a service and the ring disappeared down a grating. The happy couple adjourned to the vestry for signing the registers amid general congratulations all round.

Then it was time to face the congregation, walk down the aisle as husband and wife, to be greeted by the Brownie pack at the north door with bags of confetti. It took months to clear it all out of the Lancia. The noisy bells sounded out again while numerous photos were taken.

Then off to Peruga with Robert driving the Lancia. The tables were named after different birds. Alison, John and I gave speeches. She concealed a radio under the table to hear the latest cricket score. Once meal and speeches were over, the happy couple thanked the guests for their contributions to such a memorable day. We climbed in the Lancia which was always more difficult with the hood up to stop Bernice's hat blowing away and off to Stamford Cottage to put the Lancia to bed before retiring to Dale Brook Avenue.

The Reverend Doctor

Part 4.2 – Living Together

The Honeymoon

We decided to take our honeymoon in the autumn through various other commitments but where? An ocean cruise was right out of the question because Bernice would have been sick all the time in spite of stuffing herself with Quells. She could feel dizzy travelling at the rear of a coach or the back seat of a car (the Lancia had plenty of fresh air). I was surprised that she accepted my driving so readily. Two well travelled people wanted to go where neither had been before. New Zealand was one of the few places so we booked a month's tour with Journeys of Distinction.

After a stop-over in Singapore, we landed at

Christchurch in the South Island. Mottram friends who had emigrated to a farm near-by showed us round including the mock Gothic cathedral which was almost totally destroyed in an earthquake later. A vintage tram ride was obligatory. The advantage of a conducted tour was visits to the best sites had been arranged. Gay, a cousin of Bernice, lived in Dunedin in the South so we called on her. I heard

Signpost at the Southern tip of New Zealand

from her as I was writing this when she sent me a picture of herself at 92 in full motorcycle regalia having been taken for a special ride – a tough old girl! The short sea passage to

Stewart Island Bernice did not enjoy but it was our farthest South. Fish and chips were the special culinary delight.

Returning northwards we took perhaps the most scenic route in New Zealand over the Mackinnon's Pass to the spectacular Milford Sound and boarded the small 'Milford Mariner' for the night. Luckily the Sound is a deep cleft in the mountains so well sheltered and Bernice got some sleep. Retracing our steps, we arrived at Queenstown. We were not tempted to have a drink in an ice bar but took a steam boat round the lake to see sheep shearing at a farm. Bernice enjoyed the old houses in a sort of open-air village but I could not persuade her to try the bungee jump at Kawarau Bridge.

For both of us, the highlight of the South Island was the helicopter flight up the Franz Joseph glacier towards Mount

Cook, the highest point in New Zealand. For me it was my first time in a helicopter, for Bernice, her first time on a glacier.

We toured most of the North Island from Wellington in the south to its northern tip. I am still doubtful whether I would chose to live at Rotorua where steam came out of the roadside grids and peoples' gardens. The Pohutu Geyser at Whakarewarewa was spectacular but difficult to catch on a photo while the evening of Maori entertainment was very different from anything in our country.

We saw the Government House where the treaty with the Maoris had been signed and enjoyed the scenery in the Bay of Islands. We watched woodcarvers at work on some of the spectacular Maori carvings.

Group photograph of those on our trip

We were sad at leaving these remarkable islands once more for Singapore where we had an extra day on the South Island due to a change in flight schedules.

Further Holidays

To the reader, it could seem that we were on perpetual holiday but we both resumed our usual activities on returning to England after such a memorable honeymoon. I had to get used to Bernice with her television, something I never had. While she resumed all her Guiding activities, I took services in the local churches again. We had a sort of unwritten agreement that she would take care of domestic duties within the house, except for the attic, and I would be responsible for the exterior. But itchy feet soon caused us to consider foreign holidays.

One of the first was the Oberammergau Passion play. Although I had been many years previously, I welcomed the chance to see it again. The package tour first had ten days in the Zillertal valley so I was able to show her one of my old leading grounds, as well as buying a pair of Austrian oven gloves with their Tyrolean design of a boy and a girl. We were both deeply moved by the Passion play and as a memento purchased a dice with six different graces for use at meals. Summer was late coming that year with snow lying on the Alpine meadows. During our visit, the weather became hot; the snow melted quickly causing the Danube to flood. Navigation was closed. We did not heed the warning for future holidays.

After our experience in New Zealand where we were changing from one hotel to another every couple of days (or nights), we decided to sample river cruising. Bernice would not be seasick. We would retain the same room for the whole of the cruise. We could sit on the upper deck in the sun, watching the country slide past. We would moor up in the centre of a town or village convenient for sight-seeing. Special trips might be organised from the ship and the cuisine was reputed to be to a high standard.

A cruise from Luxor on the Nile took us south by boat first and finally by a coach guarded by an armed escort to the spectacular temples at Abu Simbel.

In the other direction, we watched camels parading round the great pyramids near Cairo and looked at many fabulous places in between. We were allocated a table in the dining room with a group from the Isle of Man. They made it clear to us novices that they had been on many Nile cruises before as well as how wonderful was their own island. Their tune changed when I gently told them that my cousin was Elspeth Quayle, a member of the House of Keys.

Our Rhine cruise was as cold as Egypt was hot. We went up from Cologne to Basel where we saw Tracey, daughter of Di Broddle, and her husband Christoph. They took us to a restaurant which should have had a view of the mountains – cloud. The outside tables were covered with white, not cloth but snow. Water in the Rhine was rising as we returned north. The level in the Rhine Canal was controlled but to rejoin the main river where the water had risen, the masts, the deck railings all had to be lowered to enable us to pass under a bridge. One evening while I was sitting by a window for dinner, I watched the water rising over a flight of steps. A pair of mallard climbed up the steps and waddled rapidly away across the car park. What did they know? We reached Cologne just in time but the cruise after ours was stranded there.

We had better weather on the Danube – magnificent castles, baroque churches and palaces at places like Vienna, Melk and Budapest. On the Seine, we started near the centre of Paris, sailed past Rouen down to Monet's gardens, the Bayeux tapestry and the D-day landings. The size of the cemeteries brought home to us the scale of casualties in both World Wars.

As land lubbers, we holidayed in the south of Portugal (more oven gloves) as well as Lisbon. We flew across the Atlantic to the Canaries but our favourite destination was Madeira (more oven gloves). The Hotel Porto Santa Maria was conveniently situated at one end of a long flat promenade and had an indoor swimming pool. While the hotel served excellent meals (often too much!), every room had a kitchenette so we could make a light lunch. The near-by castle housed one of the top restaurants on the Island while the area was noted for its small restaurants. Other shops were nearby as was the central bus station. Tours around the rest of the island could be arranged and we watched the cruise ships docking in the port from our hotel bedroom window. But for us, perhaps the main attraction was the Anglican Church where we could join in worship in an English service on a Sunday. But during these holidays, my Parkinson's condition was slowly deteriorating.

Parkinson's

'Parkinson's', Dr. Mark Roberts whispered to Bernice as he watched me walk down the corridor at the Alexandra Hospital that July 2011. I had suspected for a long time that something was wrong. I had taken longer to recover from the radiotherapy than two or three fellow sufferers I knew. I became tired very quickly. When I queried this at Mottram surgery, all Dr. Clark would say was 'It's just old age'. I asked for a referral to a neurologist. I had maintained my subscriptions to a medical insurance company so I was able to see Dr. Roberts within weeks rather than months. A scan confirmed my attempts at drawing interlocking triangles and snail spirals. Parkinson's. After the initial shock, it was a relief to know the worst.

Through seeing the decline of Auntie Poll in my youth, I knew I would have a similar fate of becoming an invalid. Bernice was finding the stairs at Stamford Cottage getting steeper while the weeds in the garden seemed to be growing larger. Having put the Lancia into as good a condition as we could, I had already decided to part with my old friend. CY 8115 was sold by auction at Buxton that summer. A fellow Lambda enthusiast purchased her to keep company with another Lambda. She has since been sold on and is still running somewhere on the Continent.

We realised that we must move into a bungalow and put Stamford Cottage up for sale towards the end of August 2011 and accepted an offer at the end of September. Meanwhile we had been searching for a bungalow and on 4 October made an offer for 261 Broadbottom Road. It had been extended at the rear into a spacious lounge and enlarged kitchen. The drawback was the steep drive up to it. Then began the frustrating months of waiting for our purchasers to find their money. In fear of losing 261, I purchased that bungalow by selling some securities and so was able to complete that transaction on 16 March. Two days later, I received the cheque from our purchasers – O ye of little faith. On 16 April, we started moving into 261 and had finished clearing Stamford Cottage on 26 April. We spent three nights in the Premier Inn during the move. A few months later, we had the kitchen modernised with a better layout and lighting. It was certainly a wise move although traumatic for me to leave Stamford Cottage after living there for so many years.

Recognition of My Achievements

'The Lord gave, and the Lord hath taken away; blessed be the name of the Lord' (Job 1,2). As so often in my life, when one door closed, another opened. It was the same after leaving Stamford Cottage. During 2011, I had been writing my *Reminiscences of the North Western Museum of Science and Industry* because I realised that there would be no record of the early days at 97 Grosvenor Street. The Greater Manchester Council was asserting that Liverpool Road was an entirely new museum, endeavouring to wipe out any memory of our achievements. While I could refer to the Annual Reports I had written and some other documents, I could not access the official records at the Town and County Halls so called this *Reminiscences*. Bernard Champness helped with the layout and publication. We sent copies to various libraries and to the Museum at Liverpool Road.

Medal of Honour

Unknown to me, two old friends were trying to secure some official recognition of my career in Manchester. They were Professor John Pickstone at Manchester University and David Higginson, President of the Manchester Literary and Philosophical Society. I was surprised to receive on 1 August 2013 a letter from the Vice Chancellor would I be prepared to receive their Medal of Honour for 'recording the industrial past of Manchester and the North West region'. A special evening ceremony was held early in 2014 but alas John Pickstone had fallen ill and died in the meantime. It was only the twenty-sixth such medal awarded. Bernice was delighted. *The Reminiscences* had helped to secure this. It was a remarkable honour.

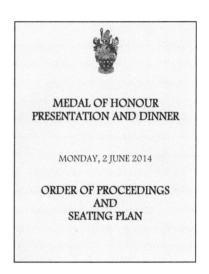

MEDAL OF HONOUR
PRESENTATION AND DINNER

MONDAY, 2 JUNE 2014

ORDER OF PROCEEDINGS
AND
SEATING PLAN

MBE

David Higginson also was able to use *The Reminiscences* to good effect in his campaign to support an application to the Prime Minister's office to secure for me some national recognition for all the work I had done to promote the history of the Industrial Revolution. He was ready to send his submission on 16 August 2013. I received a letter dated 21 November 2014 that 'The Prime Minister has asked me to inform you, in strict confidence, that... he is recommending that Her Majesty may be graciously pleased to approve that you be appointed a Member of the Order of the British Empire in the New Year 2015 Honours List'. It would be announced officially in the London Gazette on 31 December 2014. Many congratulations poured in and I was featured in the local papers.

The investiture was due to be held at Buckingham Palace in May but that presented me with a dilemma – Parkinson's. I realised that the train journey, the overnight accommodation as well as getting to the Palace would exhaust me. 'You must go'. 'You must see the Queen'. Some Mottram friends were furious that I was considering not going. I explained the situation to the authorities. What happened was truly wonderful – Oh ye of little faith.

The Investiture was held in St. Michael and All Angels, Mottram by Warren Smith, Lord-Lieutenant of Greater Manchester on the afternoon of Saturday, 6 June. Instead of sharing the Investiture with only two people as would have been the case at Buckingham Palace, the church was packed with probably two hundred people. In my short speech of thanks, I pointed out,

> *We meet today in the Church of St. Michael & All Angels which for me is very appropriate. Underlying all my work has been the trust that it was done with the blessing and guidance of God...*

> *While Parkinson's has restricted my ability to lead services as well as lecturing on the history of engineering, Parkinson's has been the reason why this Investiture is being held here today. It has brought so many together to celebrate what is the culmination of my career with the award of the MBE. So once again I thank you all for coming, especially the tea ladies, but above all, I thank Her Majesty the Queen for granting me this public recognition of my work.*

Bernice and the church tea ladies provided light refreshments afterwards. I was told quietly that I had merited an OBE, had that not been awarded to another all those many years before. For me, it was more appropriate to receive such an award at the end of my career.

Warren Smith, Lord-Lieutenant of Greater Manchester

Cancer

Soon after the triumph of the Investiture, that scourge of both our families struck again. This time it was my best beloved, Bernice. We went to Tameside Hospital on Wednesday 15 July when Bernice was told she needed a hysterectomy. After more hospital visits scans and an operation, we were told on Wednesday 2 September that cancer had been found but they thought they had stopped it spreading further. This came as a shock to all of us but we were comforted by the expectation that the cause had been removed. More scans and operations followed in the ensuing year with the hope that the subsequent treatment at Christies with chemotherapy would have stopped the disease. Our hopes were raised only to be dashed time and time again with Bernice gradually weakening. She was moved from Tameside Hospital to Willow Wood Hospice on Wednesday 3 August. Her treatment here was wonderful but we knew the end was in sight. Gill and Allison came to stay at Stamford Cottage. On Sunday 14 August, I gave her Communion and we read Psalm 23 together which brought her some peace. I returned home for a rest, leaving Gill and Allison at her side. I was rung early the following morning 15 August to hear that she had passed away peacefully.

The funeral was on Wednesday 31 August at Mottram church, the day before my 80th birthday which she had so much longed to celebrate. Family members turned out in force as did a guard of honour of perhaps fifty Trefoil members. After an ominous start, the day turned out fine. We went into church with a peal of muffled bells to find a large congregation and again Bishop Rupert said a few words. The great respect in which Bernice was held was shown in the substantial donations we were able to send in her memory to both Willow Wood Hospice and the Guides Seven Springs camping ground.

Requiescat in pace.

Funeral Service and Thanksgiving
for the life of
BERNICE PICKFORD HILLS
24th July 1942 – 15th August 2016

St. Michael & All Angels, Mottram in Longdendale
Wednesday 31st August 2016, 12:30pm

Post Script

God moves in a mysterious way his wonders to perform...
Ye fearful saints, fresh courage take, the clouds ye so much dread
Are big with mercy and shall break in blessings on your head.

Willow Wood offered a bereavement counselling for those who had lost a loved one. The Counsellor was so impressed with all my activities and achievements that she felt I should write my autobiography. I hope you have enjoyed what I have written and that it will bring blessings in your life as it has mine.

Faithful vigil ended, watching, waiting cease;
Master, grant your servant his discharge in peace.

Appendix I – Chronology

1936, Sept. 1	Born at Lee, Lewisham.
	Birth registered 14 Sept. when baptised.
1938, May 6	Mother Margaret Magdalen died of cancer.
1939, September	War declared, father joined as Chaplain, Richard went to Kathleen and Robert Tomson at Littlehurst, Tunbridge Wells.
1943 or 1944	Started as a dayboy at Rosehill School, Tunbridge Wells.
1944, Nov	Royal Drawing Society, Honours award. Five more awards up to 1950
1949, June 7	Father married Audrey Eleanor Trevelian Mann.
1950	Head boy of Rosehill School.
1950, Sept	Started at Charterhouse School.
1952, July	Oxford & Cambridge Schools Examination Board, 'O' Level passes in English Language, Latin, French, Elementary Maths, General Science. Dec. 'O' Level Greek.
1954, July	Oxford & Cambridge Schools Examination Board, 'O' Level General Paper, Greek. 'A' Level, Latin of Classical Studies, Ancient History.
1955	Head of House in Long and Cricket Quarters. Left at end of Cricket term.
1955, September	Called up for National Service.
1956, probably June	Commissioned in Royal Artillery.
1957	Army Arts & Crafts Exhibition, Eltham Palace, Highly commended in Models Section.
1957	Started as Undergraduate at Queens' College, Cambridge.
1958, November	Purchased 1924 Lancia Lambda, CY 8115.
1960, June	Cambridge University degree of Bachelor of Arts.
1960, August 20	Climbing accident on Great Gable while instructing for the Outward Bound.
1961, September	Started Dip. Ed. Course at Cambridge Institute of Education.
1962, June	Cambridge Institute of Education passed Dip. Ed. Course with award of merit for essay, 'A Critical Examination of the Outward Bound'.
1962 – 63, Sept – Mar	Taught at Earnley School, near Chichester.
1963, Summer term	Taught at Worcester College for the Blind.
1963, July	Royal Institution for the Blind Certificate in Standard English Braille.
1964, February	Proceeded Master of Arts at Cambridge,
1964, July	Imperial College of Science and Technology Diploma for thesis on Fen Drainage.
1965, September	University of Manchester Research Assistant in the History of Textile Technology.
1967	First book published as *Machines, Mills and Uncountable Costly Necessities, A Short History of the Drainage of the Fens*.

1968, July	University of Manchester award of Doctor of Philosophy.
1968, Autumn	First grant of £12,000 to establish a Science Museum for Manchester.
1968	Purchased Stamford Cottage, Mottram.
1969, October 20	Museum of Science and Technology opened by Lord Rhodes of Saddleworth in 97 Grosvenor Street with R.L. Hills as curator.
1973	Society for the History of Technology, awarded Abbott Payson Usher prize.
1983	The Museums' Association Fellowship awarded.
1983, November	Father died.
1984	Retired from the Museum of Science and Industry in Manchester on ill-health grounds.
1985	Accepted for training in the Church of England as an ordained priest.
1985	Started training at St. Deiniol's Library, Hawarden.
1987, June	St. Deiniol's Library certificate in Theology.
1987	Advisory Council for the Church's Ministry, passed General Ministerial Examination.
1987, September	Started curacy at St. Clement's Church, Urmston.
1989	Moved to Great Yarmouth.
1990	Year teaching History of Science at UMIST as stand in for Joe Marsh.
1992, September	Honorary Member of the International Association of Paper Historians.
1996, July	Elected Companion of the Institution of Mechanical Engineers.
1997, November	Passed Mountainwalking Leader Summer Scheme.
2003, April	Audrey died.
2006	President of the Manchester Association of Engineers during its 150 Anniversary Year.
2008 – 11	Warden of the Society of Ordained Scientists.
2008, August 8	Married to Bernice Pickford.
2011, June	Lancia CY 8115 sold.
2011, July 25	Parkinson's confirmed.
2012, April	Moved into 261 Broadbottom Road.
2012, June	British Overseas Railway Historical Trust Honorary Membership.
2013, January	Istituto Europeo di Storia della Carta e delle Scienzo Cartarie, Honorary Member.
2013, October	Awarded University of Manchester Medal of Honour.
2013, November	Manchester Literary & Philosophical Society, Honorary Member.
2014, July 15	John died in Eastbourne Hospital.
2015, January	Member of the Order of the British empire announced.
2015, June 6	Ceremony by Ld. Lieutenant of Greater Manchester at Mottram Church for MBE.
2016, August 15	Bernice died of cancer.

Appendix II – Curriculum Vitae

Date of Birth	1st September 1936, at Lee Green, London.

Education

Rose Hill School, Tunbridge Wells, 1945 – 1950.

Charterhouse School, Godalming, 1950 – 55.

'O' Level: Latin, Greek, Elem. & Add. Maths., Gen. Science, French, English Language, Scripture.

'A' Level: Latin, Greek and Roman History.

Queens' College, Cambridge, 1957 – 62, M.A & Dip. Ed. 1961 - 2,

Historical Tripos and Certificate of Education with award of merit.

Imperial College, London, 1964 – 65, D.I.C., Thesis on 'The Introduction of Steam Drainage to the Fens'.

UMIST, 1965 – 68, PhD. Thesis on 'Studies in the History of Textile Technology'.

St. Deiniol's Library, Hawarden, 1985 – 87. Training for ordination in the Church of England.

National Service

Royal Artillery, commissioned, 1955 – 57.

Career

Earnley School, Chichester, & Worcester College for the Blind, teacher, 1962 – 63.

North Western Museum of Science and Industry in Manchester, Founding Curator, 1965 – 85.

UMIST, Hon. Lecturer/Reader, teaching undergraduate courses for Physics, Mech.Eng., Paper Science, Civil Eng.

Imperial College, London and the Universities of Keele, Leicester and Salford, External Examiner in History of Technology and Science and Society M.Sc. courses and theses.

Manchester University Extra-Mural Department and the Workers Educational Association, teaching adult classes on Industrial Archaeology, History of Textiles, Architecture, etc. from 1966 to 1987.

Church of England, Ordained priest 1988, since then working full/ part time for the Church as well as continuing research on history of technology.

Honours and Awards *Society for the History of Technology*, awarded the Abbot Usher Payson Prize in 1973 for article published in *Technology & Culture*.

Museums Association, elected Fellow in 1983.

Institution of Mechanical Engineers, elected Companion in 1996.

Museum of Science and Industry in Manchester, made Honorary Life Vice President in 2007.

Istituto Europeo di Storia Della Carta e Delle Scienze Cartarie, Foundazione Gianfranco Fedrigoni, made Honorary Member, 2013.

Manchester Literary & Philosophical Society, made Honorary Member 2013.

University of Manchester Medal of Honour, 2014.

New Year Honours, 2015, Member of The Order of The British Empire (MBE).

Offices held in Societies at Various Times

International Association of Paper Historians, President. Now Honorary Member 1992.

British Association of Paper Historians, Chairman. Now Honorary President.

Manchester Region Industrial Archaeology Society, Secretary and Chairman. Now Honorary Member.

British Overseas Railways Historical Trust, Life Member 2012.

The Newcomen Society, Chairman and Treasurer of the North Western Branch and Member of Council.

Jodrell Bank Concourse Committee, Member.

Mottram Educational Trust, Chairman.

Manchester Literary and Philosophical Society, Member of Council and Honorary Curator. Honorary Member 2013.

Manchester Association of Engineers, Member of Council, Editor and President (2005 – 07).

Society of Ordained Scientists, Secretary and Warden (2008 - 11).

Life Member by paid subscription

National Trust in lieu of payment for report.

Royal Society for Protection of Birds.

Welsh Highland Railway Society.

Appendix III – Major Publications

Books

Machines, Mills and Uncountable Costly Necessities, A Short History of the Drainage of the Fens, Goose & Co., Norwich, 1967, p. 180.

Power in the Industrial Revolution, Manchester University Press, 1970, p. 274.

Richard Arkwright, Priory Press, London, 1973, p. 96 (reprinted twice).

Beyer, Peacock, Locomotive Builders to the World, Transport Publishing Co., Glossop, 1982, p. 302, 3rd. impression 1998.

Papermaking in Britain, 1488 – 1988, A Short History, Athlone, London, 1988, p. 249, reprint by Bloomsbury Academic Collections, 2015.

Power from Steam, A History of the Stationary Steam Engine, Cambridge University Press, 1989, p. 338, (reprinted in 1993).

Power from Wind, A History of Windmill Technology, Cambridge University Press, 1994, p. 324, (reprinted 1996).

The Origins of the Garratt Locomotive, Plateway Press, p. 40, 2000.

Life and Inventions of Richard Roberts, 1789 – 1864, Landmark, p. 272, 2002.

James Watt, Vol. 1, His Time in Scotland, 1736 – 1774, Landmark, p. 416, 2002.

James Watt, Vol. 2, The Years of Toil, 1775 – 1785, Landmark, p. 256, 2005.

James Watt, Vol. 3, Triumph Through Adversity, 1785 – 1819, Landmark, p. 287, 2006.

The Drainage of the Fens, [revision of Machines, Mills…], Landmark, p. 205, 2003, (2 edn. paperback 2008).

Windmills, A Pictorial History of their Technology, Landmark, p. 208, 2005.

Development of Power in the Textile Industry, from 1700 – 1930, Landmark, p. 254, 2008.

The North Western Museum of Science and Industry, Some Reminiscences, 2013.

Articles

Academic American Encyclopaedia, various articles.

Althin, T., *Festskrift Torsten Althin*, 1997, 'Working Machinery'.

Bibliologia 19, Le Papier au Moyen Age: Historie et Techniques, 'The Importance of Laid and Chain Line Spacing', 1999.

Bibliographical Dictionary of Scientists, Williams, T.I., Ed., A.& C. Black, 1969, various articles.

Biographical Dictionary of the History of Technology, Day, L.& McNeil, I., Eds., Routledge, 1996, various entries.

British Association of Paper Historians, Vol. 1, *The Oxford Papers*, Fourth Annual Conference, St. Edmund Hall, Oxford, 1993, 'The Use of Straw in Papermaking' and 'James Watt and his Copying Machine'.

Ibid, Vol. 2, The *Exeter Papers*, Fifth Annual Conference, Exeter, 1994, 'The Origins of Thermo-mechanical Pulp' and 'James Watt and Paper and Papermaking'.

Ibid, Vol. 3, *The London Papers*, Sixth Annual Conference, Imperial College, 1995, 'The Chelsea Mills of the Straw Paper Company', and Alan Crocker & R.L. Hills, 'Neckinger Mill Paper and Watermarks'.

The British Overseas Railways Journal, No. 2, Summer 1987, 'Thomas Walsh and the La Guaira and Caracas Railway, Part 1'.

Ibid, No. 3, Autumn 1987, 'Thomas Walsh and the La Guaira and Caracas Railway, Part 2'.

Cambridge Antiquarian Society, Vols. LVI & LVII, 1962 - 63, 'Windmill Drainage in the Waterbeach Level'.

Cantrell, J. & Cookson, G., Eds., *Henry Maudslay and the Pioneers of the Machine Age*, 2002, 'Richard Roberts'.

Chartered Mechanical Engineer, June 1975, 'Newcomen Engine of 1712'.

The Christian, Summer 1986, 'The Importance of the Bible to a Lay Reader'.

Institution of Civil Engineers, Proceedings, Engineering History and Heritage, Vol. 164, Issue EH3, 2011, 'John Rennie, Mechanical Engineer'.

Congress Book of European Paper Days, Ed. Castagnari, G., Fabriano, 2006, 'The Importance of Early Italian Paper and Papermaking in Britain'.

Deutscher Arbeitskreis fur Papiergeschichte, DAP, September 1999, 'Das 200 jahrige Jubilaum der Erfindung der Papiermaschine'.

Direct Current, Journal of the EM2 Society, No. 11, Jan. 1986, 'A Dutch Weekend'.

Early Railways, Vol. 1, Eds. A. Guy & J. Rees, Newcomen Soc., 2001, 'The Railways of James Watt'.

Ibid, Vol. 2, Ed. M.J.T. Lewis, Newcomen Soc., 2003, 'Richard Roberts' experiments on the friction of railway waggons'.

Ibid, Vol. 3, Ed. M.R. Bailey, Six Martlets Pub., 2006, 'The development of machine tools in the early railway era'.

Forth Naturalist and Historian, Vol. 21, 1998, 'James Watt's Surveys Around Stirling'.

Geigy Circle, Nos. 17 & 18, 'The Manchester Museum of Science and Technology'.

Ibid, No. 19, 'A Century of Steam'.

History of Technology, Vol. 1, 1976, D.S.L. Cardwell & R.L. Hills, 'Thermodynamics and Practical Engineering in the Nineteenth Century'.

Ibid, Vol. 2, 1977, 'Museums, History and Working Machines'.

Ibid, Vol. 5, 1980, 'Water, Stampers and Paper in the Auvergne; A Medieval Tradition'.

Ibid, Vol. 6, 1981, 'Early Locomotive Building near Manchester'.

Ibid, Vol. 18, 1996, 'James Watt, Mechanical Engineer'.

Ibid, Vol. 25, 2004, 'The Development of the Steam Engine from Watt to Stephenson'.

Ibid, Vol. 26, 2005, 'Richard Roberts' Contributions to Production Engineering'.

Industrial Archaeology Journal, Vol. 3, No. 1, 1996, 'The Cruquius Engine, Heemstede, Holland'.

Ibid, Vol. 4, No. 1, 1967, R.L. Hills & H. Milligan, 'Rescue Operations at Beyer, Peacock'.

Ibid, Vol. 10, No. 3, 1973, 'De Schoolmeester; A Dutch Papermaking Windmill'.

Industrial Heritage, Transactions 2, Sixth International Conference on the Conservation of the Industrial Heritage, 'Twenty One Years of Industrial Archaeology in Manchester, Where next?'

Industrial Monuments, Transactions 1, (First International Congress on the Conservation of Industrial Monuments), June 1973, 'The Preservation of Mill Engines'.

Ibid, Transactions 3, (Third International Congress on the Conservation of Industrial Monuments), June 1978, 'Problems of Displaying and Working Textile Machinery in a Museum'.

International Association of Paper Historians Year Book, 1980, 'Water, Stampers and Paper at Ambert'.

Ibid, Vol. 4, 1983 – 4, 'The Early Use of Wove Paper in Books'.

Ibid, Vol. 5, 1984, 'Papermaking Stampers: A Study in Technological Diffusion'.

Ibid, Vol. 6, 1986, 'The Development of the First Papermaking Machines'.

Ibid, Vol. 7, 1988, 'John Tate and His Mill'.

Ibid, Vol. 8, 1996, 'The Drive for Efficiency in Papermaking'.

Ibid, Vol. 9, 1992, 'Early Italian Papermaking, A Crucial Technical Revolution'.

International Paper History, Vol. 1, No. 3, 1991, 'The First Steam Engine in a Paper Mill'.

Ibid, Vol. 9, No. 3, 1999, 'The Bicentenary of the Papermachine'.

Istituto Internazionale di Storia Economica 'F. Datini', Prato, Italy, Vol. 23, 1991, 'Early Italian Papermaking'.

Ibid, Vol. 24, 1992, 'From Cocoon to Cloth, The Technology of Silk Production'.

The Kintyre Magazine, Vols. 41 – 43, Spring 1997 – Spring 1998, 'James Watt at Campbeltown'.

Living Economic & Social History, Ed. Pat Hudson, Economic History Society, 2001, 'The Value of Grounding in Economic History'.

Looking at Paper, evidence and interpretation, Symposium Proceedings, Toronto, 1999, 'A Technical Revolution in Papermaking, 1250 – 1350'.

McNeil, I., Ed., *An Encyclopaedia of the History of Technology*, Routledge, London, 1990, 'Textiles and Clothing'.

Manchester Association of Engineers, Transactions, Vol. 146, 2001 – 2, 'Richard Roberts, Prolific Inventor'.

Ibid, Vol. 150, 2005 - 6, 'Textiles, Temples and Paper in China & Tibet'.

Ibid, Vol. 151, 2006 - 7, 'The North Western Museum of Science and Industry'.

Ibid, Vol. 152, 2007 – 8, 'The Life and Works of Thomas Telford'.

Ibid, Vol. 152, 2007 – 8, 'The Railway Collection of the Museum of Science and Industry'.

Manchester Literary & Philosophical Society, *Selected Papers by John Dalton presented to the Manchester Literary & Philosophical Society*, Ed. K.M. Letherman & B.R. Pullan, R.L. Hills, 'John Dalton, His Life and Achievements'.

Manchester Memoirs, Manchester Literary & Philosophical Society, Vol. 127, 1987 – 88, 'Peter Ewart, 1767 – 1842'.

Ibid, Vol. 132, 1993 – 94, 'A Monument to the Industrial Revolution: The North Western Museum of Science and Industry'.

Ibid, Vol. 134, 1995 –95, 'James Watt, 1736 – 1819, Pioneer of Scientific Engineering'.

Ibid, Vol. 147, 2008 – 9, 'Dalton's Manchester, The First Industrial City'.

Ibid, Vol. 153, 2014 – 5, 'The Preservation of the North West's Industrial Heritage: a memoir'.

Manchester Region Industrial Archaeology Society, 'Starting the North Western Museum of Science and Industry'.

Manchester Regional History Review, Ed. J.V. Pickstone, Carnegie, Vol. 18, 2007, 'Richard Roberts, (1789 – 1864), pioneer of production engineering in Manchester'.

Manchester Statistical Society, 170 Session, 2002 – 3, 'Glossop: The Rise and Fall of a Textile Town, 1790 – 1950'.

Manchester Technology Association Year Book, 1970, 'The Newcomen Engine in the Manchester Museum of Science and Technology'.

Mining History, The Bulletin of the Peak District Mines Historical Society, Vol. 13, No. 6, Winter 1998, 'James Watt's Steam Engine for the Leadhills Mines'.

Museums Association Journal, June 1968, 'The Manchester Museum of Science and Technology, an Experiment in Education'.

Ibid, Sept. 1970, 'Industrial Collections in the North West', (a lecture given to the annual conference).

National Trust, 'Feasibility Study for a Textile Museum at Quarry Bank Mill', Styal, 1969, p. 33.

New Dictionary of National Biography, various articles.

Transactions of the Newcomen Society, Vol. XXXVI, 1963 – 4, E.J.A. Kenny & R.L. Hills, 'The Steam Pumping Engine at Stretham, Cambridgeshire'.

Ibid, Vol. XL, 1967 – 68, 'Beyer, Peacock & Company, Some Contributions to Locomotive Development'.

Ibid, Vol. XLIV, 1971 – 72, 'A One-third Scale Working Model of the Newcomen Engine of 1712'.

Ibid, Vol. LI, 1979 – 80, 'The Origins of the Garratt Locomotive'.

Ibid, Vol. LII, 1980 – 81, 'Industrial History through Film'.

Ibid, Vol. LVI, 1984 – 85, 'The Competition to the Turbine'.

Ibid, Vol. LVII, 1985 – 86, 'The Uniflow Engine, A Re-Appraisal'.

Ibid, Vol. LVIII, 1986 – 87, 'A Steam Chimera, A Review of the History of the Savery Engine'.

Ibid, Vol. LXVIII, 1996 – 97, 'The Origins of James Watt's Perfect Engine'.

Ibid, Vol. LXX, 1998 – 99, No. 1, 'James Watt's Rotary Steam Engines'.

Ibid, Vol. 75, 2005, R.L. Hills & D. Gwyn, 'Three Engines at Penrhyn Du, 1760 – 1780'.

Ibid, Vol. 76, 2006, 'The Importance of Steam Power during the Nineteenth Century'.

The Newcomen Society, Evolution of Modern Traction, 14 Nov. 1992, Proceedings, 'The British Locomotive Building Industry & Modern Traction'.

Notes and Records of the Royal Society, London, Vol. 24, No. 2, April 1970, 'Sir Richard Arkwright and his Patent granted in 1769'.

Ibid, Vol. 52, (1), Jan, 1998, 'John Watt's Map of the Clyde'.

North Western Museum of Science and Industry, Booklets and guides:-
> Bailey's horizontal Hot Air Engine
> Beyer, Peacock, Locomotive Builders of Gorton
> A Brief History of Papermaking
> Cotton Spinning
> The Newcomen Engine
> The 'Waterwheel' Clock
> Weaving

Open University Course, 'Technology and Change, 1750 – 1940'; R.L. Hills & K.A. Barlow, 'The Changing Face of Engineering'.

Oxford Companion to The Book, O.U.P., 2010, various articles.

Paper Focus, Vol. 2, No. 17, Feb. 1988, 'History of Papermaking in the U.K., Part 1, The First Paper Produced in Britain'.

Ibid, Vol. 2, No. 21, June 1988, 'History of Papermaking in the UK, Part 2, A New Face to Paper'.

Ibid, Quincentenary Issue, Oct. 1988, 'The History of Papermaking in the UK'.

Perceptions of Great Engineers, Fact and Fancy, Ed. D. Smith, Science Museum, 1994, 'John Rennie'.

Pioneer, Journal of the K1 Group of the Welsh Highland Railway Society, Issue 3, Summer 1996. 'Rescue at Gorton'.

Ibid, No. 4, Winter 1996/7, 'H.W. Garratt – The Man'.

Ibid, No. 5, Summer 1997, 'The Origins of the Garratt Locomotive'.

Ibid, No. 6, Spring 1998, 'H.W. Garratt's Patent'.

Ibid, No. 7, Spring 1999, 'Beyer, Peacock and the Garratt'.

The Quarterly, The Review of the British Association of Paper Historians, No. 2, August 1990, 'Some Notes on the Matthias Koops Papers'.

Ibid, No. 4, July 1992, 'The Cylinder Mould Machine, Part 1'.

Ibid, No. 5, Dec. 1992, 'The Cylinder Mould Machine, Part 2'.

Ibid, No. 7, July 1993, 'Places to Visit, : 'The Schoolmaster Mill' and 'James Watt and Papermaking'.

Ibid, No. 9, Jan. 1994, 'Light and Dark Watermarks, Part 1' and 'Christmas at Matthias Koops' Mill, 1802'.

Ibid, No. 10, March 1994, 'Light and Dark Watermarks, Part 2'.

Ibid, No. 14, March 1995, R.L. Hills & J. Reeve, 'British Paper Mills: Ruthven and Methven'.

Ibid, No. 15, June 1995, 'British Paper Mills: The Afonwen Mills, North Wales' and P. Bower & R.L. Hills, 'Prince of Wales' Feathers'.

Ibid, No. 29, January 1999, 'The Origins of Modern Paper'.

Ibid, No. 33, January 2000, 'The Bicentenary of the Papermachine'.

Ibid, No. 39, July 2001, 'The Chelsea Mill of the Straw Paper Company'.

Ibid, No. 39, July 2001, A.J. Crocker & R.L. Hills, 'Neckinger Mill Paper and Watermarks'.

Ibid, No. 41, January 2002, 'A Visit to the de Montalt Mill' and 'Some Notes on the Introduction of Chlorine Bleaching'.

Ibid, No. 42, May 2002, 'Multi-Layer Paper', and 'John Rennie, Mysterious Papermill Millwright'.

Ibid, No. 44, Nov. 2002, 'Olive and Partington, Papermakers of Glossop, Part 1'.

Ibid, No. 45, Jan. 2003, 'Olive and Partington, Papermakers of Glossop, Part 2'.

Ibid, No. 46, May 2003, 'British Paper Mills: Paper Mills at Hayfield, Derbyshire'.

Ibid, No. 48, Dec. 2003, 'British Paper Mills: White Hall Mills, Chapel-en-le-Frith, Derbyshire'.

Ibid, No, 48, Dec. 2003, 'Some Notes on Abbey Mills, Greenfield'.

Ibid, No. 52, Oct. 2004, 'Papermaking in the Manchester Region'.

Ibid, No. 54, April 2005, 'A Papermaking Visit to China'.

Ibid, No. 55, July 2005, 'Notes on Yorkshire Papermaking'.

Ibid, No. 56, Oct. 2005, 'A Visit to China in May 2004'.

Ibid, No. 57, Feb. 2006, 'The British Hand Mould'.

Ibid, No. 58, Apr. 2006, 'Remy Green's Obituary'.

Ibid, No. 59, July 2006, 'Papermaking in Hertfordshire'.

Ibid, No. 64, Oct. 2007, 'Five Drawings of N.L. Robert's Papermaking Machine'.

Ibid, No. 65, Jan. 2008, 'List of Scottish Papermakers, 1837'.

Ibid, No. 66, Apr. 2008, 'Excise Office List, 8 Oct. 1816'.

Ibid, No. 69, Jan. 2009, 'Lyng Mill No. 217, Norfolk'.

Ibid, No. 70, April 2009, 'The 1807 Act'.

Ibid, No. 71, July 2009, 'The Importance of Early Italian Paper and Papermaking in Britain'.

Ibid, No. 72, Oct. 2009, 'Paper Mills and Waterpower'.

Ibid, No. 73, Jan, 2010, 'Dutch Papermaking in the 17th Century as Exemplified by the Schoolmeester Windmill'.

Ibid, No. 75, July 2010, 'Oakenholt Mill Steam Engine'.

Ibid, No. 84, Oct. 2012, 'Papyrus, Parchment and Paper, Part 1, Early Writing Materials – Introduction'.

Ibid, No. 85, Jan. 2013, 'Papyrus, Parchment and Paper, Part 2, Early Writing Materials in the West: Papyrus'.

Ibid, No. 86, April 2013, 'Papyrus, Parchment and Paper, Part 3, Other Materials'.

Ibid, No. 87, July 2013, 'Papyrus, Parchment and Paper, Part 4, Early Writing Materials in the East'.

Ibid, No. 87, July 2013, 'Some Old Newspapers'.

Ibid, No. 88, Sept. 2013, 'Papyrus, Parchment and Paper, Part 5, The First Paper'.

Ibid, No. 89, January 2014, 'Papyrus, Parchment and Paper, Part 6, The Pouring Mould'.

Ibid, No. 89, January 2014, 'The National Paper Museum'.

Ibid, No. 90, April 2014, 'Papyrus, Parchment and Paper, Part 7, Dipping Moulds'.

Ibid, No. 91, July 2014, 'Papyrus, Parchment and Paper, Part 8, Papermaking Goes West'.

Ibid, No. 92, October 2014, 'Papyrus, Parchment and Paper, Part 9, The Triumph of Paper'.

Ibid, No. 93, April 2015. 'Chinese Wallpaper'.

Reader's Guide to the History of Science, Dearborn, 2000, various articles.

Railway Magazine, Oct. 1981, No. 966, Vol. 127, 'Novelty in Sweden'.

Ibid, May 1984, No. 997, Vol. 130, 'What a Whopper, Moving the South African Class GL Beyer-Garratt'.

Ibid, Oct. 1986, No. 1026, Vol. 132, 'An Electrifying Return'.

Railway World, Oct. 1981, Vol. 42, No. 498, 'Novelty in Sweden'.

Ibid, July 1984, Vol. 45, No. 531, 'The Railway Collection at Liverpool Road Station'.

The Red Rose Steam Preservation Society, 'The Mill Engine Collection for Liverpool Road Station, Manchester'.

Royal Society of Arts Journal, Vol. 144, No. 5468, April 1996, 'Joseph Glynn and Fen Drainage'.

Scientific Instrument Society, Bulletin No. 57, June 1998, 'How James Watt Invented the Separate Condenser; Part 1:, Scientific Background'; No. 58, September 1998, 'Part 2, The Separate Condenser'.

Ibid, Bulletin No. 60, March 1999, 'James Watt's Barometers'.

Smith, J.H., Ed., *The Great Human Exploit*, Phillimore, London, 1973, 'Motive Power Engineering'.

The Snowdon Ranger, Welsh Highland Railway Society, No. 23, Winter 1999, 'When is a Garratt not a Garratt?'

Ibid, No. 28, Spring 2000, 'The Development of the NG/G16 Design'.

Ibid, No. 31, Winter 2001, 'Proposed Electric Traction on the PB&SSR'.

Ibid, No. 40, Spring 2003, 'The Importance of K1's Firebox'.

Society of Antiquaries of Scotland, Proceedings, Vol. 131, 2002, 'James Watt and Delftfield'.

Society of Ordained Scientists, Bulletin No. 10, Winter 1994 – 5, 'The Origins of Modern Materialism'.

Ibid, No. 16, Summer 1997, 'Jesus Christ: Carpenter'.

Ibid, No. 41, Christmas 2007, 'Two Sermons on Cancer'.

Ibid, No. 42, Spring 2008, 'God Moves in Mysterious Ways'.

Ibid, No. 44, Spring 2009, 'James Watt, Conventional Christian'.

Ibid, No. 46, Spring 2010, 'Thoughts on Joseph and Moses in Egypt'.

Ibid, Winter 2016, 'Some Observations on Parkinson's & 'Parkinson's and Faith'.

Stationary Engine Research Group, Bulletin Vol. 5, No. 3, Autumn 1983, 'The Mill Engine Collection for Liverpool Road Station'.

Stationary Power, The Journal of the Stationary Engine Research Group, 1988, 'The Origins of the Compound Mill Engine'.

The Stationer & Newspaper Maker, No. 39, Spring 1986, 'The National Paper Museum'.

The Stationer's Company, 'John Tate, England's First Papermaker', lecture given on 24 Feb. 1993.

The Stretham Engine, A Brief Guide, 1965.

Technology and Culture, Vol. 13, No. 1, Jan. 1972, R.L. Hills & A.J. Pacey, 'The Measurement of Power in Early Factory Steam Driven Textile Mills'. This article was awarded the Abbot Usher Payson Prize in 1973 for the best article in Technology and Culture that year.

Textile History, Vol. 2, No. 1, Dec. 1971, 'The Manchester Museum of Science and Technology Textile Display'.

Ibid, Vol. 10, 1979, 'Hargreaves, Arkwright and Crompton, Why Three Inventors?'.

Journal of the Textile Institute, Vol. 80, No. 2, 1989, 'William Lee and His Knitting Machine'.

Journal of the Trevithick Society, No. 24, 1997, 'James Watt in Cornwall'.

XVI International Congress for the History of Science, Budapest, 1981, 'George Stephenson, 1781 – 1848'.

XX International Congress for the History of Science, Liege, 1997, Technology & Engineering, Lette, M. & Oris, M., Eds., 'James Watt's Application of Scientific Technology to Industry'.

Voornamelijk, 'Henk Voorn, An International Paper Historian'.

The Wallpaper History Review, 2004 – 5, 'Paper, Paper Everywhere: the Bicentenary of the Fourdrinier Papermaking Machine'.

The World of the Industrial Revolution, Essays from the Lowell Conference on Industrial History, 1984, Weible, R., Ed., 'Steam and Waterpower: Differences in Transatlantic Approach'.

World Pulp & Papermaking Technology, 1990, 'Five Hundred Years of Papermaking in Britain'.

Editorship

I have edited various books such as E.G. Loeber, *Paper Mould and Mouldmaker*, Paper Publications Society, Amsterdam, The Netherlands, 1982; A.H. Shorter, *Studies on the History of Papermaking in Britain*, Variorum, Aldershot, 1993. Edited with W.H. Brock; Wilfred Vernon Farrar, *Chemistry and the Chemical Industry in the 19th. Century*, Variorum, 1997 and Donald S. Cardwell, The *Development of Science & Technology in Nineteenth-Century Britain*, Variorum, 2004.

Films

In association with Courtaulds, I advised and helped in the production of:-
    'Power Behind the Spindle'
    'The George Saxon Engine at Magnet Mill'.

In conjunction with the Manchester University Audio/Visual Service, I helped to produce:-
    'The Newcomen Engine'
    '1,000 Pounds per Square Inch, Manchester's Hydraulic Power Supply'.

I made three other films for the North Western Museum of Science and Industry:-
    'Woven by Hand'
    'Hand Made Paper'
    'The Spinning Mule'.

Appendix IV – Working Machines and Demonstrations

Early Days at 97 Grosvenor Street

Textiles: two types of hand spinning wheel, broad hand loom, Jacquard hand loom, spinning jenny, roving frame, self-acting spinning mule, Leesona pirn winder, latch circular knitting machine, ring spinning frame, calico power loom, Jacquard ribbon loom, calico printing with hand blocks, Devoge card cutting machine for Jacquard looms.

Steam Power: Newcomen engine, grasshopper, vertical and small horizontal engines all run on steam, steam turbine by electric motor.

Internal Combustion Engines: Crossley atmospheric gas engine, Crossley four stroke gas engine, Petter two stroke engine.

Horsepower: a farm horse wheel could be demonstrated.

Machine Tools: Holtzappfel ornamental turning lathe, small Whitworth lathe, Whitworth planning machine.

Electric Generation and Use: Early Gramme Ring dynamo, ECC DC generator, arc lamp, various early light bulbs, Wimshurst machine, principles of electric generation, radios and loud speakers.

Optics: Telescopes which could be looked through, principles of lenses, stereoscopic photography.

Clocks: Two faced 'Waterwheel' clock, Bailey turret clock mechanism, office wall clock.

Papermaking: Clough beater for pulp preparation, small and large hand moulds for making sheets, drying apparatus.

Printing: Wood and iron hand presses, foot and power operated treadle platen presses, Wharfedale flat-bed press, guillotine.

Added after the move to Liverpool Road.

Textiles: Hand demonstration spinning mule, replica of Arkwright's waterframe, preparatory machines to prepare cotton for spinning, terry towelling loom.

Machine Tools: A restoration workshop was established in the Great Western Warehouse with some historic machine tools.

Railways: Replica 1830 carriages were built for visitor rides which could be hauled by either a steam locomotive from Agecroft Colliery or a battery-electric locomotive. A replica 'Novelty' was motorised and the Isle of Man locomotive 'Pender' was sectioned and motorised. The controls in a EM2 electric locomotive cab could be demonstrated.

Mill Engines: The five large mill engines, Haydock beam engine, Durn Mill single cylinder horizontal engine, Barnes Mill tandem compound engine, Ferranti cross compound vertical engine and the Elm Street Mill horizontal cross compound engine could be run under steam.

Internal Combustion Engines: A replica of Otto's fist four stroke gas engine was built. A Mirrless air-blast diesel engine was commissioned. A National diesel engine was linked to drive its generator.

Waterpower: The undershot waterwheel was installed with a water circulation system.

My mother, Margaret
Magdalen Hills,
remembered in stone at
Lavant, West Sussex.

IN LOVING MEMORY OF
MARGARET MAGDALEN HILLS
DIED 8TH MAY 1938
AGED 40 YEARS.

THE REV. LESLIE HILLS, M.A. M.C.
DIED 4TH NOVEMBER 1983
AGED 86 YEARS.
AND REV. ELEANOR TREVELYAN HILLS
APRIL 2003 AGED 86 YEARS

My wife, Bernice Pickford
Hills, remembered in
wrought-iron at Mottram-
in-Longdendale

Lightning Source UK Ltd.
Milton Keynes UK
UKHW05f1056060418
R1675600001B/R16756PG320558UKX4B/4/P